# JOURNEY IN BLUE
A Peek into the Workers' Party of Singapore

# JOURNEY IN BLUE
## A Peek into the Workers' Party of Singapore

Yee Jenn Jong

World Scientific

NEW JERSEY · LONDON · SINGAPORE · BEIJING · SHANGHAI · HONG KONG · TAIPEI · CHENNAI · TOKYO

*Published by*

World Scientific Publishing Co. Pte. Ltd.
5 Toh Tuck Link, Singapore 596224
*USA office:* 27 Warren Street, Suite 401-402, Hackensack, NJ 07601
*UK office:* 57 Shelton Street, Covent Garden, London WC2H 9HE

**National Library Board, Singapore Cataloguing in Publication Data**
Names: Yee, Jenn Jong.
Title: Journey in blue : a peek into the Workers' Party of Singapore / Yee Jenn Jong.
Description: Singapore : World Scientific, [2020]
Identifiers: OCN 1222952492 | ISBN 978-981-123-146-9 (paperback) |
    ISBN 978-981-123-015-8 (hardcover)
Subjects: LCSH: Workers' Party (Singapore) | Political parties--Singapore--History. |
    Singapore--Politics and government. | Yee, Jenn Jong.
Classification: DDC 324.25957--dc23

**British Library Cataloguing-in-Publication Data**
A catalogue record for this book is available from the British Library.

Copyright © 2021 by World Scientific Publishing Co. Pte. Ltd.

*All rights reserved. This book, or parts thereof, may not be reproduced in any form or by any means, electronic or mechanical, including photocopying, recording or any information storage and retrieval system now known or to be invented, without written permission from the publisher.*

For photocopying of material in this volume, please pay a copying fee through the Copyright Clearance Center, Inc., 222 Rosewood Drive, Danvers, MA 01923, USA. In this case permission to photocopy is not required from the publisher.

For any available supplementary material, please visit
https://www.worldscientific.com/worldscibooks/10.1142/12096#t=suppl

Desk Editor: Lai Ann
Design and layout: Lionel Seow

Printed in Singapore

The Workers' Party has been effective in representing the interests of Singaporeans because of dedicated and loyal party members like Yee Jenn Jong. JJ's reflections in this easily digestible book provide some insights into the workings of the WP. In the run-up to the 2020 general election, JJ shares the efforts the party undertook to persuade credible, highly-qualified Singaporeans — confident to debate in Mandarin and dedicated to the cause of growing a credible and responsible opposition — to join the party as candidates. Much work goes on behind the scenes and readers will find this book useful for perspectives that the mainstream and online media sources have not authoritatively or incompletely captured over the years.

**Pritam Singh**
Leader of the Opposition, Singapore
Secretary-General, the Workers' Party

I was in Parliament when Jenn Jong became an NCMP in 2011. I noticed that Jenn Jong and I spoke about many similar things on policies focusing on entrepreneurship and supporting SMEs in Singapore. Both of us are entrepreneurs. Jenn Jong, too, understood the issues which SMEs faced. I enjoyed most of his speeches in Parliament.

The battles opposition MPs and members have to face against the formidable PAP are tremendous. I am glad Jenn Jong has written *Journey in Blue* capturing the trials and tribulations of being in the opposition in Singapore. As he wrote, his ultimate loyalty is to Singapore and speaking against policies is not being disloyal. Reading the book, I learned about 'retail politics', of how the WP builds a relationship with voters. The book gives great insights to the WP and the life of an opposition member that Singaporeans should know about.

**Inderjit Singh**
Former Member of Parliament (1996–2015), Singapore

An interesting and insightful read about JJ's political journey. Everyone's perspective is different and there is much to learn from one another. JJ's book provided that learning opportunity, not only with his views, but also how he felt at different stages of his journey. I value the opportunity to have worked with him for the start-up community. JJ had experience in starting companies when he entered Parliament in 2011. He raised many questions about SMEs and supporting start-ups. We had regular chats on the subject, and I have learnt much from his sharing. Entrepreneurship is critical to the economy and his experience was valuable. When invited to help, JJ readily agreed to be part of the Action Community for Entrepreneurship (ACE) which I was chairing. He stayed active throughout his term and contributed well. It's been a while, but I am glad to know both of us are still active with start-ups!

**Teo Ser Luck**
Former Minister of State,
Ministry of Trade and Industry & Ministry of Manpower, Singapore
Former Member of Parliament (2006–2020), Singapore

*Journey in Blue* is an interesting reflection of an entrepreneur-turned-politician. Jenn Jong's views are personal and sincere, and give the readers a rare peek into the Workers' Party of Singapore.

**Er Kwong Wah**
Former Permanent Secretary, Ministry of Education and Ministry of
Community Development, Singapore

I met Jenn Jong (or JJ as we affectionately call him) during my term as Nominated Member of Parliament. As an NMP whose position was primarily based on my advocacy with the environment and nature conservation civil society, 'speaking for the trees' in a Parliament at a time when such issues were not so commonplace, it was comforting to me to see JJ also raising issues related to sustainability, and speaking on the bills related to the environment and energy conservation.

More than that, what is still a source of inspiration to me was his persistence in speaking up on a range of other issues, notably the pre-school education sector and concerns for SMEs, raising many questions, and when not satisfied with the answers, he pointed supplementary questions to the political office-bearers. It was apparent to me that he was not only serious about holding the government's feet to the fire. More importantly, and certainly beyond merely criticising what he considered gaps in the system, I was also impressed by the proposals that his speeches contained to raise standards for the betterment of the areas he was passionate about, some of which, interestingly, later saw the light of day in government policies.

*Journey in Blue* provides not just a rare insight into an MP's experiences in the highest law-making body of the land; it is a searingly honest account of the challenges and obstacles faced by a politician from an alternative party not many Singaporeans are privy to in a country which, until only recently, is not used to the value of diverse voices in Parliament.

**Faizah Jamal**
Former Nominated Member of Parliament (2012–2014), Singapore

JJ, who helped to open the door to my own involvement in WP, has consistently been a passionate and committed leader in his tireless outreach on the ground, week after week, house after house, block after block, general election after general election. This is a detailed personal account of his journey so far with the WP and it provides a colourful glimpse of his experience and observations in his journey.

**Dennis Tan**
Member of Parliament, Singapore

Yee Jenn Jong has been my comrade-in-arms in the Workers' Party for almost 10 years. I still remember our first meeting during a house visit in East Coast GRC when he first participated as a volunteer. Since then, we have gone through many of the exciting ups and downs in Singapore's recent political scene together.

We were fielded in adjacent constituencies in the 2011 general election — he in the now-defunct Joo Chiat SMC and I in East Coast GRC — and subsequently in the 2015 and 2020 general elections, when he contested in Marine Parade GRC. We served together for several years in the WP's Central Executive Committee and in the 12th Parliament of Singapore, where we were seated almost next to each other as Non-constituency Members of Parliament.

While many of our experiences have been similar, JJ offers a perspective that reflects his unique experiences in this journey. *Journey in Blue* provides an important primer for any aspiring politician who wishes to contribute to Singapore through an opposition party like the WP. It is a story of grit, hard work, disappointment, and hope — all of which can be expected when one throws in one's hat into Singapore's political arena.

Through all this, JJ has proven himself to be a man of integrity, who fears God and cares for the people around him. He has been a man whom I am proud to call a friend.

**Gerald Giam**
Member of Parliament, Singapore

Our Pledge as Singaporeans enjoins us to build a democratic society. To realise this, Singapore needs a responsible, able, and electable Opposition so as to balance and offer an alternative to a ruling party that is more dominant than in any other industrialised electoral democracy. I would encourage Singaporeans to read Yee Jenn Jong's frank and wide-ranging political memoir. I hope that his insights from the trenches help Singaporeans to better understand the lived experience of those striving to build a responsible political alternative in Singapore. Jenn Jong's memoir movingly details not only the challenges facing the Opposition but also the satisfaction arising from taking the more difficult path to serve one's country.

**Leon Perera**
Member of Parliament, Singapore

Anyone who wants a glimpse into a political journey less travelled should read what JJ had encapsulated in this book. A well thought-out and frank take on his life-changing decision to serve the nation from the other side of the fence.

**Png Eng Huat**
Former Member of Parliament (2012–2020), Singapore

This is no ordinary reflection on a political journey. JJ has provided a rare glimpse into the backrooms of a small and upcoming WP seeking to find its voice to represent Singaporeans in a very tough space dominated by a behemoth that had performed well to provide for the country. This is a fascinating story about a group of resilient personages finding common purpose but ever vulnerable to the curse of democratic politics: egoism.

**Daniel Goh**
Associate Professor, National University of Singapore
Former Non-constituency Member of Parliament (2015–2020), Singapore

I knew JJ before he entered Parliament as we are both entrepreneurs in the same field of education technology. Even though we might disagree politically, we bonded over our common interest in business. If Singapore is to develop as a society, political competitors need to also be able to be friends. This is the only way for our society to remain cohesive. This book by JJ is important in this respect as it shows how a successful Singaporean does not necessarily have to embrace the establishment, and instead chose to enter opposition politics.

**Calvin Cheng**
Former Nominated Member of Parliament (2009–2011), Singapore

Jenn Jong and I were both part of the 12th Parliament of Singapore, he as a Non-constituency MP and myself as a Nominated MP. Besides this, we both share a penchant for writing and a belief that Singapore and Singaporean politics would be better with an informed electorate that is educated and interested in the mechanics, issues and personalities that drive our political system. The world we live in is becoming increasingly complex, and Jenn Jong's writings over the past decade, as well as his latest book, serve an important function in explaining part of the political process to readers. He brings politics to life through his vivid anecdotes and storytelling. I hope he inspires more of those who have entered the political arena, regardless of which side they chose, to tell their stories and share insights on a vital aspect of our society.

**Nicholas Fang**
Former Nominated Member of Parliament (2012–2014), Singapore

Having contested against the ruling party's candidate at two general elections, my time as an opposition politician coincided with Jenn Jong's journey in blue, which he has recorded in this excellent book. Among those I have met and gotten to know along the unique and arguably hostile pathway of Singapore politics, Jenn Jong stands out. He is a man motivated and energised by his conviction and commitment to the cause for greater democracy for Singapore. When the later generation reaps the victories sown by this generation, it is because of people like Jenn Jong who tirelessly toiled and worked the ground over long years, that the seeds could be nurtured to fruition. I commend Jenn Jong for his purposeful resolve and courageous perseverance despite the odds. I call on the younger generation to draw inspiration from his exemplary spirit.

**Jeannette Chong-Aruldoss**
Candidate for Mountbatten SMC, GE2011 and GE2015

Different facets of the Singapore Story are now emerging, and this latest book, *Journey in Blue*, is an important account from the opposition frontline.

Most Singaporeans will know Yee Jenn Jong as the man who first shot into the limelight on election night in 2011, when he came within a whisker of beating his PAP opponent on his first attempt — no mean feat at all in Singapore. Yet his political journey has been anything but accidental, and he has served with distinction in Parliament and in many other roles.

Disarmingly candid, Jenn Jong offers insights that should be read by anyone interested in the workings of the Workers' Party. *Journey in Blue* is Jenn Jong's story, as well as a masterclass on opposition politics in Singapore.

**Loke Hoe Yeong**
Author of *The First Wave: JBJ, Chiam and the Opposition in Singapore*

Jenn Jong's *Journey in Blue* is a gem of a political biography. It is delightfully well-written with a simple, modest, yet penetratingly pithy and hard-hitting candour.

It tells the inside stories of Jenn Jong's political career with the Workers' Party over the last 10 years and three general elections. Both the author's and the WP's experiences are covered including key successes and failures, the historical euphoria of the first opposition victory deposing two PAP ministers in Aljunied GRC in 2011, the travails of AIM and AHPETC, dark days post-2015, the WP's controversial yet distinctly successful leadership transition, and finally its hard-won electoral vindication in GE2020.

Through all these, Jenn Jong's humble yet incisive analysis, remarkable entrepreneurial ability, steadfast bipartisanship, and pragmatic objectivity shine through. This gives the reader a clear-eyed, yet first-hand insight into the hardships and resolute behaviour under fire of the home-grown, deeply grassroots connected political leadership and values that have made, and will continue to make, the WP such a formidable opposition party.

This volume is a finely detailed and hard-nosed account of the real political struggles undergone by Jenn Jong, WP veterans, and the promising volunteers-turned-politicians who in the end and in spite of all odds, rose to the occasion to create a more democratic polity. And in the course of their trial by fire, one can discern the motivation and mettle worthy of leading a future government of Singapore.

**Yeoh Lam Keong**
Former Chief Economist, Government of Singapore Investment Corporation

# Foreword

The Workers' Party (WP) is today the most successful opposition party in Singapore, where the People's Action Party (PAP) has been in control of politics and government since 1959. In good times and bad, a resilient WP has been able to maintain viability, relevance, and vitality in a dominant party system, democratic in form but uncompetitive in practice.

The PAP claims, reasonably, that it is not the ruling party's job to make things easier for the opposition. And yet, this claim belies its sustained efforts to make life very much harder for any party that dares to challenge its pre-eminence. The playing field is anything but level.

Therefore, to say that the WP is the most successful opposition party in these circumstances is to say a lot. In the 2020 general election, for instance, it was not only able to retain control of Hougang SMC and Aljunied GRC but did so with significantly bigger margins. Additionally, it won Sengkang GRC with candidates who appeared youthful, diverse, articulate, and empathetic, but no less credentialed than many in the PAP. In fact, the WP actually won 50.5 percent of the votes totalled from constituencies that it contested, which means that if we exclude constituencies it did not contest, the WP narrowly beat the ruling party.

But what has the WP had to do in order to become successful? Even as it argued for a "First World Parliament", the WP had to restrain itself from expressing any ambition larger than simply increasing the strength of opposition voices in Parliament for the purpose of enhancing parliamentary checks and balances. It had to stay firmly within the ideological middle-ground and appear as pragmatic (even as technocratic) as possible, offering technically-proficient policy alternatives that do not suggest radical ideological difference. Compared to parties like the Singapore Democratic Party (SDP), which offers a more differentiated and pronounced ideological alternative to the PAP's globalised neoliberalism, the WP seems like a tinted-blue-mirror image of the PAP, no doubt more inclined to advance worker interests in trade-offs with corporate ones than the ruling party would, but still broadly accepting of the PAP's hegemonic ideological foundations. The WP had to grow without frightening an electorate that has never seen an alternative to the PAP government and that readily imagines how things would simply fall apart if the PAP were to be de-throned in a 'freak election'.

In such strategically and tactically challenging circumstances, the prospects of the WP would depend on cautious expansion, ego management, members' loyalty, strong leadership, strict party discipline, and carefully orchestrated public communication and image cultivation. Not surprisingly, even as the WP's social media campaigns have become extraordinarily effective in signalling authenticity and appeal, the public continues to know very little about what actually goes on within the party.

And that is one reason why I welcome Yee Jenn Jong's book, which promises a peek into a party whose every move is calculated and calibrated. But it delivers more than just a peek.

Jenn Jong's account of what he saw and what he did over his decade-long involvement in the party, particularly the five years when he served as a Non-constituency Member of Parliament, opens the reader's eyes not only to the backstage of political theatre, but also to the on-stage stories and myths that both attract public fascination for current affairs and politics, as well as degrade the ideals of democracy to crude notions of disloyalty to Singapore when considering the meaning of opposition and opposition-supporters. The book helpfully seeks to dispel many such myths that have arrested Singapore's political development.

Jenn Jong candidly shares some very revealing impressions he has had of many key figures in the WP leadership as well as his parliamentary and constituency colleagues. Along with rich descriptions of the mechanics and dynamics of opposition-party life, these impressions form a valuable collection of character sketches that may help explain the reasons and motivations behind what have sometimes seemed rather surprising, and at other times even frustrating, turns of events.

If we assume that Singapore's electoral system will become more competitive and evolve over time into something like a two-party system, where the WP has just as much of a chance to form the government as the PAP, then we the electorate will need to understand deeply what the WP as the ruling party might look like in the future. For gaining such deep understanding, Jenn Jong's book will become a vital resource in the expanding scholarship on Singapore's political development.

**Professor Kenneth Paul Tan**, PhD (Cambridge)
Lee Kuan Yew School of Public Policy,
National University of Singapore
Hong Kong Baptist University
Author of *Singapore: Identity, Brand, Power*
(Cambridge University Press, 2018)
& *Governing Global-City Singapore: Legacies and Futures After Lee Kuan Yew* (Routledge, 2017)

October 17, 2020

# Preface

This book reflects my personal opinions and journey. I do not speak on behalf of the Workers' Party (WP).

I will share my experience and roles during the 10 years of my involvement with the WP of Singapore. I was fortunate to have been part of the major breakthrough in the 2011 general election (GE2011) when the opposition party won its first Group Representation Constituency (GRC), Aljunied GRC. These 10 years took me through a period of working at the highest level of the party, serving as a Non-constituency Member of Parliament and a member in the party's top decision-making Central Executive Committee from 2011–2016, taking part in three general elections, and assisting in many other areas of the party's work. I speak from the viewpoint deep in the battlefront as the party underwent major transformations and suffered big attacks from the ruling People's Action Party (PAP), and yet still managed to make some breakthroughs.

Why am I writing this book?

To many outsiders, the WP may be a black box. Whether one hates or loves the WP or simply does not care, the impressions are often formed from what we read in the media or from hearsay.

I was once such a person. I had long supported the party secretly from afar, cheering from the sofa of my home when Low Thia Khiang, former secretary-general of the WP, unexpectedly won Hougang Single Member Constituency (SMC) in 1991. I followed news of the party in elections and how its members performed in Parliament. I followed the unfortunate disqualification of the late J. B. Jeyaretnam from Parliament in 2001. I did not know anyone from the party. I only understood their roles from what I had read. That was until I took an unexpected big leap to thrust myself upon the party shortly before GE2011 and managed to be selected as their candidate for Joo Chiat SMC.

From then, my understanding of the party grew deeper and I treaded the deep waters of Singapore politics.

Many Singaporeans have a stereotyped understanding and misinformed impressions of the party. I share a few of the many personal experiences that convinced me as to why I should write this book.

During one of our house visits between 2015 and 2020, I chanced upon a father and his two sons, then studying in a primary school, outside the Marine Parade Public Library. I chatted with the father for a while. By chance, I met the same person a week later at a business event. He told me that after our group had left, one of his sons had asked him who we were. He told his son that we were from the Workers' Party, an opposition party. His son asked him, "Then why are you talking to them? They are from the opposition. They are bad people."

Ouch. The gentleman quickly added that he corrected his sons that being in opposition does not mean bad. Having an opposition is part of the democratic process, where parties contest for the right to represent the people through elections. Thankfully, that gentleman was enlightened.

Another person, a friend who had actively helped in my 2011 and 2015 general election campaigns, told me that her son, then in the Gifted Education Programme, was once asked to write an essay on a local politician they admired. Of all people, her son chose to write about me. I had spoken to him during the election and he had even attended two of our rallies. The teacher asked the boy to rewrite his essay, because Yee Jenn Jong had failed to win in the general election. Therefore, he was not a real politician.

The boy, then just 11 years old, refused to rewrite and argued his reasons on why I should be considered as a politician. The teacher relented and allowed his essay.

In the "Class Notes" project that former *The Straits Times* journalist Bertha Henson started with undergraduate journalism students prior to the 2020 general election (GE2020), one of the writers Ethan Tay wrote a piece titled "I've never liked the Workers' Party".[1] In his work, he described the youthful perceptions that he had formed of the WP — that we were out to find faults all the time with the government and that we even bullied the PAP to prevent them from doing their work. His perceptions changed when he was tasked to follow our activities and report about our work. After weeks of following the WP at first hand, the concluding remarks of his piece read as follows:

> *"This WP I know now is nothing like the party I watched on television screens. They seem to have a quiet humility, taking knocks as they come, like the saga over the town council finances which looks like it will be dragged out through the coming general election.*
>
> *…*
>
> *They say you should never judge a book by its cover, or that the proof of the pudding is in the eating. Likewise, I've learnt not to form my judgement based on just what the media brought to light.*
>
> *My youthful perceptions of the opposition have changed. I actually have some admiration for them now."*

After GE2020, I had breakfast with former Nominated Member of Parliament (NMP) Nicholas Fang. He shared that an acquaintance had told him during the campaigning how good he thought Jamus Lim, a new WP member who was part of the team that won Sengkang GRC, was, yet in the same breath also asked what was the difference between an SMC and GRC. His friend had supported the WP without understanding much about even the basics of Singapore's political

---

1  Ethan Tay, "I've never liked the Workers' Party", Class Notes, March 29, 2020, https://www.ourclassnotes.com/post/i-ve-never-liked-the-workers-party

system. I replied that I have seen supporters who supported us without question and even treated opposition candidates like heroes. However, I added that I had also encountered many who would similarly support the PAP without any understanding of our political system as well, and viewed all opposition candidates as troublemakers without even attempting to find out more. We agreed that Singapore can benefit from greater political awareness.

I hope this book can help to achieve a better understanding of what it is like in the alternative camp. They say that history is written by the victors. Inside and outside of Parliament, I had called for more meaningful political education for our youth. A common version of political education is what the winners want you to know. I hope this book can give readers a glimpse of what it is like to be an opposition politician, regardless of whether we win elections or not. I hope this book can open up Singaporeans' understanding of the role of alternative voices and why we need to build strong alternatives to have a more resilient democratic system.

I shall attempt to present the WP members as I know them, even with their shortcomings, as all humans have.

I wish to thank Andrew Fong for linking me to Chua Hong Koon of World Scientific Publishing. It started with a casual meet up with Andrew after GE2020. I had met Hong Koon before, when he was with another publisher. During 2013–2014, I had written an earlier book that was a compilation of my popular blog pieces and speeches. Although I explored options of publishing that book, I was personally not completely satisfied with the content, so I decided to abandon the project.

When the outline of this book was accepted, I wrote non-stop for three weeks to produce the first draft of all 10 chapters. Many thanks to the professional team at World Scientific for bearing with the many changes I had to make along the way. A big thank you to Yap Keng Ann, a faithful volunteer since 2011, who had diligently kept many of the photographs of our campaigns. I did not even know he had been storing stuff somewhere on a cloud storage over the many years. I also wish to thank Tan Ke-Yang for the photograph of my speech at Temasek Junior College, and the photographs of the WP rally in Simei during the 2015 general election.

I wish to thank Professor Kenneth Paul Tan, Loke Hoe Yeong, Elgin Toh, and others for their many helpful comments on earlier drafts. Nevertheless, any shortcomings or errors in the book are mine.

I also wish to thank Shirley Soh, an art lecturer from LASALLE College of the Arts, for her advice when I suggested that I wanted to paint an abstract piece for this book. Many thanks to Chen Yi Quan for working with me on my artistic interpretation of 'Journey in Blue', and my daughter Grace Yee for the doodle of this journey. I have included various art pieces relevant to my journey in this book as well.

All my net proceeds from the sale of this book will go towards the community causes that I have initiated and still continue to support. Some of these causes include the food distribution programmes that are described in this book.

I write this book for all the wonderful people who had partnered alongside me in this unexpected journey in blue. Many volunteers served without any expectations of rewards. I was privileged to have committed comrades in Parliament together with me. I write this book for my closest family members, especially my father and my wife, both of whom had initially strongly objected to me taking this journey, but have since transformed to become my strongest supporters.

**Yee Jenn Jong**
August 2020

# Contents

**Foreword** ................................................................................................ xiii

**Preface** .................................................................................................. xvi

**Part 1: Journey Before Blue**

**Chapter 1.** Life Before Blue ........................................................................ 4
My Early Years ........................................................................................... 4
Growing Up in Singapore ............................................................................. 6
For College, For Nation ............................................................................... 7
Defending Singapore and the People's Action Party ........................................ 9
A Politics Too Extreme ............................................................................... 11

**Chapter 2.** Taking the Leap ....................................................................... 13
An Active Interest in Policies and National Events ........................................ 13
The First Move .......................................................................................... 19
Fears and Objections .................................................................................. 24

**Part 2: Journey in Blue**

**Chapter 3.** The Battle for Joo Chiat ............................................................ 32
Overcoming the Unsteady First Steps .......................................................... 32
Nomination Day ........................................................................................ 37
Developing and Delivering My Message ...................................................... 41
Engaging the Press ..................................................................................... 46
Polling Night ............................................................................................. 50

**Chapter 4.** Parliament .............................................................................. 55
The Non-constituency Member of Parliament Position ................................. 55
Baptism of Fire .......................................................................................... 57
Policy Work .............................................................................................. 59
Pushing Early Childhood Issues via Parliamentary Processes ......................... 64
Pressing Issues via Parliament ..................................................................... 77
The Population Blue Paper That Nearly Was Not to Be ................................ 89
Fireworks in Parliament ............................................................................. 93
Farewell to Parliament ............................................................................... 103
Leader of the Opposition .......................................................................... 106

xxi

**Chapter 5.** Engaging the Community ... 113
Workers' Party on House Visits! ... 113
Aljunied-Hougang-Punggol East
Grassroots Events and Outreach ... 119
Meet-The-People Sessions ... 122
Bricks in Blue ... 128

**Chapter 6.** The Battle for Marine Parade GRC ... 133
A Disappointing Electoral Boundaries Review Committee
Report ... 133
Assembling the Team ... 137
The WP's Way ... 142
The Campaign ... 146
Analysis of the GE2015 Results ... 150
Responding to an Attack by *The Straits Times* ... 153

**Chapter 7.** The Second Battle for Marine Parade GRC ... 157
After the 2015 General Election ... 157
A COVID-19 General Election ... 160
Making the Most of Limited Ground Campaigning ... 162
Analysis of the GE2020 Results ... 166

**Chapter 8.** A Peek into the Workers' Party ... 174
Leadership and Structure ... 174
Powered by Volunteers and Members ... 179
Retail Politics ... 183
The By-elections of Hougang and Punggol East ... 190
Leadership Renewal ... 202
Myths, Perceptions, and Questions about the Opposition ... 207

**Part 3: Reflections**

**Chapter 9.** Whither Singapore? ... 218
Sharing the Field? ... 218
The 2011 and 2017 Presidential Elections ... 224
Political Education ... 237
Political Office ... 243
Opposition Unity ... 250
A United Singapore ... 253

**Chapter 10.** Concluding Words ... 258

# Part 1

# Journey Before Blue

# Chapter 1
# Life Before Blue

## My Early Years

I am the third child in my family; my elder brother and sister are two and four years older than me, respectively. My parents were Chinese language teachers. Life was not easy for them as teachers' pay was quite low. My father came from Gopeng in Perak, Malaysia, and my mother came from Muar in Johor, Malaysia. Both had come to Singapore even before Singapore's independence. They came looking for jobs as teachers and met each other in the then Teachers Training College, now known as the National Institute of Education.

My parents had difficulties looking after two young toddlers, my elder siblings, while coping with their jobs. It was the 1960s, a difficult time for Singapore in terms of economic opportunities and occasional race-related riots. As such, when I was born just a few months before Singapore's independence in 1965, my parents made the difficult decision to send me to my paternal grandparents in Gopeng. My grandparents were happy to take me in. I spent the first two years of my life in Gopeng, a sleepy town about 20 kilometres south of Ipoh, a tin mining town that was losing its importance with the decline of the tin mining trade.

I was too young to remember much. I could have been quite well liked in the neighbourhood because whenever I returned to Gopeng, even in my early adult years, many neighbours still remembered me fondly. It was also in Gopeng where I picked up Cantonese from my grandparents.

I was born with a hole in the heart, a condition known as ventricular septal defect. The hole is in the wall (septum) that separates the heart's lower chambers (ventricles). This defect allows oxygen-rich blood to leak into the oxygen-poor blood chambers in the heart. My heart has to work harder than a normal healthy person to get oxygen to the rest of my body. As a result, I could not participate in vigorous activities as I would become breathless faster than others.

The defect was found after I had gone to Gopeng. I had to travel back to Singapore from time to time for medical check-ups. The doctors did not recommend any operation, because it would have to be an open-heart surgery and the risk of something going wrong then was quite high. For much of my life, this defect has not bothered me. I have been a relatively active person since birth. Although I was not allowed to take part in physical education (PE) classes, I loved to play football and run around in school during recess time and after school until I became too breathless. Once, in Primary Six, a temporary teacher took over the PE class and selected runners for the school's sports day. I took part in the selection race for 100 metres and was shortlisted for further training. I returned home and proudly told my father, only to have him scold me instead. My track and field career ended as quickly as it had started.

My earliest childhood recollection was when I was brought home from Gopeng to stay with my parents in their house in Opera Estate in Siglap — the first and only house they had ever owned. My father told me that his in-laws had advised him not to keep paying rent when they were previously living in a rental place as they should get a permanent house, especially since my mother was expecting my elder sister. So they invested in a small terrace house in a new part of Singapore at that time. Back then, directly behind our house, Chai Chee was still a *kampong* (traditional village) with pig and vegetable farms. The Housing and Development Board had not even been formed then.

For some reason, even though I was only about two years old, I vividly remember stepping into the house with its cement floor and spartan furniture. I recall my parents telling me that this would now be my permanent home and I had to get along well with my brother and sister.

## Growing Up in Singapore

And Singapore did indeed become my home, where I lived, played, studied, and worked.

I grew up in a Singapore that suddenly became an independent country, no longer a part of Malaysia. My parents were Chinese teachers in Chinese schools that were then the hotbed of so-called communist or socialist activities. Politics was a taboo topic for my parents. They had seen their colleagues lose their jobs or even detained. The first time I knew how my parents voted was in the 2011 general election, when I was a candidate in the constituency where they lived!

Life was quite frugal when I was young. There was the mortgage to pay and five mouths (later six when my younger brother came along) to feed in the family. Once in a long while, we would be treated to a visit to the *pasar malam* (night market) that was nearby, or to the movies.

Kindergarten for me was first at Kong Hwa School, where my mother was teaching. Later, I was transferred to the kindergarten at the Church of Our Lady of Perpetual Succour near our house because my father had learnt that English was to be the main language medium in Singapore. My parents could not teach us English, so the next best option would be to send my brothers and me to English schools. The nearest was St Stephen's School, which was where my primary education took place. My sister had already started school at Kong Hwa School, so she attended Chinese-medium schools all the way till college, whereas the rest of us went to mission schools where English was the main medium of instruction.

Although always active, I was a relatively good student and stayed in the top classes throughout primary and secondary schools. I joined the St John's Ambulance Brigade in secondary school because I had mistaken that it was compulsory to join a uniformed group. Being small in physique and with a medical condition, I thought joining the least vigorous uniformed group would be better for me.

I never expected much from my extra-curricular activities (ECAs, today renamed as co-curricular activities or CCAs) because there always seemed to be stronger, better, and more confident peers than me. I was one of the smallest in class and in my ECA. Somehow, I passed my first non-commissioned officer course in Secondary Two despite failing badly and scoring the lowest in my marching and commanding the squad as I had scored very well in all my written papers. That began my accidental path towards leadership positions. Each year, I was promoted due to my good scores in written tests. I rose to become Sergeant in the St John's Ambulance Brigade in St Patrick's School. It was my first taste of a leadership position.

## For College, For Nation

For my tertiary education, I enrolled in Temasek Junior College, just a 10-minute walk from my house. The motto of the school was, and still is, "For College, For Nation". The greater freedom I experienced in college and my unwillingness to reject friends led me to join one ECA after another. Soon I found myself taking part in four ECAs, including being the president of the Computer Club. I joined my classmates who wanted to run for council elections and was voted into the 6th Students' Council, my fifth ECA. I took part in various competitions at the college and national levels and even won the college first-aid competition and a national team programming competition.

For many people, junior college (JC) is a short two years of their life and oftentimes not memorable. For me, JC was the time I opened up and developed greater confidence in myself. It shaped many of my perspectives in life and led me to champion for education, which is what I have been actively advocating both in work and later in Parliament. My enjoyable two years in college inspired me to give back by volunteering to serve after I had started work, first as president of the College Alumni and later concurrently as member of the College Advisory Board.

Beyond school, I was actively serving in many areas in church during my teenage years and early adulthood. When I was in National Service (NS), I volunteered to be an officer with the St John's Ambulance Brigade, where I spent a great part of my weekends outside of NS doing training or events for the Brigade. Later, it was an active four years of hostel life at Raffles Hall at the National University of Singapore (NUS) and in the Boys' Brigade, as well as a host of involvements in various committees following my graduation.

Due to my medical condition, my vocation in NS was as a clerk in the Systems and Computer Organisation (SCO), which later became part of today's Defence Science and Technology Agency. One month into a boring clerical routine, I was given an opportunity. SCO had ordered a laboratory full of microcomputers but there was no one assigned to manage them. I was given a challenge: within five days, I was to figure out how to use a plotter device that was lying around. I managed to complete an impressive report detailing its useful functions with beautiful charts produced with the plotter in a far shorter time than allocated. Although still officially designated as a clerk, I was given a new job function within SCO. I ran the computer laboratory for a year, training officers and soldiers on how to use computer applications. When SCO needed programmers for the microcomputers they had purchased, I was roped in to become a programmer and systems analyst, continuing in this role for the remainder of my NS. It was an interesting two and a half years of NS in the early days of the Singapore Armed Forces' computerisation efforts.

My entire education took place in Singapore. After I had graduated with a Computer Science degree from NUS, I became a tutor there while continuing my postgraduate studies. I was a Doctor of Philosophy (PhD) student at NUS, but I found that I was more interested in the business world. So I left NUS midway through my PhD candidature to join the then Trade Development Board (Enterprise Singapore today) and pursued a Master of Business Administration with the Nanyang Business School in the Nanyang Technological University.

I share these experiences because I observe that today, our education system is so fixated on grades, with parents pushing their children for top grades. In this new age of the Fourth Industrial Revolution, our education cannot solely be about grades. Education has to develop the child holistically and provide students with the opportunities to become resilient and adaptable. Good results are important, but more important than that is to develop confidence in the child. My parents, being teachers, pushed me in my earlier years to study hard. I would be punished if I did badly in spelling or in my tests, so that became my motivation to study initially. I eventually made it through university on an Oversea-Chinese Banking Corporation scholarship. However, it was my active involvement from my schooling years that led me to serve in various voluntary roles, often concurrently. Being involved in the community and special interest groups gave me the confidence later to embark on launching my own start-up, and to eventually join politics. Those who knew me in my earlier years in primary and secondary school were surprised that I had transformed from being a timid person to one willing to step into the fire of opposition politics.

### Defending Singapore and the People's Action Party

When I was working for NUS in 1992, I was sent to Tokyo on a work trip to present a research paper I had written for a seminar. One evening while in Tokyo, I met an elderly American man in the hotel lobby. He had worked and lived in Singapore in the 1980s. After finding out that I was from Singapore, he declared that Singapore was no different from North Korea: we were brainwashed by propaganda and Lee Kuan Yew, the first Prime Minister of Singapore, was ensuring a family succession like in North Korea.

I found myself defending Singapore against his allegations. I insisted we have free elections and that although Lee Hsien Loong is the son of our founding Prime Minister and even if he was to be the future Prime Minister, it would be by a fair process within the ruling political party.

We parted that evening, he more convinced that Singapore had brainwashed our people, and I convinced that he was just the typical proud American who wanted their system of democracy imposed on every country in the world.

Growing up in Singapore, I had been through our brand of National Education and was exposed mainly to our state-owned media. When the alleged 'Marxist Conspiracy' arrests took place in 1987, I was still a university undergraduate. Also known as Operation Spectrum, 16 individuals were arrested under the Internal Security Act and detained without trial. They were accused of using communist ideas to go against the government. I was apathetic to the arrests and took the government's stand at face value. Like most Singaporeans, I had gleaned my news from the mainstream media and did not investigate any further. It was only after I had joined the Workers' Party that I got to know and speak to people who were detained under the so-called Marxist Conspiracy and listened first-hand to their viewpoints. They may be socialist in their beliefs but none of those I had met sounded like they had any Marxist or subversive agenda to push.

I recall voting for the People's Action Party (PAP) in my first general election when I had come of age. I based my vote on the strength of what the government had achieved economically for Singapore. I had great respect for our first-generation leaders for having transformed Singapore. Also, there was not much to choose from among the opposition candidates at that time. The qualifications of those candidates were usually far from those of the PAP's, the latter who would generally be the incumbents with track records to show.

## A Politics Too Extreme

I was becoming increasingly uncomfortable with the way key members of the opposition were treated. I disliked the rough treatment of J. B. Jeyaratnam, Francis Seow, Tang Liang Hong, and others after each general election. Even though I was still inclined towards the PAP for their track record, I would cheer when I saw good opposition candidates doing well or when they had won. I admired the guts of the voters in Anson, Hougang, and Potong Pasir for defying the ruling party and was envious that they had good candidates to choose from.

I felt that the PAP's policy of upgrading housing for votes was extreme. Intellectually, I could not support it. It was a blatant use of taxpayers' monies to further a political party's goals. I had supported the PAP for how they had transformed Singapore economically, but I found it increasingly difficult to vote for any party that uses undemocratic means to entrench themselves in power. In fact, I felt so strongly over this that in the 2006 general election, I wrote in the forum pages of *The Straits Times* to argue for this policy to be stopped. Then Minister for National Development, Mah Bow Tan, gave what was a typical and unsatisfactory reply. The summary of this letter can be found in the next chapter.

I was also uncomfortable with the way our democratic processes were manipulated through the Group Representation Constituency (GRC) system. A GRC is a type of electoral division or constituency in Singapore that is represented by a team of multiracial candidates, rather than by a single candidate in a Single Member Constituency (SMC). It was started in 1988 as a way to ensure minority race representation but grew to become an obvious gerrymandering strategy.

As a voter, my frustration was that I often found it difficult to vote for someone on the alternative slate if I was not confident to see the person running the constituency or governing Singapore. As I spent more time abroad and read more widely, I began to understand how different political systems functioned. I became unconvinced that only the PAP could have the A-team and that Singapore is good only for one team. As an entrepreneur, I believe that in business, we need competition to force dominant companies to stay innovative and to be tuned to consumers' needs. So too in politics. We need to have credible competition for the PAP. I believed that Singapore has enough talent for more than one team. Given the way that the PAP had decimated the opposition and injected fear into the system, it might take a long time before capable people can overcome the fear factor to step forward.

# Chapter 2
# Taking the Leap

## An Active Interest in Policies and National Events

I found that I love to write, and could write relatively well. My first published letter in the forum pages of *The Straits Times* was in 1993, when I was frustrated that the challenger to the late Ong Teng Cheong, former Second Deputy Prime Minister, in our first presidential election seemed like a highly reluctant candidate.

My letter argued that the late Chua Kim Yeow, Singapore's first accountant-general, needed to be convinced himself that he was the best person for the job. He had instead said that Ong was "a far superior candidate" and that he was persuaded by the late Goh Keng Swee, former Second Deputy Prime Minister, and Richard Hu, former Minister for Finance, to take part in the contest. I had felt disappointed with his lack of effort and urged him to have more drive.

The day after my letter was published, *The New Paper* reported on my letter and several other writers followed suit in the forum to similarly urge Chua to put up a more serious fight. He did, and that must have prompted some alarm in the government because on polling day itself, *The Straits Times* published an editorial by a senior writer giving his take on why he would vote for Ong. Ong won as expected, but the score probably worried the People's Action Party (PAP) as the winning margin was not impressive.

I was then a *Time* magazine subscriber and even had two letters published by the magazine, written under my pen name, Jeremiah Yee.

I wrote extensively to the forum pages of the *Today* newspaper and *The Straits Times*. Back in those days, there was no social media. Writing to the forum pages was my avenue for expressing my views and pushing for change.

Some of the later letters I had written before becoming a parliamentarian are summarised below. After I had entered Parliament, it was better that I use Parliament, party platforms, and social media to make my proposals. Hence, my writings to the forum pages became much fewer. In Parliament, I continued to pursue the issues I had raised in the forum pages, especially those which I felt had not received a serious response.

1. **The Straits Times (ST) Forum June 16, 2006: Strong case to upgrade opposition wards**

    In this letter, I had expressed surprise and disappointment with then National Development Minister Mah Bow Tan (ST, June 11, 2006: "Upgrading for all wards, but PAP ones first") over the government's change of tone to this divisive and short-sighted policy. Earlier, Senior Minister Goh Chok Tong had said that the government could consider if a request for funds was submitted by Hougang member of parliament (MP)-elect Low Thia Khiang.

    I reminded the government of its promise that by 2015, all constituencies would be upgraded and hence the upgrading-for-vote strategy would soon start to work against the PAP. Already in the 2001 general election, upgrading had proven to be not an important issue, as evidenced by the results in Hougang and Potong Pasir — two single member constituencies (SMC) where the opposition had won. Ground feedback seemed to show that it was costing the PAP votes, even in other constituencies, as it was seen as an unfair use of the nation's resources.

    Mah later replied to four people together — Chua Mui Hoong, Basant Kapur, Sylvia Lim, and me via *The Straits Times* Forum (ST, June 17, 2006: "Upgrading is a unique programme by

Government"). Chua had written a commentary in *The Straits Times* while Kapur, Lim, and I had written to the forum pages, all of us urging the PAP to rethink their votes for upgrading policy. His reply was that upgrading is over and above the basic obligations of the government, funded by budget surpluses. Given limited resources, it had to prioritise upgrading to those in PAP constituencies.

2. **ST Forum May 18, 2010: Death of Goh Keng Swee**

   In the letter, I shared my surprise that my children, who were then still schooling, did not know who Goh Keng Swee was. Neither did they know who S. Rajaratnam was when he died in 2006. I suggested that current affairs and political education in school should be better covered in schools.

3. **TODAY Voices July 6, 2010: Why not liven up MRT cabins legally?**

   I wrote in response to the Mass Rapid Transit (MRT) graffiti incident where two individuals had vandalised and spray-painted a train. While the breach of security could not be tolerated, I urged the authorities to find ways to allow street art in an organised manner. This would make Singapore more interesting and creative, like the colourful street art in some global cities.

4. **ST Forum August 14, 2010: Don't tie down talent**

   I responded to then Minister-in-charge of Entrepreneurship, Lee Yi Shyan, to share my thoughts on the issues Singapore faced in promoting entrepreneurship. I pointed out that one of the problems was that we did not have the right culture for Singaporeans to be entrepreneurs and for entrepreneurs to be creative and globally competitive. I went on to list various reasons and approaches the government could take if we wanted to seriously develop an entrepreneurial Singapore.

On the same theme of entrepreneurship, in 2004, I had responded to then Senior Minister Lee Kuan Yew on his idea of releasing civil service scholars into the workforce as entrepreneurs (ST Forum June 15, 2004: "Entrepreneurs from public sector: Quality, not quantity"). A section from the letter is reproduced below:

*"My fear is that in its enthusiasm to meet SM Lee's objective of sending up to half of its scholars into the private sector as entrepreneurs, the public sector will create mini government-linked companies.*

*Reluctant scholars may be pushed into starting businesses tied to the apron strings of these organisations and be given easy contracts to get their businesses started.*

*Singapore would have created many entrepreneurs but of the wrong type. They would not succeed outside Singapore, or even in Singapore without support."*

5. **ST Forum 10 March 2011: Level the playing field for private and voluntary welfare organisation (VWO) preschools**

    I responded to then Minister of State for Education Masagos Zulkifli, who had said a planned $290 million investment by the government in the preschool sector would help keep preschool fees affordable, and contribute to upgrading centres and programmes.

    I pointed out a huge disparity in government support for the then two anchor childcare operators, National Trades Union Congress (NTUC) and PAP Community Foundation (PCF), with that of their support for other VWO or privately owned centres. I argued for a change in the government's mindset and policy in how they should support the preschool sector. (Preschools later became an issue that I pushed very hard for when I entered Parliament, a few months after this forum letter was published.)

Besides writing to forum pages, I was invited to participate in two government policy committees. The first was in the mid-2000s when the company I had founded, ASKnLearn, was active in providing information and communication technology (ICT) education to students. The then Infocomm Development Authority had wanted to stem the declining interest in computer science studies by students and had set up a national infocomm education workgroup. Over the one-year period that I was on the committee, we looked at various ways to promote ICT education to school-age students. After the recommendations were made, my company continued to be an even more active participant in ICT education in schools.

From 2007–2009, I was a member of the REACH policy workgroup on Education and Human Resource. REACH is the official Singapore Government feedback unit. It was a committee consisting of education professionals from both the private and government sectors.

The scope of the work of the REACH committee was very wide. I recall that at the first meeting, we were deliberating on which aspect of education or human resource development we should focus on during our term. Many ideas were bounced about. One topic was early childhood, and I shared a story. My wife had recently unexpectedly met an ex-senior teacher of a childcare centre we were previously operating. The teacher had more than 10 years of experience in childcare and had attained the Diploma in Leadership, qualifying her to be the principal of a centre. However, she instead chose to enter the masseur trade. Her starting basic pay was higher than her last drawn salary as a senior teacher.

Christine Chen, founder president of the Association for Child Care Educators and then president of the Association for Early Childhood Educators, who was also part of the committee, with many more years of experience in the early childhood industry than me, affirmed my experience with more stories about how poorly supported the industry was at that time. Many teachers and principals were leaving the profession. It was difficult to hire good locals.

I enjoyed my time working with this dynamic group of very experienced individuals. REACH provided secretarial support. We had access to high-level civil servants and even political office-bearers. We interviewed those from the kindergarten and childcare sectors, from those at the operating level to the top policymakers. We made several bold policy proposals which we believed were sorely needed at that time. These included having one government agency to oversee both childcare and kindergartens and having the Ministry of Education run some kindergartens and offer better funding support to make the industry a viable career for locals. All the difficult, but I felt necessary, reforms were turned down. We were granted a closed-door meeting with a senior policymaker before our paper was published for them to explain why the ministry could not accept most of our proposals.

For the record, post-2011 general election (GE2011), many reforms were made to government policies. The preschool sector was one that was reformed. Our proposals were then all fulfilled, some in slightly different forms. What had earlier been rejected with explanations as to why they were difficult to be executed could actually be done when there was a will to do it and a commitment to allocate resources.

In the course of my work as an education entrepreneur, I dealt with policymakers as well as those executing policies on the ground. My experiences serving in the policy committees and in private conversations with policymakers left me convinced that Singapore had become too cosy, that those at the top had become risk-averse. This would not augur well for Singapore at a time when we needed to be nimble and bold. I felt that only strong competition would make the government listen more closely to real issues on the ground.

## The First Move

I had sold ASKnLearn, the company which I had founded, and left it in 2009. Ninety percent of our business had been with the government. I felt that I could only watch politics from the sidelines when I was running a business with nearly 150 employees, whose jobs were dependent on the government sector for business, and with other shareholders to whom the company was accountable.

Even though I was interested in the alternative camp, I did not personally know anyone active in the opposition parties. Also, there were only two political parties then that matched my moderate views of opposition politics and were structured to be able to push the PAP in the elections. The PAP would only take the competition seriously when the opposition is able to push them where it matters the most, i.e., in winning seats in Parliament. I only considered the Workers' Party (WP) and the Singapore People's Party (SPP). I decided against the SPP as it was not clear to me what the transition would be like after its chief, long-time MP Chiam See Tong, whose health was already declining, stepped down.

I felt that the WP seemed to have a better plan at developing itself beyond the key person and then-only elected MP, Low Thia Khiang. In 2006, some of the candidates had credible professional credentials. I was also quite impressed with how the party took the aggressive hitting and baiting over the James Gomez incident and came out of it stronger. Gomez, a former WP member, had accused the Elections Department of losing his minority-race candidate's application form during the 2006 general election. This turned out to be a false accusation after closed-circuit television footage showed that he had instead placed the form in his briefcase. He, together with Low and Sylvia Lim, was questioned by the police but eventually let off with a stern warning. The leadership seemed to be disciplined enough to avoid being trapped by the PAP and landing candidates into future troubles. Publishing its manifesto detailing the party's stand on key policy areas also gave me clarity as to whether I subscribed to their stand.

The only person I knew in opposition politics was Tan Tee Seng, whom I had met through my business dealings. I did not even know back then that he was one of those detained in 1987 under the alleged Marxist Conspiracy, until he surfaced as chairman of the Reform Party at the end of 2010 and I had read about it in the news. Over the few years that I had known him, he had never even talked about politics with me. Tan did text to ask me to join the Reform Party after he became its chairman, but I was not interested.

For me, it was either the WP or nothing.

I contemplated writing to the party many times but hesitated because there was so much that I did not know about them or what it might imply if I became active or even a future candidate. As GE2011 drew nearer with more and more media reports, I became increasingly interested but stopped short whenever I started to write something.

Finally, on February 24, 2011, the Electoral Boundaries Review Committee (EBRC) report was published. Joo Chiat was left as an SMC. I had lived in, or just at the boundaries of, the SMC my whole life. I felt confident that I knew how voters in the almost-entirely private estate might be persuaded and how to manage the campaign if I were the candidate for the opposition. Still, it was a tall order on how to approach the WP so late in the game.

On the morning of February 25, 2011 as I read the coverage of the EBRC report in the news, I hesitated no more. I whipped up a self-introductory email and sent it to Low Thia Khiang and Sylvia Lim, the then secretary-general and chairman of the WP, respectively. They were the two most prominent faces of the party at that time and their emails were publicly available on the WP website.

As I had expected, nothing happened. It was the Budget period and nearing the general election. Both Low and Lim would have been too busy and they must have had other emails from random people like myself introducing themselves out of the blue. Why should they even be interested in me, even if I had some decent professional credentials.

I am an entrepreneur. Instinctively, we know we have to make things happen rather than to wait for things to happen. I had waited far too long to make my approach. Any delay would mean that it would be too late for anything to happen for me in GE2011.

So, on the evening of Saturday, February 26, 2011, I texted Tan Tee Seng and asked if he knew anyone in a senior position in the WP whom I could contact directly. He suggested then Treasurer Eric Tan. I forwarded the email I had written to the WP to Tan Tee Seng, who passed it to Eric Tan, along with my mobile phone number.

I received a call from Eric Tan that same evening and he arranged to meet me on Monday, February 28. My wife was around when he called. Only then did I tell that I had written to the WP. She replied, "Ha ha. That's a good joke." I showed her the email and her expression changed.

She joined me, her crazy husband, for breakfast with Eric Tan at the Holland Village hawker centre on the following Monday. We got down to business almost right away, introducing myself and talking about politics. I indicated that I was willing to help and be considered as a candidate, particularly for Joo Chiat SMC. It was a good and long conversation. We found that we knew common people. His uncle was the late Robert Tan, former principal of Temasek Junior College. I was president of the alumni when Robert Tan was principal of the College.

### Journey Before Blue

I felt sure that given my sudden introduction to the party and the short time leading up to GE2011, the WP would want to do all sorts of rapid checks on me. Eric Tan did exactly that. He told me some time later that soon after our meeting, he spoke with his uncle, who had only nice things to say about me.

Shortly later, I received an email from the late Jane Leong, a WP Central Executive Committee member and trusted close aide to Low. As it turned out, she also knew many from the so-called Marxist Conspiracy group including Tan Tee Seng and his wife. I was certain that she, too, and others were checking on my background. It helped that I had some public profile then, having been featured in news articles a number of times for my business-related matters and my constant writing to the forum pages.

I was invited to meet with Low that same Wednesday, and my wife joined me. She still could not quite believe how fast matters had moved since Saturday. It was past 10 pm as we waited until he finished his last case of his regular Meet-The-People Session and we talked for some 40 minutes.

For the first time, I was meeting face-to-face with someone for whom I had cheered from afar in 1991 when he first won Hougang SMC. Here was someone whom I had followed in the way he discharged his constituency and parliamentary duties and held on to the SMC one general election after another despite all sorts of challenges like upgrading for votes and votes lobbying by top PAP leaders.

There were no airs. Just a humble man doing what he believed he needed to do for Singapore. He must have had a long day, yet he still had the energy and sharpness of mind as he engaged with us. The meeting was very casual, at the void deck of Block 310 in Hougang. I asked about his motivations to be in politics and he asked me to read the article, "Overcoming the Deafening Silence" written by Nanyang Technological University student reporters in 2009. That same night after I went home,

I found that the article was a good read. In the article, Low described his frustrations regarding various issues with the PAP government in his younger days and with the one-sided nature of reporting that silenced public opinions. He wanted to make a change in society despite knowing the uphill challenges he would face. These sentiments resonated with me. I believed Low sensed my wife's great apprehension and also my dilemma of wanting to step forward yet being afraid. Too many things had happened to some members of the opposition in the past. I did not want anything unforeseen to happen to my family or myself.

Meanwhile, with GE2011 likely to be called soon, I was asked to join the East Coast team and help with campaigning. That was welcomed because I had no clue what campaigning was like. I wore the closest blue I could find to the WP's colour and joined in for about a week in various parts of Simei and in the private housing areas in Changi. Everything felt strange to me.

Within two weeks, I was told that the party was prepared to field me as candidate for Joo Chiat SMC, given my knowledge of the place. I found out much later from Eric Tan that the party was expecting Joo Chiat SMC to be merged into Marine Parade Group Representation Constituency (GRC), so they were focusing more on East Coast GRC post-2006. Only one visit was made since the last general election to Joo Chiat SMC. When the EBRC report was published, my letter was also sent out to the party the next day and I then quickly barged my way in. I believe that if I had waited a few more days, Joo Chiat SMC would have been allocated to another person and it would have been difficult for the party to allow me in.

This was in 2011. I was rather surprised myself at the speed in which I came to be offered the candidacy. Given where the party is today, anyone trying to get in at such short notice would definitely not be successful. In 2011, the party was growing and taking on more areas to contest. Finding suitable candidates was still a challenge then. It helped that several senior members of the party knew people who knew me, and they could quickly verify my motivations and suitability. My meetings with Eric Tan and later with Low also paved the way for the accelerated passage.

In 2011, others also tried to approach the WP close to GE2011 about the same time that I did. Eric Tan told me that an entire group leaving the Reform Party had wanted to join the WP. There were several of candidate calibre among them. I was told that the deal they had offered was to come in as an entire group or not at all. Knowing Low, that was surely a non-starter for bargaining with the WP. I was also told that others tried to join but positioned themselves as heroes for the opposition movement. That was another non-starter with the WP. The WP that Low had sought to build up after taking over as secretary-general in 2001 was to build up the party as a team. In politics, there will always be people believing that their ways will save the opposition cause. Low knew that personality politics would divide the party. He would rather pass up on such people, even if they had strong professional credentials, than to risk breaking up the party because of those driving the party in different directions. Low was a strict disciplinarian, as I found out later in my journey in blue.

## Fears and Objections

I was offered the candidacy in quick time, but accepting it was far from smooth sailing.

My wife was totally unprepared for this. I had misjudged her willingness to be involved. We had done quite a lot of crazy and risky things as a couple. We left our jobs and started ASKnLearn in 1999 when our youngest and third child was just a few months old and our two daughters were still in preschool. We sank our entire savings into a risky start-up. I figured that if anyone could take risks, she would be the one.

Although I would sometimes talk about politics with her in the past, it was always about others or about some policies which I did not agree with. I was busy with my business till 2009. Even after 2009, I started other ventures but on a smaller scale. I did not imagine that I would end up as a candidate for an opposition party, so I had never broached this subject with my wife. As an entrepreneur, I knew that if I never tested anything, I would never know if it was possible. My approach in February 2011 was to reach out and understand what it was like inside the WP. Of course, I was hopeful that perhaps they might need someone like me whom I felt fitted the profile for Joo Chiat SMC. Then, everything happened too fast.

I told her that the WP had offered me the candidacy. I was totally unprepared for her response. It was more than just a simple "No". The emotions were too strong for me to describe in this book. The fears which the PAP had instilled in ordinary people about what could potentially happen to them if they contested against the PAP was so real. I was stuck. I had pitched myself so well to the party and got myself the position I had wanted. My wife refused to give me her blessings, which would have meant that I had to embarrassingly turn down the party. I tried unsuccessfully for several days to sell the idea to her.

The clock was ticking away. Eric Tan had given me an ultimatum from the party to accept by a certain date as there were other candidates to whom they could offer the position.

I tried one final move. I knew my mother-in-law was a staunch supporter of Lee Kuan Yew. I told my wife that she might want to let her mother know and see what she had to say. It was the only card I had left to play. I did not know what the response would be. The next day, my wife told me to go ahead. Her mother had told her that if this was what I had wanted, it would be good for her to support me. Although my mother-in-law continued to firmly support the PAP, she also understood that it was important for my wife to stand alongside with me.

I struck while the iron was hot in case my wife changed her mind. I immediately returned my form to join as a member of the WP. I also arranged to discuss with the party how I should commence my campaigning in the SMC. I will describe that journey in the next chapter.

I thought I should also let my parents know as they had always been so cautious about politics, having lived through the turbulent years when socialist and communist activities were rife. I wanted to wait a bit longer till I had started campaigning as I did not want them to make me change my mind.

So, after I had commenced some quiet house visits and before I was to be officially introduced to the public for the first time, I told my parents that I would be contesting in the upcoming general election. My father's first response was, "So the PAP invited you?" I told him I was to be the WP's candidate and that I would be contesting where they were living.

His response was strangely a very muted "Ok." I even asked if he could be an assentor for me on nomination day, which he did not object to. All candidates need at least six voters residing in the constituency to be assentors on nomination day.

After my conversation with my father, I was introduced to the public that same Sunday, April 3, 2011, following a visit to a market at Yishun. A few candidates-to-be and I sat with Low at a coffeeshop, to the glare of photographers and reporters. After the event, reporters approached me to take down my contact details. I was featured on television, radio, and in print news that day. My phone was flooded with text messages from friends.

My parents' reactions were delayed. A few days later, my father called to plead with me to drop my candidacy. It was really painful to have to reject him. My mother was not comfortable. It took a while for reality to sink in. Seeing me in the news must have opened up old fears. They did not wish any harm to fall on me. I could only assure them that I would be really careful about what I would say to avoid any lawsuits. It was too late to walk away. My father apologised that he could not be my assentor as my mother was not comfortable if he became part of the process. I told him that it was all right as we had enough assentors. Actually, I did not have enough assentors then.

Another interesting set of stories I will share is that I also consulted people on the PAP's camp during the process of coming forward to the WP. Ironically, I knew several senior people aligned to the PAP through my work and other involvements. I knew no one in the WP then.

One individual whom I consulted was Er Kwong Wah. He had been permanent secretary in the Ministry of Education and the then Ministry of Community Development before retiring early from the civil service. He was also active in several grassroots organisations in very senior positions. I knew Er through work: he was a founding director of the company I had started, ASKnLearn. He laughed when I had tea with him to tell him of my intentions. He shared that he had personally recommended a few people to the PAP in the past, some eventually becoming ministers. Er described what working in the community would be like. It was nothing glamourous. You will hear lots of complaints. Er did not discourage me. In fact, he wished me well. I continued to be in close contact with him after joining politics and continued working with him on new projects.

I also met with David Wong, who had served very actively under George Yeo, former cabinet minister and a rising star in the PAP, and had helped in many of Yeo's election campaigns. Many years back, Wong had invited me to help at Kembangan Community Centre (CC) to give a series of talks to the residents. I even met Yeo and received a letter from him, thanking me for helping with the CC. Wong was also once the chairman of the People's Association (PA) Youth Movement Central Executive Committee. He had given me a form to join the PA's youth group back then when I had started helping at Kembangan CC. However, I never filled up the form.

I asked to meet Er and Wong because I wanted to understand what politics would be like before I fully commit to push for my candidacy with the WP.

Wong offered to set up an immediate meeting with Yeo, which I politely declined. If I had wanted to, I had access to political office-bearers whom I had met earlier. I never saw myself to be wearing full white. Wong also shared what it would be like to be a backbencher MP, not exactly glamourous too. He wished me well and we remained in touch after my entry into politics. When we parted, I recall he told me that I would do well in the election. At the minimum, he expected me to become a Non-constituency Member of Parliament.

I am sharing my journey because there remained such fears holding people back even though they genuinely wished to offer themselves as part of our democratic processes in the alternative camp. It is also definitely not good for Singapore if people who can and wish to serve are held back because of fears expressed by people around them. That was in 2011. I believe the situation is much better now after several general elections: there are fewer lawsuits, opposition activists are not forced to live in exile, and the WP has gained some ground. My candidacy was nearly stopped twice. It is not true that there cannot be candidates of good qualifications in the alternative camp. The hatchet had been very sharp in the past.[1] This fear had to be gradually broken down.

---

1 Quote from Lee Kuan Yew: "Everybody knows that in my bag I have a hatchet, and a very sharp one. You take me on, I take my hatchet, we meet in the cul-de-sac." Lee Kuan Yew, "In quotes: Lee Kuan Yew", BBC, March 22, 2015, https://www.bbc.com/news/world-asia-31582842

# Part 2
# Journey in Blue

# Chapter 3
# The Battle for Joo Chiat

## Overcoming the Unsteady First Steps

I had joined the Workers' Party (WP) when preparations for the 2011 general election (GE2011) had intensified. The candidates for all the constituencies to be contested by the WP were mostly confirmed and had already started their campaigning. The active party members were all busy and involved in different teams by the time I was ready to start my campaign.

After I was given the permission to be the likely candidate for Joo Chiat Single Member Constituency (SMC), Low Thia Khiang asked if I had an election agent in mind. My response was, "What's that?" I had no idea what a campaign should be like or what logistics were required. He thought for a while and said that he would send a member to me.

The next day, Low arranged a meeting at his Hougang Town Council office. A long-haired and skinny man by the name of Shaun Lee was with him. Lee looked more like a rock musician than a serious campaigner. I learnt that election agents are to help candidates with the planning and coordination of election activities so that candidates can focus on campaigning. Lee had helped out with the National Solidarity Party in the 2001 general election and then with the WP in the 2006 general election. He was just nine years old when J. B. Jeyaretnam had won in his constituency of Anson in 1981. Lee's late father was a big WP supporter and had hosted Jeyaretnam and his campaigners with drinks and snacks at his house during the Anson by-election. His mother had been a volunteer for David Marshall when he was leading the Labour Front. Lee had thus become interested in politics from a young age. He considered his political views left of centre.

And so, my campaign started around the third week of March with just Lee and myself taking some general party brochures. I chose to start my campaign in Siglap right on the street where I lived. To Lee's credit, he appeared for our first visit with his hair cut short even without my asking.

Even though I had spent a week campaigning with the East Coast Group Representation Constituency (GRC) team before this, everything was so alien. What was I to say to the residents? How do I introduce myself? The party's strict order was that prospective candidates could not say that they would be standing in the constituency. There are two good reasons for this. First, the party reserves the right to change candidates even at the last moment as it deems fit. No one should expect that they must definitely be fielded where they were told to cover, even if the party had agreed in principle with the person on where the candidacy should be. Secondly, this was to keep the People's Action Party (PAP) guessing as to who the candidate(s) might be as the PAP might adjust their deployment if they knew ours.

The restriction of not letting people know that I would be the candidate left me with little to talk about with residents. I also could not publicly ask for volunteers on social media as I could not give any indication that I would be a candidate. We had expected the elections to be called within one to two months, which left me with little time to cover the entire Joo Chiat SMC. I had promised Low that I would cover the entire constituency at least once. It looked like a big challenge even though I had decided to take leave from my business to focus on campaigning daily from early April. I had no helpers other than Lee and did not even know what to say and how to campaign. I did not know people within the party, so I did not know where to ask for help. I only had a Facebook account which was not very active then. I did not have a blog page yet either.

I called friends, my ex-staff from ASKnLearn, and family members. I wanted to campaign daily and we needed many helpers so I would not be walking alone, and we could knock on more doors at a time as it took too long for residents in private houses to respond to visits.

I tried to imagine how a Joo Chiat voter would find me online. It would be through Google search by my name. What would they see on the first page and what would the first few links be?

I decided that I should manage my online presence. I had been featured online from forum letters I had written but these do not show up easily in a Google search because they are hidden in the database of newspaper websites. I decided to quickly beef up my online presence on social media. I immediately created my blog site. I listed my old forum letters and wrote one or two blog articles per day to flood the site. I tidied up my LinkedIn profile, updating it with all the latest and relevant credentials, always bearing in mind how a savvy online voter might view me.

I think my strategy worked. Within a week, my blog site showed up on the first page of Google when searching by my name. I wanted readers to feel that I was a logical person with good policy ideas and therefore would make a good parliamentarian. I was new to Facebook as I had only created my Facebook page midway through my campaigning when I found a volunteer who guided me through this.

I began to draw in a steady stream of new volunteers, mostly from Lee's and my own network. I still had not figured how to make my house visits effective. I felt that I was saying all sort of things but was not able to articulate why residents should vote for the WP. More than a week had passed in my campaign. In 2011, the party only had a general briefing session for all candidates and some guidelines on campaigning, hardly enough for a newbie.

Then, one evening, Yaw Shin Leong, the then organising secretary of the party, called me and asked if I needed any help with how to pitch for my house visits. He came late that evening to my house, after his own campaigning ended, at around 11 pm. Yaw was someone always full of energy and was then already well-established with the party despite being just in his mid-30s. He had joined the WP in 2001, was politically ambitious, and had worked his way up the party ranks.

We role played. Yaw acted as the resident and I, the candidate. His experience showed. He would point out every fault — handshake not firm enough, hand was released too fast; I was not direct to the point; I did not sound sincere enough; and so on. We went on for about half an hour.

That session left me with much to think about. I thought about my own experience as an entrepreneur. I had many real-life experiences in business when I had to make short and impactful pitches in unexpected situations, literally in under a minute, to arouse the interest of someone important. In business, these short pitches were to make the other person grant me a proper meeting so that I could have more time to sell my ideas or products, or pitch for funding.

That night, I formulated my 20–30 seconds elevator pitch which I would apply to every single person I met, whether at home or in coffeeshops. I might vary it depending on the crowd, location, or age profile of the person I met, but essentially, my pitch went something like this:

> Hi, I am Jenn Jong from the Workers' Party (later it became 'prospective candidate for the Workers' Party' closer to nomination day and 'candidate for the Workers' Party' after nomination day). I started my career teaching computer science at the National University of Singapore and I am now an education entrepreneur. I have lived and studied in schools here since young. I believe Singapore needs a stronger alternative and we need your support in the election.

The pitch was meant to trigger further talking points, from which I would flexibly adjust to see how I could engage in further conversation in areas that the resident wanted to speak about. Some wanted to know more about my professional background, some asked what I meant by a stronger alternative. Others were interested to learn that I lived in their neighbourhood.

I also organised the volunteers, who were steadily increasing in number to sometimes over 10 per visit. I would observe which volunteer could engage with residents better and put them in charge of a small team. Depending on the number of volunteers each time, I would split the teams to cover different areas near one another. The lead engager would do the pitching and if the residents wanted to see me, they would send a text message and I would make my way there as soon as possible while moving in between teams near each other.

I felt that this was one aspect I handled well in GE2011. By evolving an effective short pitch and managing the volunteers well, we combed through the entire SMC and managed to cover all available areas, other than condominiums and apartments that we could not visit. We wrote to all the large condominiums and managed to get nearly half of them to agree to us visiting the residents. We visited every condominium that granted us visiting permission within the six weeks of campaigning. I started about the same time as Charles Chong, my opponent in the PAP. I recall at the end of March 2011, when I was on an earlier-scheduled short business trip to Kuwait, I read in an online *The Straits Times* article that Chong would be replacing Chan Soo Sen as the PAP candidate in the SMC.

I started with only one member from the party. By the end of the campaign, I still had hardly any WP members helping, most of them busy elsewhere. The Joo Chiat SMC volunteers were initially friends, ex-staff, and family members. As we moved along, I recruited anyone who enthusiastically supported me when we met, if they had time to join in. That included Dennis Tan, Member of Parliament (MP) for

Hougang SMC. He was (and still is) a resident of Joo Chiat SMC. Tan turned up on nomination day to support the WP candidate for his SMC. We had a mutual friend at the nomination centre. Seeing his enthusiasm, I invited him to join our campaigning. That evening, he donned blue and joined in. His wife and himself helped almost on a daily basis throughout the remainder of the campaign. They were eloquent and I trusted them to help with engaging residents.

Even some from the People's Association grassroots organisations jumped camp. A former classmate who was previously holding a very senior position in the Joo Chiat grassroots had left the Citizens' Consultative Committee not too long ago. He became an informal advisor and linked me to others in the community. A former student of mine from my first job as a tutor in the National University of Singapore, Yap Keng Ann, was previously a member of one of the Telok Kurau Neighbourhood Committees. Upon reading about me through the press, he dropped me an email. We met up and he joined our campaign actively, and helped all the way through till the 2020 general election.

By the end of my campaign, we had over 40 regular volunteers. Sometimes we had as many as 15–20 at a time. A few, like Tan, joined the party after the general election.

I remain grateful to Yaw for helping a rookie like me in politics get started. It was a short but very effective 30 minutes of guidance. He was a seasoned campaigner and I was a new candidate, eager to learn how to do the visits effectively. The campaign time was too short to make too many mistakes. Drawing on the experiences I had from my business practices, I adapted my campaign.

## Nomination Day

On nomination day, all candidates, their election agents, and assentors were required to report at the Hougang Town Council office. From there, buses had been chartered to ferry everyone to the nomination centre together. For every general election, there would be nomination centres spread across the island, each handling the nomination for several constituencies. This practice of assembling everyone together early in the morning on nomination day had been started even before I joined the party. It could have been some bad experiences in the past in which a candidate failed to show up or assentors coming late or not showing up that likely prompted this practice.

At the nomination centre, there was a legally trained person scanning through all our forms to ensure they had been filled in correctly. Details of all candidates and assentors were checked against their National Registration Identity Card. The WP left nothing to chance after facing problems in the past over nomination forms.

Approaching nomination day, there was strong public speculation as to where Low would be fielded. The decision to put Low in Aljunied had been kept under wraps. Very few people in the party knew with certainty and most of the candidates were not told. Such information was strictly on a need-to-know basis.

Prior to nomination day, Yaw was campaigning with Sylvia Lim, Pritam Singh, Chen Show Mao, and Muhamad Faisal Manap in Aljunied. Low was campaigning in his home turf of Hougang. However, I had strongly suspected that a switch would be made. No one told me, but little bits of tell-tale evidence, and even the party's slogan "Towards a First World Parliament", led me to the conclusion. We cannot have a First World Parliament with just a couple of elected MPs. Low is adept at reading political sentiments. He had long wanted to see the party expand beyond just himself as the sole elected MP. The year 2011 was a good time to go for it. Ground sentiments were apparently weak for the PAP, but they did not seem to know it then. Anger on the ground had been strong. In any case, given my short runway to the election, I was very focused on my own campaign and had little time to think about battles elsewhere.

# The Battle for Joo Chiat

The press knew that we would be gathered at the Hougang Town Council office, as had been the tradition of the WP in the past. Photographers, television cameramen, and reporters had camped outside the office waiting to report on our deployment.

The bus for Joo Chiat SMC was probably the first, or one of the first, to leave the Hougang Town Council gathering point and bring us to Tao Nan School where the nominations would be announced. My team was the only one from the WP going to Tao Nan School. Before we departed, Low got onto our bus, said some words of encouragement, then alighted the bus.

The last buses to leave were for Aljunied GRC and Hougang SMC. That was obviously to keep the PAP guessing where Low would be fielded.

I recall that I had already reached Tao Nan School early and was waiting in the Nomination Hall. The PAP teams were there already. Tao Nan was the nomination centre for Marine Parade GRC, Joo Chiat SMC, Mountbatten SMC, and Potong Pasir SMC. I chatted with the candidates for the PAP and the opposition parties. Singapore People's Party's (SPP) Lina Chiam and National Solidarity Party's Jeannette Chong-Aruldoss and Nicole Seah were also at the centre.

I was watching the television broadcast by Channel News Asia at one corner of the hall. Senior Minister Goh Chok Tong, candidate for Marine Parade GRC, was standing quite near me watching, too. Then the news reported that Low was in the bus with the rest of the Aljunied team and Yaw was heading out on a bus as the sole candidate, which of course meant that he was going for Hougang SMC. The nomination centres for both of these constituencies were different. I distinctively heard Goh Chok Tong mutter quite loudly, "How can he do this?" I believe he was referring to Low's move to Aljunied GRC because I remember telling myself in my mind, "Why not?" I never quite understood what Goh meant. I thought that the PAP intelligence would have figured out that Low would make that big move. The PAP's Aljunied GRC team already had two full ministers and a senior minister of state. There was not much that the PAP could do to strengthen the slate anyway.

Nomination paperwork went through smoothly, and our forms were pinned onto the noticeboard for all to view and to challenge if any details were wrong. One of the assentors from the SPP team approached me excitedly and told me that something was wrong with Charles Chong's form. I went to take a look. I could not quite remember exactly what it was, I think it was some cancellation made or some parts were handwritten and other parts were typed out for one of the assentors. I did not think there was anything wrong, so I did not take any action. Furthermore, Chong had the full 10 assentors on the list. Even if one was to be disqualified, he still had more than the minimum of six. In fact, I recall that I only had eight assentors. For various reasons, a few of my friends who had earlier agreed to be assentors told me a few days before nomination day that they could not make it. Since I already had more than six, it did not matter. My father had told me that if needed, I could just call him, and he would immediately drive over and become my assentor. However, I did not want to ask him to fill in the remaining slots given his earlier apprehension of me being a candidate.

At 12.30 pm, all the nominations in our centre were accepted. I could now officially go to voters and say, "I am the candidate for the Workers' Party in Joo Chiat SMC." Before that, we were strictly not permitted to say so. However, close to nomination day, when we were already campaigning hard daily, I told residents that I was the "likely candidate" since the press had already picked up the story of me walking the ground. I did so because I felt that voters would not take me seriously if I visited and I was not even the candidate. One of the most common questions residents would ask when I met them before nomination day was, "Are you the candidate?" At least, I could say I was the "likely candidate". Some would then reply, "You mean you don't even know you will be the candidate?" My reply to that would be, "It will be confirmed on nomination day. We want to leave the PAP guessing." Low certainly did keep the PAP and the media guessing.

## Developing and Delivering My Message

All along, I had been thinking seriously about how best to get my message across to the electorate. After Yaw's brief coaching session in early April 2011, I was determined to work on my personal branding. I decided that I needed to pitch consistently, whether at rallies, in my blog, when engaging with residents one on one, or with the media.

From the elevator pitch I had shared earlier, one could guess how I branded myself — as a local boy who did reasonably well in his studies and career, eager to contribute to a more resilient Singapore by having stronger alternative voices in Parliament. It went well with the party's slogan — "Towards a First World Parliament". Whenever I campaigned near a former school of mine or where I had lived, or if I noticed a child wearing a school uniform which I was familiar with or was from my alma mater, I played these up as talking points.

Below is a blog post I wrote to accompany the video of my speech on nomination day. It illustrates the branding I had decided on and consistently adhered to throughout the campaign:

> I am the Worker's Party representative for Joo Chiat SMC. I have been a Joo Chiat resident all my life — in Opera Estate, Telok Kurau and now Siglap. I studied in St Stephen's, St Patrick's and Temasek Junior College. My wife studied at Haig Girls, Tanjong Katong Girls and Victoria Junior College. My three children had all studied at schools located in Joo Chiat. My parents taught at schools around Joo Chiat.
>
> I have explained in my earlier blog post why I have chosen to be an alternative voice under WP. I believe Singapore should have strong alternative voices and a credible alternative party for the long-term insurance of Singapore. Joo Chiat is passionately my home, and home to my parents and many classmates and friends. It is therefore my great pleasure to contest in Joo Chiat as I have much at stake in Joo Chiat. At

Joo Chiat, we already have good parks and beautiful homes. I hope we can add a new dimension to it, by having a spirit that makes Joo Chiat the pride of Singapore. As an entrepreneur for the last 11 years, I have built up organisations from scratch. My youth and entrepreneurial spirit will help me push initiatives from the ground up in Joo Chiat.

I will do whatever it takes to fulfil my job as a full-time MP if elected. I look forward humbly to your support.

To further entrench myself as the local boy, I targeted the coffeeshop owners. I made friends with several. Some were openly distributing my flyers. My parents visited a coffeeshop at Jalan Tua Kong one afternoon and the owner gave him my flyer and told my father to vote for me! Of course, my father proudly proclaimed, "That's my son!"

My father, from being apprehensive of my involvement, volunteered to join us when I campaigned in the estate where he lived, and where he had spent 50 years of his life. He accompanied me to visit neighbours. We asked neighbours to tell neighbours.

In each general election, there will be star candidates. In 2011, it was Chen Show Mao and Nicole Seah. Then there was the big move by Low into Aljunied GRC. I felt that I had to figure out how to get media attention. I believed that being featured by the media was important. However, the WP has restrictions when it comes to engaging with the media. Ask any political desk reporter and they will tell you how frustrating it can sometimes be to get quotes from WP candidates. As a strict disciplinarian, Low controlled this well. Pritam Singh has continued this practice as the current secretary-general. I can understand why. With many candidates, there is a need to control how we engage the media because any weak link or mistake can be quickly exploited by the PAP. The party wants to control how it drives the overall campaign. And in 2011, the stakes were high because the party took a gamble in taking Low out of Hougang SMC. The attacks would be fierce because the PAP would not want to lose Aljunied GRC, and with it two ministers and a senior minister of state.

I believe that Joo Chiat SMC was not a constituency the WP had expected to win or to do well in. I was a late addition to the team, without any political profile. At the start of the campaign, I read various political analysts' comments. None listed Joo Chiat SMC as a hot seat. In the busy campaigning to secure Hougang SMC and Aljunied GRC, the WP key leaders only had time to lend their support to a few of the hotly contested areas. I was provided with one member, Shaun Lee, for whom I was grateful for, to jumpstart my campaign. Joo Chiat SMC was not one of the areas which Low or Sylvia Lim visited during the whole campaign. There was supposed to be one visit by them, but it was cancelled because they had to focus on Aljunied and Hougang.

I honestly did not mind as well. I was new to the party. I did not know what was normal nor what I should have expected from the party. I felt voters would want to consider the candidate for their constituency more than whether Low or Lim campaigned with me. I expected nothing other than to be fielded, to have some speaking slots at the rallies, and to have some support for putting up banners and posters and support in preparing the candidate profile. The candidate profile was to be mailed or delivered to each voting household. Gerald Giam, then a WP candidate for East Coast GRC and current MP for Aljunied GRC, was kind enough to permit me to use a software he had written to merge the names from a household into one mailing label per household. Each candidate had to see to the distribution of their own candidate profile to voters.

My speaking slots at the rallies were limited. I was told from the start that I would have three slots out of the eight nights. Joo Chiat SMC did not have any good rally sites, so the party did not pick the designated site for the SMC to be its rally site at all. I spoke twice within the first six nights at Serangoon Stadium and Bedok Stadium. My third and final speaking slot was to be at Bedok Stadium again on the final night of the campaign. Then, the day before that Bedok Stadium rally, I was informed in the afternoon that the party wanted the final night of the campaign to focus on the key battlegrounds. I either had to speak that night at the Sengkang rally site or I would have no more speaking opportunities.

Naturally, I was rather disappointed. I was not sure if any Joo Chiat residents would be attending the rally at Sengkang, which was far away. I was also not prepared because I was still doing visits that afternoon and my original speech was not due until the next evening. I had wanted the final speech to focus on things I would do for Joo Chiat residents. Nevertheless I decided to accept the speaking slot at Sengkang.

Public speaking had never been my strength. It was made worse by the lack of preparation for that last speech. I had no experience with election speeches. My first two speeches were passable but weak compared to those of seasoned speakers. I hastily drafted a speech for the evening, listening to the advice of a couple of volunteers who were with me that afternoon. None were familiar with Singapore's elections. One of them pointed me to a United States politician's impressive speech at a conference hall and asked me to follow that style. I wrote a speech that was far too long and not appropriate for the Singapore rally crowd. Candidates had to send our speeches to Jane Leong for vetting before delivery. I duly submitted it but it was quite close to the rally time. When I reached the rally site, Leong had managed to just glance through my speech. She gave me a few quick pointers, for which I did instant amendments.

That speech haunted me for quite a few days to come. Midway through the speech, the crowd was getting restless. I did not give them any punchline to cheer at for long periods. I spoke about how I wished to develop the neighbourliness spirit and the importance of family values — not the best topics to deliver in a rally. It began to rain and the crowd started jeering. I had to try to figure out which part of my speech to cut off while looking at a crowd of 20,000 or so restless people. I did not know where to hide myself that night. It was an embarrassing lesson, but I never again gave a bad rally speech after that. I have learnt that one will need to keep rally speeches short and sharp, packed with some good punches in between driving home key points in a logical manner. The press will pick up only short sound bites. Points rebutting our opponents for comments they had made make for the best punchlines. In the 2015 general election, several of my rally punchlines were well-reported in both the mainstream and social media, such as the one in response to Emeritus Senior Minister (ESM) Goh Chok Tong on his rooster story. Goh had said that the WP was like a rooster boasting that its crowing every morning caused the sun to rise, a reference to the opposition claiming that there had been policy shifts post-GE2011 because of their work. I rebutted that the rooster "crows every morning because it's morning and it's time to wake up. The rooster is telling the people, 'Hey, wake up', that's what the WP has been telling the PAP, that's what you, the citizens of Singapore, have been telling the PAP".[1] I had to learn the hard way what a rally speech was supposed to be like.

Overall, I think I did decently in my message to Joo Chiat voters. The Party's message of "Towards a First World Parliament"[2] also resonated well with middle-ground voters. The WP had called for a greater number of credible and elected opposition MPs to insure Singapore against a possible future failure of the ruling party. Credible elected opposition in Parliament will allow an alternative government to form in times of crisis or need. A significant number of elected opposition MPs will also ensure that the government will be held to account, explain, and justify to Singaporeans their decisions and policies in a meaningful way. In the later chapters, I will further discuss this function of checks and balances that the WP strove to provide with the breakthrough of GE2011.

---

1   Ng Jing Yng and Kelly Ng, "WP's aim is to wake up sleeping Govt: Yee", Today, September 3, 2015, https://www.todayonline.com/ge2015/wps-aim-wake-sleeping-govt-yee

2   "WP: Move towards First World Parliament", AsiaOne, April 28, 2011, https://www.asiaone.com/News/Elections/Story/A1Story20110429-276277.html

## Engaging the Press

The previous section covered how I consciously planned my message to Joo Chiat residents, targeted to build on my strengths. This was probably the most successful part of my campaign.

The problem with a ground campaign was that no matter how hard we tried, it was impossible to reach many residents. In the six weeks of campaigning, I covered every house that was accessible and even condominiums that allowed us access. I even had time to spare in the final two days to cover Opera Estate a second time. In GE2011, we knocked on every door that could be reached and rang every bell that we could ring. Yet, many residents were not at home. Not all would go online to search me out.

The mainstream media would have been the best. However, there were star candidates and important key battlegrounds. I knew I was not the type to be a star candidate nor was Joo Chiat SMC a contest the media were very interested in. I was also a new candidate in a party that had strict rules about how and when we could engage with the press. There was to be strictly no press engagement unless permitted by the party, and any engagement would be carefully controlled. How was I to get my message to as many as possible?

In my work as an entrepreneur, I courted the press. I ran a start-up. We had no budget for advertising. We ran on a shoestring budget. I did not hire any public relations agency to engage with the press. I did everything myself, and it worked quite successfully.

My start-up at that time, ASKnLearn, was in the news many times. Give me access to a reporter with interest in our line of work and I can spin a story. I put myself in the shoes of journalists and figured what would make a story for them, and for us. In my work, I mostly chose not to feature our company, but to feature our clients, the schools. When we felt that we had an interesting project with a story to tell, I would write the story in such a manner as to interest the reporter and get the school to contact them. Then when the story was featured, we would make a copy and stick a sentence at the bottom of that copy that said, "ASKnLearn is proud to have supplied the technology used at X school." Reporters generally would not feature us, a commercial company. They were more open to feature a government school or students doing something interesting. Once in a while, if the journalist was more generous, we found our name mentioned inside the article. The school and the teacher-in-charge got the credit for doing something novel. We got ourselves featured indirectly and we would take that article and show it to another school, tempting them to engage us because X school had used our solution. We pitched to prospective clients that these solutions were innovative enough to be featured. I made friends with reporters covering education technology news.

I had to use my experience more discreetly and discerningly because there were rules to go by and the WP was famous for being strict on this. I recall, at our first briefing for candidates before our campaigns started, we were told not to contact the press and not to invite them to our house visits, unless it was an event organised by the party. We were not to let them know that we would be candidates. I remember asking at that briefing, "What if the reporters were lurking around, saw us doing our visits, and approached us or the residents?" I was told that we cannot stop the press from spotting us, speaking with residents, or speculating if we would be candidates and where we would contest in. We should, however, refrain from speaking with them.

A few days after I was formally featured on April 3, 2011 after the market visit in Yishun, I got an accidental break. I had planned a visit to Opera Estate. My wife and I were driving to the Kembangan Mass Rapid Transit station to pick up some volunteers. We were early. I turned into one of the small dead-end lanes in the Frankel Estate so that we could use that extra 10 minutes or so to engage with as many residents as we could.

I had just stepped out of my car and was only at our first house when lo and behold, a *The Straits Times* reporter, Chong Zi Liang, approached us and greeted me. He asked if I had seen Andrew Kuan around. Kuan had announced that he was interested to be an independent candidate in Joo Chiat SMC. *The Straits Times* had sent Chong to check on potential candidates who might contest there as there might be a three-cornered fight.

I thought to myself, "I am going to be the candidate for this constituency, and you can be the first to report this. Wouldn't this be a more interesting story than an independent who will unlikely contest eventually?"

I told him, "No, I am a resident in Joo Chiat myself. I have not seen Andrew around yet."

I also told him that I just happened to be there because I was early and would be picking up my volunteers to visit another part of Joo Chiat. He asked where we would be at. Since I was not the one who called the press and Chong happened to spot me doing my house visits, I decided to be flexible with the rules. After all, having spotted me, he might already be writing something on this so I might as well better angle the story for him. I proposed that I could drop him off near where we would be if he promised not to come too close when we engage with residents because we did not want to scare the residents with a journalist around. And he should not photograph the residents. He replied that he would speak with just a few residents after we leave.

Opera Estate would make a perfect story too, because that was where I had grown up.

So Chong got his story that day, titled "WP Newcomer Visits Homes in Joo Chiat". He was the first from the media to figure out that I was the likely candidate for WP in Joo Chiat SMC, just days after I first surfaced in a WP-organised media event. Chong had also included a phone interview with Kuan in that article. As a new candidate, I got a sizeable feature in *The Straits Times*, and with the branding that I had wanted — that I was a local boy likely to come back to contest in my home ground. The report came with a coverage of my business and educational background, together with a quote of why I had joined the WP — to help in building a credible team to challenge the PAP. The article also mentioned my blog as I was hoping he would, because I had told Chong to read my blog to find out more about why I had joined WP. I was hopeful that might drive voters to search up my blog where I had already published a number of my previous writings and new opinion pieces, and had also included hyperlinks to news that had featured me in my professional career.

As the campaign went on, the press got wind of the contest getting warmer. *The Straits Times* contacted me and said they would feature my opponent, Charles Chong, and would also give a similar-sized article for me. The party cleared that request. I picked my spot for the interview — the coffeeshop next to Siglap Centre at the heart of the SMC. It was also near where I was living.

We had a good interview. I took the chance to direct the answers towards the branding that I had wanted to create. After the interview, my volunteers and I crossed over to the four low-rise Housing and Development Board (HDB) flats to start our next round of visits. There, at Wong Clinic, I met an elderly nurse. As I passed our brochure to her, she said that she remembered me. She had worked there for some 40 years and said that I was often running around in my pyjamas as a young kid whenever I was there to see the doctor.

I immediately called the reporter who still at the coffeeshop. I told him that he should speak with the nurse. He did. The next day, the story opened with what the nurse had told the reporter about me running around in my pyjamas as a child at the clinic. Wong Clinic was as old as the only HDB flats in Joo Chiat SMC, built after a devastating fire in Siglap in the 1960s. If there was one shop which long-time residents in Siglap knew, it would be Wong Clinic. *The Straits Times*' article was quite long and covered me as the local-boy-made-good. It featured the success of my start-up that was eventually sold to a public-listed company, and my desire to come back to be the voice for Joo Chiat residents.

Towards the last few days of the campaign, the party leadership allowed us to engage directly with the press as we deemed appropriate. I doubt any of the other candidates did. On the other hand, I immediately contacted Channel News Asia and took the chance to rebut some estate upgrading promises by Charles Chong.

I understand the party's apprehension with the mainstream media. Low viewed them with suspicion because of the type of politics that he had to go through in his political life. He had seen how the media could become the tool to discredit a candidate. I was mindful of why the party had these reservations but I felt that if I had to make a breakthrough in Joo Chiat SMC, I had no choice but to find a way to engage people through mainstream media. And engagement was not just about the number of times I was featured in the news. As opposition members, we may not be able to fully control how the story may eventually turn out. Still, if we wish to engage, one should be mindful to craft the answers carefully to bring out the message that you want to convey. Overall, I was quite happy with how the press had featured me in 2011.

## Polling Night

GE2011 was my first election. I did not know what to expect. I started without many expectations but was confident that if I created a strong enough message and reached enough people, a breakthrough might be possible. We pushed really hard, campaigning daily for six weeks non-stop. By the end of the campaign I had worn out a brand-new pair of shoes and lost five kilograms.

The toughest day was a weekend in which Neptune Court gave us permission to visit in the morning, and Villa Marina in the afternoon.

Both were large condominium projects. By the end of the day, my legs ached so badly, especially from climbing down the stairs. That day, we knocked on more than 1,400 homes. By evening, I could barely walk. The next morning, we were up again for more visits.

As the campaign went on, I became increasingly more confident. I was quietly hoping for an upset win. The operator of a coffeeshop in Siglap, whom I got to know well and supported us strongly, would give me bookies update each time I was there. It went from a non-contest at the start to an almost 50-50 prediction on the eve of polling day. I did not know what to make of these odds, but I knew that we just needed to keep pounding the streets.

The night of polling day was a seesaw of emotions. There were nine polling districts in Joo Chiat SMC. The votes were close. The WP won in four of these polling districts; the best performing one was where my parents lived. However, we lost badly in one district. That sank my campaign.

The initial count was that I had lost by exactly one percent. Ng Swee Bee, who was coordinating the results for the party, had texted me to ask for an update. I replied, "Sorry, we tried very hard, but we still lost by one percent." I called for a recount, which was allowed if the result was within a difference of two percent, but I knew it was pointless. I had observed the counting process. Errors were extremely rare. In fact, in the recount, I lost another six votes.

With a heavy heart, I drove to Hougang Stadium where all WP candidates and supporters were gathered and waited for the results. When the results were announced, I had to give a Thank You speech on stage. It was a very hard and emotional speech to give. The journey had been amazing, truly. I started with just one WP member assigned to help. Shaun Lee worked very hard, too. More and more volunteers came as we pushed along. Many worked hard. I ended my speech with the challenge to the PAP — "Keep Joo Chiat, and I will be back."

Of course, they never did.

Below is a post I made right after the narrow defeat. It sums up best how I felt that night:

> My journey continues on
>
> (May 8, 2011)
>
> Dear voters of Joo Chiat SMC, dear Singaporeans
>
> As you now already know, I have lost narrowly in Joo Chiat SMC. I had wanted badly to win it for all the supporters who walked tirelessly with me, who blasted emails and phone calls to lobby for support, who gave selflessly of their time and money, and for all the residents I have met who cheered me on. I accept the results and urge Joo Chiat residents to work with Charles Chong as the elected MP for the common good of residents.
>
> My political journey officially started only 2 months ago when I was first accepted as a member of the Workers' Party and then accepted as their likely candidate for Joo Chiat. It was not that I was not interested in politics before this, but my fear for my business and my family led me to delay my formal entry as a member of a political party until I was certain of myself. I had followed political developments in Singapore for a long time, written to the forum pages of the newspapers, sat on government committees recommending policies and served in many community activities. These have gradually led me to my conviction that there is a need for a credible alternative voice and a need to move out of my comfort zone to be part of the change process.
>
> It has been an incredible 2 months. As a political rookie, I had to learn to overcome my fears, learn how to engage with residents, how to speak at rallies, how to organise supporters

around me and how to organise a campaign. There were mistakes and hiccups but I am proud of the way we close ranks and overcame whatever problems that came our way.

We did well. I know many residents have been won over and have come out openly to declare their support for our Joo Chiat campaign, despite whatever mistakes I may have made. We swung many voters. I believe I had lost because there is still a large silent majority who have fear in them; fear of their votes not being secret, fear of the uncertainty of an alternative party running the constituency and fear of losing whatever benefits the ruling party can give to them.

My journey has just begun. It will not stop with this narrow defeat. In whatever capacities available to me, whether as an active citizen or through the political processes, I will continue to push for improvements to our political system so that there will be a fairer Singapore, there will be true democracy and there will be channels where your voices will be effectively heard. I will continue to propose ideas which I believe can improve our lives and better shape our economy.

Once again, I like to thank all the supporters and residents who have given me their confidence and I look forward to your continued support.

I had my pluses and minuses in GE2011. In an SMC, a good ground campaign, sufficient time, and a conscious effort at relaying a strong message to voters can be effective. I sometimes wonder what would have happened had the Prime Minister (PM) not made that apology late in the GE2011 campaign. Several ministers had come under fire for their reluctance to acknowledge growing problems in their ministries. As a result, the PM gave a rare apology in a public rally, which *The Straits*

*Times* had called "remarkable for its [...] humility".³ It was probably targeted at Aljunied GRC residents, whom the PAP felt they were losing. I met some Joo Chiat residents after GE2011 who told me that the apology by the PM swung them back to the PAP. They felt that they should give the PAP a chance to prove that they were prepared to change.

Middle-class voters residing in private estates are especially susceptible to vote swings, as I learnt at first hand after observing the voting patterns over my three elections. They cannot be threatened with estate upgrading as these do not apply to private housing. Voters were angry in 2011 because they deemed the PAP to have been arrogant and deaf to voices on the ground. Common issues I had heard during campaigning included spiralling healthcare costs, expensive public housing, high cost of living, large influx of foreigners competing for jobs, and poor public transport. The apology by the PM had softened some hearts. Joo Chiat SMC was never expected to be won by the opposition. I eventually lost by 388 votes, or one percent of the popular vote. It was a vote swing of 14 percent from 2006.

However, I must add that the most important factors for any candidate to do well in an election are the party's branding and the general sentiment of voters. If I were in any other opposition party, I would not have done as well. And the mood on the ground in 2011 was distinctively against the PAP. The PAP had focused too much on economic growth. The strong gross domestic product rebound in 2010 could have misled them. Still, the PAP's brand was the strongest. There was a strong pool of silent voters who will just go with the PAP brand. It would take a lot of groundwork, positive media presence, great speech delivery, and good credentials to win them over, even in the most conducive of sentiments for the opposition.

---

3   Raju Gopalakrishnan and Kevin Lim, "Singapore PM makes rare apology as election campaign heats up", Reuters, May 4, 2011, https://in.reuters.com/article/idINIndia-56766220110504

# Chapter 4
# Parliament

## The Non-constituency Member of Parliament Position

My score was the second highest of the losing candidates in the 2011 general election (GE2011). Lina Chiam from the Singapore People's Party lost by an even slimmer margin in Potong Pasir Single Member Constituency (SMC). To make it to nine opposition parliamentarians as provided by the Constitution at that time, there would be three Non-constituency Member of Parliament (NCMP) positions offered: one to Chiam, one to me, and another for the Workers' Party (WP) team who had contested in East Coast Group Representation Constituency (GRC) to decide.

Whether I accepted the post also depended on the party. The Central Executive Committee (CEC) would meet to decide after we received our letters from Parliament informing us of the offer for the positions.

A few days after polling day, there was the counting of votes from overseas voters. It would not have mattered because overseas votes were too few to change the outcome. I went anyway to show appreciation to those who made the big effort to travel to vote.

At the counting station, while waiting for the boxes to be opened, Low Thia Khiang suddenly approached me and asked if I knew a certain person. A poison pen email was sent to him after the polling results, warning the party not to take me as the NCMP as I might soon be sued over something that I had allegedly said in the course of my work many years ago.

I knew the person and the circumstances. I told Low what I knew and the legal advice I had gotten from various lawyers at that time. The lawyers were confident that there was no case. Furthermore, the time period for any legal action to be taken had already long lapsed. Anyway, I assured Low that if it ever became an issue, I would defend vigorously.

On the morning before the CEC meeting, Low invited me to his home. We chatted about the campaign, if I wanted the NCMP position, if I planned to contest in future elections, and about other things in general. I told him that I would accept the position if the party allowed me to and yes, I would contest in the next election, health permitting.

I was not in the CEC. So, I waited at home for the result. I received a call from Sylvia Lim after the meeting to inform me that the CEC had voted to support my acceptance of the position. I asked about the other NCMP seat. Lim informed me that it went to Gerald Giam, and that Eric Tan had resigned from the party as a result of this.

Tan had been my first point of contact when I tried to join the WP. I understudied in the East Coast GRC team briefly before my candidacy for Joo Chiat SMC was decided upon. Tan was the leader of the East Coast GRC team. He had pushed for my candidacy with the WP. I had also met Giam during those visits and also spoke quite a bit with him during the campaign period even though we were contesting in different constituencies. Giam came across as a serious thinker and was very committed to the opposition cause. He gave me a book he had earlier published, which captured many of the blog pieces he had written earlier. Giam had been an active blogger, as deputy editor for *The Online Citizen*, and also ran his own blog site. The articles were well-written and were useful insights for me as I started my own blog.

I had mixed emotions. Both were good guys. Between the two, I felt that Giam had more reasons to be an NCMP even though Tan was the team leader. Giam was much younger; youth is useful in opposition politics. Being in the opposition against a very dominant ruling party, NCMPs may find it difficult to win the next election. It might take more time to make the breakthrough. While Tan had good experience and knowledge of the finance world, Giam came across to me as more well-versed in a wider range of issues, as illustrated by his blog pieces. Giam's grasp on diverse issues would be more advantageous for the WP as it sought to build on the breakthrough via parliamentary performance in the 12th Parliament. With heightened expectations of voters, the WP will be expected to take on the ruling party and offer policy ideas across all ministries.

I asked Lim if the party wanted me to reject my NCMP offer so that Tan could take up the position instead. She replied that there was no need. There was no turning back. Tan had immediately called the press after the CEC meeting to announce his resignation.

I had a chat with Tan after his resignation. I heard and understood his point of view. We left matters as they were.

After the CEC meeting, I accepted the offer from the Parliament. At the next CEC meeting, Chen Show Mao, Pritam Singh, and I were co-opted into the CEC as the party felt that all parliamentarians should be involved in the highest decision-making body. I was assigned the position of deputy treasurer. Some months later, I became the treasurer after Yaw Shin Leong left the party.

## Baptism of Fire

The WP entered the 12th Parliament with a team of eight: six elected Members of Parliament (MPs) and two NCMPs. The People's Action Party (PAP) made up 81 of the 87 elected members, still an overwhelming number.

The nation's presidential election was due in August of 2011. Parliament would not sit until the new President had been elected. Hence, Parliament started only in October that year, a long delay from polling day of May 7.

I was not an elected MP, so I did not have constituency nor town council work to busy myself with. I used the time waiting for Parliament to convene to read up more and write more blog articles. The team looked to Low and Lim for guidance on how to ready ourselves with Parliament matters. Parliament also conducted briefings and a tour of the facilities. The library seemed like a cosy place. It was a place I would come to use quite a lot over the next four years.

All of us spoke when the 12th Parliament was opened with the President's Address as it was our first session in Parliament. Low had advised us to speak on the topics that we were most interested in and that would likely be areas we will focus on during our parliamentary term. We were also advised that the opening session of Parliament would likely have more lively debates as the PAP would take the opportunity to size us up, especially with an unprecedented number of opposition MPs.

I spoke on education and developing a resilient and innovative economy, with special attention to our small and medium-sized enterprises. Indeed, during the four years in Parliament, I spoke quite extensively on these areas, particularly in education which I was most familiar with.

I was not sure what to expect. I prepared for some potential questions from the PAP MPs, but I must have been quite bad at spotting questions. None of what I had prepared for were raised. Instead, five PAP office-bearers, Heng Chee How, Tan Chuan-Jin, Sim Ann, Lawrence Wong, and Lim Hng Kiang all rose to speak, mostly questioning me over issues I had raised about the economy.

I thought I did reasonably well, considering that I was totally unprepared for these questions. The questions came fast, one after another. I did not even sit down after answering each. My exchanges with them were covered in the mainstream media the next day. I recall the advice that former Nominated Member of Parliament (NMP) Calvin Cheng had given me when we met briefly for lunch before Parliament had convened. He said that if you wish to be in the news, take on the office-bearers.

Similarly, when the PAP backbenchers wished to be reported, they took on the top opposition members. In the opening Parliament session, our 'star catch' of GE2011, Chen Show Mao, was also subjected to questioning from the PAP MPs after his speech.

That first session started my active participation in the 12th Parliament. I spoke very often and raised questions across a wide range of topics, which I will elaborate on in subsequent sections. I took pride in doing thorough research for my speeches. I may not be the most natural at delivering speeches, but I found that I could handle rebuttals decently well. I speak better off-the-cuff and especially when the topics are those that I am familiar with.

With my own more intense maiden speech experience, I was not surprised by the attention which Jamus Lim, a WP MP elected into Parliament after the 2020 general election (GE2020), received in the opening session of the 14th Parliament where seven PAP MPs responded to his speech, including Senior Minister Tharman Shanmugaratnam.

## Policy Work

We were only a team of eight. We could hardly call ourselves a Shadow Cabinet. Each of us were assigned some ministries to anchor, where we would track bills, file questions, and make proposals related to those ministries. We were further assigned other ministries to back up another WP MP. I was assigned education and trade & industry as my primary ministries. If I recall correctly, I was to be back up for transportation and healthcare. I might also have been given social & family (Ministry of Social and Family Development (MSF)) to cover as a backup too — I cannot quite remember now but I was fairly active addressing issues in MSF and various other ministries as well. As an NCMP, I was not provided with an allowance for a legislative assistant (LA). LAs are to help parliamentarians with policy work and constituency work. Only elected MPs are provided with such an allowance. The allowance is only

$1,300 a month per LA. It would not be enough to hire a professional full-time LA. The LAs to the WP MPs were all part-timers.

We were asked to see if we could form our own pool of volunteers to help us with our area of policy work. After each general election, there would be a multitude of volunteers. Many still wanted to continue helping even after the general election. Jane Leong assigned volunteers to us based on our areas of focus. I also tried to find my own. I had a good number of volunteers in my teams. I called for various sessions to brainstorm issues. I soon realised that policy and research work was not for everyone. There were many who could tell me what they felt or heard or complained about certain issues. Solutions often could not really be found from them.

Instead, I turned to my own sources. Being quite deeply involved in education, preschools, and running businesses, I found that my best source for insights and solutions were from practitioners in the industry. They were not necessarily opposition supporters. I called on them for information and to bounce off ideas. My 20 years of experience in the education industry came in useful as I had friends and acquaintances who were active at the operating level and even at the policy-making level. My best research came from private tea sessions with them, promising to keep their identity confidential if they did not wish to be known. The most informative people were those who had already left the ministries where they had been holding important positions prior to leaving. Some of my best parliamentary questions originated from casual discussions with people on the ground. Some also gave me the background stories on how various policy decisions were reached when they were with the ministries.

My first parliamentary question came from a chat with a friend who was running a large private education institution. I wanted to know if there were interesting issues I could raise. His advice was, go ask how many Singaporeans were enrolled in private schools for higher learning and I would be surprised. I did, and indeed I was surprised to find that

41,000 Singaporeans were enrolled in private institutions of higher learning in Singapore. This was a very large number considering that Singapore had a cohort of around 40,000 born each year. That figure excluded the number of Singaporeans studying overseas as the government did not track such figures. A large percentage of the population desired higher learning. As such, increasing the number of places for Singaporeans in autonomous universities then became one of the issues I championed.

I must have done a decent job at covering the two ministries which I was given. Some months later, Low added a third — the Finance Ministry, which he felt was not sufficiently covered. Bills in this sector were even harder to fathom. Some required specific deep industry knowledge before you could speak intelligently on the issues. I took it on anyway.

Back on the topic of policy volunteers. I eventually stopped the meetings because the sessions became talk shops. They were good for general feedback but I was struggling to cope with three ministries plus two others, on top of my day jobs. I needed to be more effective and focused.

I recall in March 2012, there was a bill called the Energy Conservation Act, a dry topic under the Ministry of Trade and Industry. I dreaded speaking on this because if you did not have the knowledge and understanding, you could easily be made to look foolish. There would be much to read up on. Then I saw some wonderful research notes circulated to us by Daniel Goh, an associate professor from the National University of Singapore. Apparently, Goh had joined the WP not long ago as a volunteer and unknown to me, Low had been getting him to organise a research team. Goh divided volunteers into different teams for different areas and each team was kept small, but effective, as they would be people who could offer ideas and do relevant research. That was the early days of the 'policy group'. Over time, I believe more were recruited and more policy research areas opened up.

Gerald Giam and I spoke on the bill, with excellent inputs from the new policy group. From time to time, I would rely on them. Sometimes notes came back as pointers and data. Sometimes the research was so well-written you could extract a good part of it to be used in your speech. It was also helpful to have the new policy group keep an eye on issues that we could raise as parliamentary questions or speak about during the annual Committee of Supply debates on the ministries. Committee of Supply debates are held after the Budget debate in late February or early March each year, stretching for over a week and covering a wide range of topics. Extra help by volunteers of high calibre to monitor areas we could speak about or debate on policy ideas was always welcomed.

Low was ever mindful of expectations being set too high. We never called ourselves the Shadow Cabinet nor announced this publicly. I would have suffered from the workload of covering three ministries plus support in another two or three ministries if I had to be the Shadow Cabinet to so many ministries. We also did not want to raise too high expectations about our policy group. The PAP has ministers and junior ministers, plenty of them to spread across the ministries, working full-time as office-bearers. The PAP has access to 120,000 full-time public servants. Their backbencher MPs sit on Government Parliamentary Committees to shadow different ministries. They are given access to policymakers and data. We often had to fight hard for data from the ministries when such data was not available in the public domain.

In my opinion, our policy group of volunteers served two important functions:

1. MPs received better support from the more qualified volunteers working under the leadership of Goh, who had lots of experience in organising research.

2. Policy teams became a recruitment base for future candidates. We could see at first-hand how they conducted research and their level of maturity in policy matters.

Dennis Tan, Leon Perera, He Ting Ru, and several others, and of course Goh, were some of those from our policy teams who impressed me. After 2015, I was no longer deeply involved with policy work for the party as I was no longer in Parliament. I stepped in only when MPs needed specific help in areas which I was familiar with. I cannot comment on the policy helpers post-2015. I am sure many of the new candidates in 2020 were originally helping with our policy work. A few members in the GE2020 Marine Parade team were active in the policy groups.

Even with a more organised policy team, I personally wrote every single one of the many speeches I had delivered during my four-year term. It was my personal choice. I would feel strange if I had to deliver a speech someone wrote entirely for me. Writing was something I enjoyed anyway.

It was useful to have people of good intellect you could bounce ideas off or do research with. I maintained my own network of industry professionals whom I tapped for industry-specific policy ideas or issues. I went about specifically recruiting more experts whenever I met new people whom I thought would be useful for our policy work. Giam operated in such a manner too. We often shared our network of experts as I was back-up to the ministries he was covering. We would sometimes organise tea sessions with industry experts. Many were happy to contribute their expertise since it was infrequent and informal. They could see that we did not come from the point of trying to disrupt the government. We genuinely wanted to spar with industry experts to polish our policy ideas so that we could push the PAP. We also wanted to hear from practitioners if our ideas would work.

After the 2015 general election (GE2015), I continued to do my own independent research and wrote on areas that interested me. From time to time, I cross-checked mostly with Giam or Perera to make sure my proposals would not contradict things that the party may have been saying or planned to say. My source of information continued to be from industry professionals, whom I found very useful and whose advice were very effective.

## Pushing Early Childhood Issues via Parliamentary Processes

There were great expectations by Singaporeans. The WP had campaigned on the slogan, "Towards a First World Parliament". After a honeymoon period, some were calling for more fireworks in Parliament. Some were saying that we did not speak up enough. Some wanted us to propose motions or even bills.

It was very tough for the opposition to put forward bills that are to become law when passed. There are many technical considerations and the need for careful legal drafting. It would be greatly preferred to have the civil service support for this. When there were the rare private member's bills, these came from PAP backbenchers. I am sure they received good legal and legislative support from the relevant ministries so that their bills could be accepted without amendments by the government.

Private member's motions are possible and even NMPs had proposed motions. One can be quite certain though that if the WP proposed a motion, the PAP would pounce on it and amend the motion to try to make it backfire on us. They had amended motions raised by others before and made them look bad. In 2016, Low had to use a private member's motion to get Goh to fill in the NCMP seat vacated by Lee Li Lian as she had declined to take up the position. As expected, the motion was amended by the PAP. Early in the current 14th Parliament, Sylvia Lim, supported by He Ting Ru, already raised a full motion to call upon the government to review the fairness, access to justice, and independence of Singapore's justice system following the widespread uneasiness over the way foreign domestic worker Parti Liyani was deemed to have been treated under existing justice processes. During the debate, the motion was amended by PAP MP Murali Pillai and the WP was unable to vote in support of the amendments as it fundamentally altered the original motion's call for review. I expect that the WP may raise more full motions in the current and future Parliament terms. Of course, when it comes to voting, the PAP would outnumber the opposition and will continue to amend motions raised by the latter. Even if some NMPs voted with us, our motions would be voted out. Nevertheless, motions can be a good platform for vigorous debates.

Low had seen much in Parliament. He did not favour us raising full motions, nor was there an occasion during my time in Parliament when we felt a serious need to use that platform. I sensed too that Low was carefully evaluating us during the 12th Parliament. Seven of us from the WP (including Lee Li Lian) had entered Parliament. We were not gagged. We could raise questions, speak on bills, and make proposals during the annual marathon Budget and Committee of Supply debates.

To protect ourselves and to be consistent as a team, we shared speeches and the intended parliamentary questions with one another in advance. Low would usually be the most active to comment on our draft speeches during my time in Parliament. My perspectives on issues improved by taking his comments into account, not only regarding my speeches but also those of the others. Having a good perspective is important for a politician. I contributed my fair share of commenting on the speeches of others when they touched on topics that I was familiar with. I was glad to have additional eyes commenting on our speeches to make sure that we did not expose ourselves to unnecessary attacks.

I used the Parliament processes a lot. In 2015, shortly before the general election, a news website did a tally and reported that I had the highest speech count among all male parliamentarians. Yet I sometimes still meet people who ask why I was so quiet in Parliament. Most of what we say in Parliament is not reported in mainstream media unless there is something interesting or there has been an interesting engagement with political office-bearers or across the bench. To be fair, many things which PAP backbenchers had said were not reported either. There is limited airtime and print space in the mainstream media.

Instead of a full motion, adjournment motions can be useful for raising an issue. For adjournment motions, the MP can speak for up to 20 minutes on an issue and a political office-bearer will have up to 10 minutes of reply. No debate is allowed after the political office-bearer's reply.

One of the issues I had focused on early in my parliamentary term was reform for the preschool sector. I had been active in that sector previously. During my position in the REACH policy workgroup from 2007–2009, we dug deep into issues from this sector and made various bold and radical proposals. The government was not prepared to accept many of our proposals as they were deemed too disruptive and difficult to do. Before I had entered Parliament, my forum letter published in *The Straits Times* to push for reforms in the early childhood sector was brushed aside by the government.

Now in Parliament, I could force some attention on the issues which I considered needed to be seriously addressed. I raised many parliamentary questions. These were either to obtain data or to force a discussion on the topic. After several months, Low felt I was spending too much time on this and it could be misconstrued by the public that I was trying to benefit my businesses which were in education.

After GE2011, the elected MPs had to run the Aljunied-Hougang Town Council. They had fortnightly lunch meetings, which Giam and I were invited to join later. Even though both of us were not in the operations of Town Councils, the rest must have felt that this was a good platform for us to understand more about Town Council operations and to also use it as a platform for general discussions.

After Low's email telling me to tone down raising questions on early childhood, I used the next lunch session to explain to him why I had been asking these questions. After our lunch, I had a private discussion with him. I realised that like many Singaporeans, he also did not quite understand the differences between the operations of kindergartens and childcare centres. The PAP Community Foundation (PCF) kindergartens had to be subsidised as they were unprofitable. The PCF and National Trades Union Congress (NTUC) childcares were profitable, and they enjoyed huge subsidies and many advantages over other operators. Demand for childcare was rising and that of kindergartens falling. There were many structural issues governing how our preschools were run. I explained the problems and the solutions I was proposing, and Low listened intently. At the end of the session, he said, "You should file an adjournment motion on this."

That conversation was in mid-August 2012. The next Parliament sitting would be on September 10. The request for an adjournment motion had to be filed at least three working days before the next Parliament sitting. If there were two requests, then there would be a ballot to decide which would be permitted. There could only be one adjournment motion per sitting.

My adjournment motion would be heavy on policy proposals. The time to prepare was short but I wanted to push it out. I sensed that the government was relooking many matters in the industry but had not made any significant announcements yet. If there was a time to make the pitch, it should be immediately so that the WP could contribute towards policy changes.

I have attached my speech below. The data I presented came from both the public domain and from my earlier parliamentary questions. I argued for structural reforms to the sector. Halimah Yacob, then Minister of State for Community Development, Youth, and Sports, gave her 10-minute reply, most of which derived from standard answers defending the high standards of our centres and the investments by the government in the sector. She did not really reply to some of my points because she would not have known what I had wanted to say beforehand.

Over the next two to three years, major changes were indeed made to the sector. I continued to push for what I had proposed and added even more suggestions along the way. Many of what I had proposed in the adjournment motion, from my other parliament speeches and also proposals from my involvement in the REACH policy workgroup during 2007–2009, were eventually implemented by the government, some in slightly different form. Essentially, the government had acknowledged the need for major structural reforms to the sector and to provide significantly more resources. Only once, in response to my persistent questioning, then Minister for Social and Family Development, Chan Chun Sing, said that the ministry was looking at various proposals made by members of the House, including those raised by me. That was the only time in Parliament that I received a public acknowledgement that my suggestions were being considered. However, privately in the Parliament tearoom, I would sometimes have office-bearers, including then Deputy Prime Minister Tharman Shanmugaratnam, speaking to me further about what I had raised in Parliament.

Tharman is a gracious person. When he thought that my speech made sense, he would tell me so in the Parliament tearoom. In one of my Budget speeches, I had called for consolidation in our industries. The buzzword that year was productivity growth, which many members spoke on. I felt that one of the ways to push up productivity could be to nudge companies to consolidate so that there would be economies of scale. I called for the Finance Ministry to improve on their incentives to encourage mergers and acquisitions. At the end of all the speeches of that Budget, in the tearoom, Tharman saw me, came over, and said that my speech was very interesting and stood out for having focused on the need for consolidation. It was good to note that he was listening.

Several months later, the Ministry of Finance proposed various new incentives to facilitate mergers and acquisitions. Not all the incentives were in the form that I had suggested but they were of the same intent: to help industries consolidate.

Not all of our speeches were fiery. In fact, most supported the government's initiatives while offering new ideas on the execution.

> Adjournment Motion, September 10, 2012 — Transforming the childcare sector
>
> Mr Speaker, I like to add my suggestions for reforms to the childcare industry even as the government is looking at how to boldly transform this sector.
>
> I wish to declare that a part of my business supplies products and services to preschools. I have also previously managed and owned child care centres but have no longer been doing so for the past 7 years. This proposal is to improve the industry to benefit consumers. It will not benefit my business.
>
> I will first speak in mandarin.
>
> 新加坡的托儿企业开始于70年代。当时，只有几家私人运营商和非盈利运营商。
>
> 四到六岁的孩子可被幼稚园或托儿所照顾。托儿服务包括学前教育。但由于幼稚园的学费较低，幼稚园成为大多数家长为儿童提供学前教育的首选。
>
> 到了90年代，由于有更多双薪家庭的产生，托儿企业开始发展起来。在过去十年里，它的发展更急速。在工作场所开设托儿所变得常见。在2004年初，有651间托儿所。到了今年6月，这数目增加到987间。 在这期间里，托儿所招收的儿童人数从38,455名增加到75,456名。许多组屋新镇里的托儿所供不应求，有的报名后甚至要排队等一年以上。
>
> 包括婴儿护理在内,托儿所目前照顾近9万名儿童,跟幼稚园的9万三千名学生差不多。幼稚园登记人数在过去的十年里逐渐减少。依这个趋势来看，托儿所在数量

上将快超越幼稚园了。因此，托儿所会在我们社会中扮演重要的角色。

在2004年初，托儿所平均的全日学费是每月572元。到了2008年底，学费增到699元。目前，平均学费为831元。

2008年，政府增加托儿服务费用的津贴。全日学费每月的津贴从150元增加到300元，从以上数据来看，我们可看到的是在津贴增加的同时，托儿所的平均学费也同幅度增加。如果我们分析私人托儿所的学费，我相信其学费的增长超过政府津贴的增长，因为它们的租金和劳工成本增加得很快。今天的早报就提到私人托儿所租金的困难状况。

在最近的连氏基金(Lien Foundation)调查，90%的托儿服务使用者认为，学前教育是昂贵或非常昂贵的。该调查还指出一个严重问题：托儿学费高使到夫妻不想要更多的孩子。

我们是否可能有大众化，价格合理，良好的托儿服吗？我认为可以。现在，我用英语来解释。

In the child care industry, there are many private operators, most with one or a few centres while several run chain stores.

We also have non-profit operators, dominated by NTUC First Campus and PCF Sparkletots. They are called Anchor Operators, so determined after an exercise in 2009. The criteria used included: (a) $5 million paid-up capital, (b) non-profit and (c) without any religious or racial affiliation.

Anchor Operators function mostly from HDB[1] void decks, at rents of between $2 to $4 per square metre as disclosed by MCYS[2]. For a typical centre of 400–500 sqm, this means monthly rent

---

1   Housing and Development Board
2   Ministry of Community Development, Youth and Sports

of $1,000 onwards. They receive generous set-up and furnishing grants for each new centre. In addition, Anchors get recurrent grant for manpower development and learning programmes which is estimated to go into $30 million per year.

MCYS publishes upcoming new centres from HDB and SLA[3]. From its website, I see just a few centres available to private and non-profit operators. Yet at the opening of the 100th NTUC centre in October last year, NTUC declared it will open 50 new centres over the next 2 years, which is one every fortnight. PCF too had been growing just as rapidly in the last three years. Just five years ago, PCF was a small child care player. Today, it is number 2 with 90 centres, just behind NTUC. The many new centres by these two do not match the very small number of published centres for non-profit operators. Are they given unpublished quotas?

We are told that the role of non-profit and Anchor operators is to bring cost down while maintaining quality.

Sir, there is no magic in non-profit or in Anchor Operators. The lower fees they provide can be matched by private operators. I will now demonstrate that if private operators get the same benefits as non-profit and indeed the Anchor Operators, they have shown that they could match the fees of non-profit peers.

Financial modelling for child care is straightforward. The main start-up cost is renovation, fitting out, and investment in resources. Set-up cost can be high, running into several hundred thousand dollars per centre.

In a typical centre paying competitive rents, manpower and rent account for some 80% of all ongoing operating costs.

---

[3] Singapore Land Authority

Private operators function from landed houses, commercial and government-owned buildings or purpose-built HDB void decks. Tenancy is often subjected to bidding. When tenancy expires, there is usually open bidding or adjustments to market rate. Competition has caused rents to be in excess of $10,000 to even as high as $40,000 per month in recent tenders.

Anchor Operators get choice new sites regularly at highly subsidized rents. They receive start-up, furnishing, maintenance and recurrent grants. These give them huge operating benefits over competitors.

The difference in monthly rent between non-profit and private operators can be $15,000 per month or more. Divide $15,000 by a typical centre enrolment of 75 children. That works out to around $200 cost advantage per child per month. With setup grants, Anchor Operators need to provide less for amortization of investment. They get ongoing grants to defray costs. Yet with these cost advantages, non-profit's median fees is currently just two hundred over dollars lower than that of private operators. We can find private centres whose fees are not much higher than that of Anchor Operators. Are Anchor Operators with all these cost advantages, really doing enough to keep fees affordable?

Sir, there are other industry data to support my claim.

In a parliament reply this year, MCYS disclosed that EtonHouse, a premium operator with fees of $1,500 per month, charges only $728 per month at its Hampton Preschool. The centre is a collaboration with PCF. PCF secured the site at low rent, and can enjoy other grants. EtonHouse is responsible for programme delivery, set-up and pedagogy. According to a speech by Mr Wong Kan Seng in 2009, EtonHouse manages the centre and was selected because PCF wanted to work with a private operator that could deliver 'high quality programmes'.

While there could be variations in operations compared to a typical EtonHouse's centre, the fact is, EtonHouse could deliver 'high quality programmes' at less than half of its usual fees when it operates at a void deck that enjoys subsidised rents and grants.

In the 1990s, government buildings started to provide for workplace childcare. There was an interesting practice then to charge $1 or other token monthly rent for purpose-built child care facilities which catered to children of staff working in the building. Bids were called. I noted that in open competition, these sites went to established private players whose own centres charged in the mid to upper price range.

The condition for low rent then was that fees for children of staff in the buildings must be kept low. Premium private operators could match prevailing fees of non profit operators.

Today, costs are escalating due mainly to rent and manpower. Manpower cost affects all in the industry. Anchor Operators with recurrent grants can better retain staff, head-hunt from other centres and deal with rising costs. Rent is steadily rising in our competitive market.

This has caused fees to rise. Out of pocket payments by parents in many private centres today are higher than before subsidies were increased in 2008. MCYS has no control over fees. Centres just need to give 'ample' notice to parents, which MCYS recommends as 3 months, and then fees will go up.

The government has announced new measures for the industry. While they may be initiated with good intent, I fear it could end up creating more unfair competition, destroying the diversity and innovation in our current system.

I have a proposal to bring costs down while pushing for quality and diversity — child care as a public good with private partnership through contestability.

I noted that in delivering public goods such as transport, the government has pumped billions in rail and bus investments without expecting pay back from private operators or charging infrastructure at market rent to them. We were told this is to bring the cost of public transport to a level that people can accept.

If we wish for young working couples to be able to afford child care and be encouraged to have more children, then we have a case to use a public good's approach for child care.

Government can build and lease out centres at managed low rent. All its existing sites can come under the model. Based on answers in Parliament, there are 290 void deck centres for non-profit and 176 for private operators in void deck and JTC[4] buildings, and another 52 in government buildings. That's 518 centres, roughly 52.4% of all child care in Singapore. With 200 more centres to be built mostly in government-controlled spaces, the share of sites under government's control will rise.

Old schools, disused community centres and other SLA spaces can be purpose-built by the government into mega child care facilities, even housing different operators under one roof. Childcare generally should be within 2–3 km of workplaces or homes. Many small void decks in new flats are not ideal for child care, limiting options in new towns. We can have mega child care sites as long as we ensure there is easy access by parents, with roads and parking well planned.

We can utilise unused land parcels next to primary schools.

---

4   Jurong Town Corporation

There are small plots around some primary schools which are not big enough for meaningful commercial projects. We can tap on infrastructure of the primary schools to add new preschool facilities. This will make use of unutilised space, save on infrastructure costs and cultivate exchange between preschool and primary school.

The government can negotiate as main tenant with large private landlords for sites as a bloc to supplement their bank of child care sites. It can work with property developers who get additional Gross Floor Area when they set aside preschool space at cheap rents and let the government use the space for any type of operator. We should actively pursue all options to increase the state's child care bank to cater to the mass market.

How do we allocate these centres? Rather than have more Anchor Operators, I have another suggestion.

The Anchor Operators concept has skewed the market. It is like giving a boxer super gloves and energy boosters while tying the hands of the competitor and asking them to fight each other. The stated objective for Anchor Operators was to "develop childcare operators that will set the benchmark for quality and affordable childcare services."

It may have allowed Anchor Operators to achieve higher quality as they get resources, economy of scale, and certainty of their leases. Is it fair to expect other operators to keep pace? Other operators get little or no state funding. They hesitate to invest, worried if others will outbid them for their centres at each renewal, which will wipe out sunk investment. New HDB sites are so few compared to unannounced sites for Anchor Operators. Anchor Operators could lure their staff away with scholarships. Instead of encouraging other operators to step up, it can cause some to think short term and extract as much out of their investment while they can.

We can apply contestability. Contest clusters of sites openly based on concept rather than on rent. This was done before, when government building sites charged token rent and selection was on other factors such as quality and fees.

There is no need for a one-time selection of new Anchor Operators which will strengthen only a select few and weaken everyone else. Worst, it may become impossible for new operators to enter the market, killing off future innovation. We need active competition to raise standards and to continuously drive innovation.

Recurrent and other grants should apply to all qualifying participants as long as they meet strict selection criteria on fees and quality. There should be no differentiation between private and non profit operators. We already know what the current Anchor Operators can do with the support they had been given. Why have we been limiting ourselves to think only selected non profit players can bring cost down? Let's open up and see how all others, including private operators can better that in terms of price and quality, if given similar support. I believe fair competition may even force current Anchor Operators to better their pricing, ultimately benefiting consumers.

New operators can surface from time to time. Small operators may band together into economic groups to better compete.

Contestability will drive diversity and quality. Operators cannot increase fees without approval. The government will regain control over the fee process to ensure affordability.

Government can better direct its key programmes. MCYS had found it hard to get private operators to go along with some of its programmes, such as SPARK. Last month, we were told only 115 preschools had attained SPARK accreditation, of which just 39 were private operators. This is way below the target of 85% of all centres to be SPARK-tested by 2013, a figure established by Minister of State for Education, Mr Masagos in November 2010. We can allow only SPARK-accredited operators to contest these sites.

There may not even be a need for state-run preschools. The call for nationalisation was made by many frustrated with differing standards and high costs. We can improve quality even at the low-cost segment by having a critical mass of centres available in this public-good model, and the state regulate to steer quality and pricing. It can designate some centres for the low-income group by packaging centres for different market segments in each tender exercise.

While this proposal is in the context of child care, it can also be used for kindergartens.

In summary, I am calling for child care to be a public good with fair contestability of sites at managed rents for all types of operators, with tighter control of fees and quality by the state. This will benefit Singaporeans as fees will drop industry-wide while preserving diversity and driving up quality and innovation. I hope the government can carefully consider this proposal.

## Pressing Issues via Parliament

Prior to being in Parliament, I had used the forum pages of newspapers to spotlight issues. I doubt the government takes them seriously. I also made proposals through government policy workgroups that I had participated in. These were given more serious responses. My experience though, is that if you agree with what the government was doing or had planned to do, they will gladly take your suggestions as affirmation.

When things were too challenging to do, even if necessary, you would be ignored. The preschool reforms I had cited in the previous section is one such example. Post-GE2011, the government did everything that they had earlier said they would not be able to do, and did even more.

Parliament is the highest platform in the country for law and policy-making. Even though we were outnumbered by the PAP, as opposition members we could effectively use Parliament to spotlight issues. The PAP would not acknowledge any mistake they had made or credit the opposition with any U-turn it made. Yet embarrassing data or issues could force some back-end work and quiet changes.

Some MPs, including the PAP backbenchers, are more persistent in forcing a harder look into issues. I had raised many issues during the 12th Parliament. I cite a few examples below to show how I had used question time and speeches in Parliament to force attention on these issues:

- Foreign scholarships
- Student care centres for all primary schools
- Unreasonable junior college examination standards
- Social enterprise hawker centres
- Legislation to address transboundary haze
- Through-train primary to secondary schools

**Foreign scholarships**

There had long been murmurs on the ground that we have been too generous with foreign scholarships and that the quality of many foreign scholars was not good. My own investigations talking with my contacts lecturing in our local universities revealed alarming stories of some foreign scholars who could not even attain third-class honours. How could Parliament be used to get facts and force a review? I decided to test this out early in my parliamentary term.

There was not much data on this publicly. In January 2012, I asked the

Ministry of Education (MOE) for the number of foreign scholars in our schools and universities, what percentage of them graduated with second-class (upper) honours, and what percentage completed their contractual bond period to work in Singapore.

I had decided to use second-class (upper) honours as a gauge of the quality of foreign students we were fully funding.

The answer that came back was strangely about the number of Association of Southeast Asian Nations (ASEAN) scholars. Nowhere in my question had I asked about ASEAN scholars. The figure was not high. Perhaps whoever prepared the reply might have felt that some Singaporeans may not mind Malaysians, Indonesians, and others from nearby countries coming to Singapore on scholarship because a good number have stayed here permanently after graduation and had even taken up citizenship. I figured the issue must then be the scholars from non-ASEAN countries.

Refusing to give up, I asked at the next Parliament sitting for the number of non-ASEAN scholars. It turned out to be a much larger number. And if one were to study the figure carefully, the answer was worded as the number of scholarships awarded out each year to foreign students. One has to read deeper into the answers. Scholarships tend to be for four years for the full duration of studies. I estimated that foreign scholarships at that time could have cost Singapore in the region of $144 million a year in total.

My questioning also revealed that 67 percent of the foreign scholars graduated with second-class (upper honours). Then Senior Parliamentary Secretary for Education, Sim Ann, justified that it was a good number compared with 32 percent of locals who graduated with second-class (upper) honours.

The Internet soon became abuzz with discussions.

(i) How could we compare the foreign scholars who were fully covered in cost to study here with the mass of local graduates, most of whom have to pay their way through universities? The better comparison would be with how foreign universities fund Singaporeans to study there; or to compare with our Public Service Commission (PSC) scholars. I believe Singaporean scholars in top foreign universities or our PSC scholars who do not maintain a grade point average equivalent to at least second-class (upper) standard during their studies will face a great risk of being kicked out. Surely our expectations were set too low?

(ii) The amount invested seemed high, especially when matched against the quality of some of these foreign scholars.

Subsequently, I followed up with additional parliamentary questions and speeches in later sittings. MOE continued to defend their policy. However, from my investigation with insiders in MOE and in our autonomous universities, I found that changes were made to the policy. After a couple of years, I noticed that the number of foreign scholarships was cut down, particularly from China and India. In fact, some hostels in our schools catering mostly to foreign scholars became quite empty. I stopped asking questions on this since change had been made. Whether my questions had forced any change or whether MOE had already earlier decided to cut down the numbers, I would not know.

## Student care centres for all primary schools

I had also called for student care centres to be located in all primary schools. MOE then had planned for 40 percent of primary schools to have such facilities. I was sure the demand would be very high. Childcare customers of yesterday would be the student care customers of today. Childcare demand had been very strong for several years. Children will continue to need care facilities in their early primary years. Having centres within schools would be most ideal.

Dissatisfied with an earlier MOE response to my question on this matter, I did some quick investigations. I called many existing student care centres located in schools to check on their vacancies. None had vacancies. Some waitlists were as long as more than 40. A few centres told me not to bother to be put on the waitlist. I used the 2014 Committee of Supply debate on MOE to present my findings.

Two years later, MOE announced that all primary schools would have student care centres by 2020. Perhaps MOE already had planned to increase the numbers. My method of quick research may be unconventional, but I felt it did highlight the pressing issue.

**Unreasonable Junior College examination standards**

One day, to my horror, I found that a mid-tier junior college (JC) failed half their students at the Year 1 (JC1) promotion examinations. Those who did not fail too badly could go for supplementary examinations. Still, after the supplementary lessons, around 200 JC1 students would be retained each year. I felt that this did not align with the MOE's direction to place less stress on grades but to have a more holistic education. I shared this data with a vice principal of another junior college and she, too, was shocked that the failure rate could be so high. Both of these colleges had about the same General Certificate of Education Ordinary Level cut-off point for student intake. Yet one retained more than 20 percent of its students and the other under five percent, the latter being the more typical rate.

I filed a parliamentary question asking for failure rate at JC1 level. I followed up with a short speech during the Committee of Supply debate on MOE. At the Parliament tearoom, I met then Senior Minister of State for Education Indranee Rajah who had just officially replied me on my speech. I told her why I felt strongly that using a high failure rate to push students was not right. I told her I was very sure of my data and which junior college it was. However, I said that I would not raise this issue again in Parliament. I had stated my stand and it was for MOE to decide if that was right.

The next year, I checked again with my sources in the junior college. The failure rate had dropped dramatically to be the same as that in other colleges.

## Social enterprise hawker centres

I did not file any speeches with regard to the Ministry of the Environment and Water Resources (MEWR) in 2013. Back then, NCMPs were entitled to a maximum of only 18 minutes of speaking time across all speeches during the Committee of Supply debates, across all ministries. I would usually deliver around nine speeches, spread across, at least, the three ministries that I was tasked to track, and maybe in one or two more ministries. Approximately 3 to 3.5 minutes were for 'long' speeches, usually when I had several implementation ideas to propose. Some speeches were only one minute long, such as my earlier query about JC1 examinations, which I simply wished to flag as an issue for the Ministry to reply to.

I would have wanted to speak about the social enterprise hawker centre (SEHC) model that the MEWR was about to implement, except that I had no time left in my allocation. Parliament's practice was that after all the scheduled speeches had been delivered by the MPs and the reply had been made by the minister, if there was time left, MPs could raise their hands to ask questions.

I was lucky that day. There was time left and the chair of the session allowed me to pose a question. I expressed concern that if we gave too much autonomy to the operators to impose rents and other charges to hawkers, when these operators have a significant market share of the hawker centres, we might face monopolistic behaviours that would impose high operating costs on hawkers. Hawkers would in turn impose higher food prices on consumers.

Why did I sound the caution about the operators, who would have to be social enterprises (SEs)? I had seen the reality of how SEs had run other public goods in the past. Call them whatever we wish, SEs will still want to make surpluses. When they dominate the market, monopolistic behaviours can set in.

Hence, I sought the assurance of the minister to monitor the way SEHC will be operated. Then Minister for Environment and Water Resources, Vivian Balakrishnan, gave his assurance in Parliament that his ministry would keep a tight watch over the way hawkers would be charged.

Fast forward five years: in 2019, the issue became a national debate when food blogger K. F. Seetoh revealed details of high rental charges and ridiculous terms and working hours that hawkers had to abide by.

Much online debate ensued. Many Singaporeans were angry that commercial operators were allowed to form SEs to manage hawker centres with burdensome terms for hawkers compared to those at hawker centres under the management of the National Environment Agency (NEA). Hawkers seemed to be imposed with many other costs beyond the actual rental.

The negative publicity forced NEA to stop operators from imposing some onerous conditions, allowing for early termination with smaller penalties, shortening required operating hours of hawkers, capping the fines that SEHC operators could impose on hawkers, and providing improved feedback channels for hawkers.

In this incident, it was a famous food blogger whose online publicity forced some firm actions by the authorities for the betterment of the poor hawkers. As a backbencher, I felt that my role then was to force some commitment from the government to pay attention to potential problems that could arise in the execution. I had no powers to audit the government thereafter. They will be accountable for what they had committed to. This incident also highlighted flaws in our policy planning. Policies look beautiful on paper. I am a business practitioner. I have seen issues with SE models with other public goods. Career policymakers may not anticipate such issues. Prominent former top civil servant, the late Ngiam Tong Dow, once said in a public forum that civil servants must walk the ground first before making policies.[5] Indeed, it would be good for policymakers to spend more time on the ground to better understand how a policy is to be implemented.

**Legislation to address transboundary haze**

Nobody likes the haze. Once in a while, Singapore suffers from severe haze from large fires in our neighbouring countries. These happen outside of Singapore but affect us terribly. There had been not much that Singapore could do, other than urge our neighbours to do more in their home countries to put out the fires and punish culprits who were responsible for the fires.

I happened to be in a discussion via email with former NMP Ivan Png when the issue of our annual haze cropped up. We discussed the possibility of having laws in Singapore to punish local companies in other countries. Singapore does have some laws that cover jurisdictions beyond Singapore, such as punishing Singaporeans for paedophile crimes even if these were committed overseas. While laws with transboundary reach are a rarity, we felt that Singapore should find ways to punish offences related to transboundary haze committed overseas.

I raised the issue first through Parliament questions in 2013 and later as a speech during the Committee of Supply debate on MEWR in 2014.

I was surprised to find that five months later, MEWR proposed the Transboundary Haze Pollution Bill, incorporating what I had suggested about providing powers to Singapore authorities to punish overseas

---

5  Kelly Ng, "Civil servants must walk the ground first before making policies", Today, July 10, 2015, https://www.todayonline.com/singapore/civil-servants-must-walk-ground-first-making-policies-ngiam

companies or individuals guilty of causing transboundary haze that affected Singapore. Naturally, I spoke during that debate to support the bill.

**Through-train primary to secondary schools**

One issue which I took on right from my entry into Parliament was examination stress and the excessive meritocratic system based primarily on examination results. I spoke about it in my maiden speech. Finding the solution to this difficult balance of meritocracy and stress was challenging.

The Primary School Leaving Examinations (PSLE) is a sorting examination that students sit for at the age of 12 at the end of their primary school education to determine the academic stream and secondary school the child would be allocated. In Singapore, schools have become so differentiated after years of branding and streaming that sadly, many parents see the PSLE as a do-or-die milestone.

I quickly set about to find out how the WP could contribute towards a solution. Doing away with the PSLE is difficult. Most Singaporeans know no other way to settle the allocation of school places. Some insist that such examinations are absolute necessaries, no matter how stressful.

I wondered if a through-train integrated school from primary to secondary was possible. So far, we only have several elite secondary to junior college integrated schools. Entrance into these schools were based mostly on the PSLE results, with some leeway for direct school admission where students may gain admission into schools based upon their strengths in specific academic areas, or their athletic or musical talents.

In speaking with a former senior official at MOE, I was interested to learn that around the time that MOE was planning for secondary to college integrated schools, an aided school with primary and secondary sections once made a proposal to MOE to run such a primary to secondary programme. However, the proposal was rejected by MOE. I learned from this friend the objections that MOE had at that time.

I believe a balance could be found. We could start with a small number of such integrated schools. To prevent shifting the stress to the preschool level, we could exclude top secondary schools from the scheme so there will be no through-train backdoor to top schools. It has to be started with neighbourhood schools. I considered various other implementation issues and then wrote a speech to be presented in the 2012 Committee of Supply debate.

As with all our speeches, I submitted my speech to all WP parliamentarians prior to my scheduled presentation. Low's comment was that it was a major proposal and I should first clear it with the CEC, unless it was already in our earlier manifestos, which meant that it would have been cleared by the CEC before. Low felt that not everyone in the party's highest decision-making body may agree with it. Any speech in Parliament by a WP MP will be taken to be the party's position and we will have to stand by it later.

I seized upon the following statement in our manifesto of GE2011 and quoted it to Low:

> "Taking the Primary School Leaving Examinations (PSLE) is a stressful experience for children and parents alike. At a tender age of 12, a young pupil has to face the most important examination of his pre-adolescence life — an examination that may affect his entire future. We should study the feasibility of a primary-secondary integrated programme." (WP Manifesto 2011, page 31)

The manifesto was vague. It acknowledged the huge stress at a tender young age but did not offer a concrete solution. It asked for a study on the feasibility of the integrated programme. I reasoned that my speech would be a practical execution of an idea the WP had already mooted.

Low accepted my argument. I went on to deliver the speech, the content which is provided below.

A year later, in the Committee of Supply debate of 2013, PAP MP Denise Phua and NMP Laurence Lien also made similar proposals. Phua even followed up on another occasion with an adjournment motion on the same issue, with almost similar execution ideas. It was good to note that I was not alone in wanting to push this. I also spoke again on this in the Committee of Supply debate of 2013, 2014, and 2015 because I believed passionately in it. Each time, I added more implementation suggestions on how to make it feasible. I championed this to be in the WP's manifesto of 2015 and spoke about it in one of my GE2015 rally speeches and at a doorstop interview with the media. If I were in Parliament again, I probably would have continued to raise it every year!

To date, the plan has yet to be executed by MOE. I had surfaced it for discussion and several other MPs have since suggested it too. The purpose of sharing it in this book is to show the process in which I had used to advance a proposal within the party's rules for making new policy suggestions.

> Speech during Committee of Supply debate (Ministry of Education), March 8, 2012
>
> Mr Yee Jenn Jong (Non-Constituency Member): We started the Integrated Programme (IP) in 2004 to allow higher ability secondary school students to skip the "O" levels into the "A" levels or its equivalent. I wish to propose an alternative IP, from primary one to secondary four. The current system puts huge pressure on students, parents and teachers in primary schools to prepare for the PSLE. Various Members in this House, including myself, had spoken on the excessive pressures in our school system. A Straits Times article last month reported more parents taking their primary school kids to see psychologists after doing badly in school tests, some as young as Primary 2.

The purpose of PSLE and other major exams appears to be to sort students into different streams and into different schools. Our highly competitive examination-driven system has resulted in high dependency on tuition and drilling for exams rather than education for the joy of learning.

Sir, I understand this is a difficult and emotive issue as there are parents who may feel a competitive system is desirable. However, there are parents, like myself, who can accept that our children need not fight to be in the best schools. The current system offers us no choice at all because of the dreaded consequence of the child doing badly in a major examination at aged 12. Many parents feel their child's future is determined by the PSLE. Many private schools globally already through-train students from primary to secondary, including overseas schools based on the Singapore curriculum. Some of these schools have done well in international tests despite not subjecting students to standardised examinations at Primary 6. Finland switched to such a through-train system nationwide with encouraging outcomes. Its PISA[6] test scores are comparable to Singapore's.

I would like MOE to consider piloting primary through secondary IP schools with the same level of funding per student as any Government or aided school. With such schools, primary education need not be focused on grinding out results just for PSLE and schools can spend more time on values-based education. The post-primary section will eventually prepare students for a recognised examination, namely "O" levels, "A" levels or even the International Baccalaureate. By that time, students are more mature and better able to handle stress. Existing school groups may opt to run such a programme. There

---

6   Programme for International Student Assessment

are already aided schools in Singapore with affiliation schemes where the majority of primary students enter the affiliated secondary schools. Such schools have long histories and are trusted education brands. They are potential candidates to kick-start the programme. MOE has implemented holistic assessments since 2010. The experience of holistic assessments can be incorporated to ensure the rigour in learning throughout the years of studies in such pilot schools.

Sir, I believe we have the calibre of management and teachers in Singapore to achieve this. I hope MOE can do a serious study on making this option available.

## The Population Blue Paper That Nearly Was Not to Be

In January 2013, the government issued the Population White Paper, titled "A Sustainable Population for a Dynamic Singapore".

The paper was released on January 29, 2013. It was to be debated in Parliament on February 4, just five days later!

The paper evoked strong sentiments among Singaporeans. They were already feeling congested in Singapore and feeling unfairness in employment due to the large number of migrant workers. The paper had called for an even higher population projection and many more migrant workers.

It was an important paper to debate. The WP had to put up a strong response. Many eyes were watching us.

All WP parliamentarians met. By then, Daniel Goh had a small team of capable volunteer policy helpers. They were doing some background research on the population issue earlier. We discussed our broad approach and what each MP would speak on. All of us had to speak. As with all our major debates, we planned our main points of attack and the planks of our defence. During the heat of debates, MPs needed to constantly fall back on our core principles to avoid being waylaid by the opponents.

Goh was to work on number crunching to see what alternative model we could come up with. Our options were either to oppose the white paper or to come up with our alternative model, including our own population projections. Bear in mind that we only had five days before Parliament was due to convene. We would need to have prepared our model and debated internally well before delivering it as a speech in Parliament.

At our first meeting, which was called immediately after the paper was released, Goh presented some models the team had been working on. There were some discussions and confusion over how our models worked and their implications. In my professional jobs, I had dealt a lot with numbers and spreadsheet projections. I was able to follow Goh's modelling perfectly during the meeting. As such, Low tasked me to be the coordinating person on behalf of the MPs with Goh. There were too many technical terms thrown up during the meeting. It was not productive for the MPs to be spending time on technical discussions.

The complexity was because there were many dimensions. One had to look at mortality rate, birth rate, labour force participation rate, female participation rate in the workforce, population profile by age ranges, and so on. These had to be linked with economic targets. While the government white paper had its model for us to check against, these were high-level presentations of information. There were still many assumptions and decisions we needed to make, and what sources of data we would rely on.

Having Goh and the policy team was a godsend. I had to be the gatekeeper to fully understand our model, the data and assumptions behind them, and what the implications were. We had to leave it to the MPs to work out how to do their presentation. Our model had to be defendable. Low constantly reminded us that if our model was based on wrong data or wrong calculations, the policy people on the government side would quickly tear it apart. Then the focus would not be on what the MPs had to say, but that the WP could not do projections correctly. If we had based our speeches on our model and the modelling was faulty, we would be finished. Low cited the example of the Singapore Democratic Party (SDP) being hauled to a Parliament Select Committee in 1996 over false data about the government's healthcare spending, for which Chee Soon Juan, secretary-general of the SDP, and some SDP colleagues were fined for Contempt of Parliament. We had to ensure that our model and data were correct.

We arrived at our population figure of 5.6–5.8 million by the year 2030 based on immediate zero foreign manpower growth and various population forecasting data and scenarios of labour force participation rate and total fertility rate.

While dealing with number crunching with Goh, I also had to handle my speech. I had to be confident as I explained our computation and what the implications were to our MPs. The topic was quite technical. I sensed that Low was beginning to lose confidence in our modelling. I recall at one meeting quite near to the Parliament sitting, I was still having to explain how our model worked. Low remarked something along the lines of, "Hello, so late already and we are still not sure about our model! Better get this right or we will be finished!"

I recall that just after, Goh sent me a new computational model. He felt that we could be even more aggressive in our projections without many implications on the economic targets by changing some population assumptions. I took a look and suggested that he should not even present the new model to Low, who would have totally lost confidence in us and would call off any presentation of our alternative model. Our MPs would then revert to just poking holes at the PAP's model without any substantial alternative on our end. Goh agreed with me, saying something along the lines of, "That's why the technical people leave it to the politicians to do their job."

You can imagine my relief when we went through the several days of intensive debate on the paper. No one questioned the accuracy of our model. The debate was on the philosophical aspects of the economic model that we should have and hence the accompanying population implications.

Shortly after the debates, Goh and team presented the 'Blue Paper' titled, "A Dynamic Population for a Sustainable Singapore". The presentation and explanations were excellent. I felt so proud of it. The more technical people in the WP had been pushing for the party to publish our own policy papers. We had to start somewhere. The population debate, though we were given an unfairly short time, was a good place to start.

For several months, that mountain of data still resided in my head. I recall Tan Chuan-Jin, then Minister for Manpower, spoke about the government trying to keep our foreign worker population to around 33 percent of our total workforce. I rose to question him because the PAP's own model in the white paper projected that foreign workers could grow to 40 percent in one of the scenarios. He agreed with me, saying that when he spoke about this target of 33 percent, he was referring to the current decade till 2020. Beyond that, it would depend on the success of Singapore increasing its workforce participation rate and growing workers' productivity. Indeed, I vividly recall that our local workforce was expected to hit its maximum in 2020. Beyond that, the number of locals completing their studies and entering the workforce was projected to be fewer each year than those retiring. We would have a shrinking local workforce. There was no way that the figure could be kept to 33 percent.

Since our Population Blue Paper, the WP has occasionally published other policy papers on issues such as redundancy insurance and the WP's alternatives to the Voluntary Early Redevelopment Scheme for selected HDB precincts aged 70 years or more. I believe the WP will continue to issue more policy papers in the years to come.

## Fireworks in Parliament

After GE2011, at our first meeting, for the WP parliamentarians, Low and Sylvia Lim were sharing what to expect in Parliament and also highlighted some technical aspects of Parliament. One of the things I vividly remember was Low telling us that he did not get into big fights with the PAP all the time, maybe about three times for each Parliament term. I guess this was a key difference between Low and the late J. B. Jeyaretnam, the first opposition MP elected since independence, and previous secretary-general of the WP. Low did not believe in opposing all the time. The WP would only oppose when we needed to, as the government needed to get on with doing its job of running the country. And when we did oppose, the fights could get ugly, depending on what the issues were.

A friend who is an observer of politics described Parliament as a modern-day gladiator arena. Instead of fighting with weapons and fists, we use words. Winning or losing is how the public perceives the debates.

Yes, we had some fights during my time in Parliament.

The first was over ministerial salaries in 2012. We deliberated and came up with our alternative model for computing salaries and listed our key points of disagreement with the PAP. However, I would not classify this as a big fight. While we voted against the proposal, exchanges were not that fiery.

The Population White Paper debate was closely watched by Singaporeans. Coming after the electoral losses by the PAP to the WP in GE2011, and later in the Hougang and Punggol East by-elections, the PAP wanted to score on this. There was significant unhappiness on the ground with the PAP. All the WP MPs spoke during the debate against the motion and our speeches drew rebuttals from both the PAP political office-bearers and backbenchers. Several other parliamentarians also expressed great concerns over the direction indicated by the Population White Paper.

Low called for a vote on this at the end of five days of intense debate. Parliament procedures allow for any member to call for a division, that is, to vote on the matter at the end of a debate. The call must be supported by at least five members. The vote was called to record our objection to the motion as well as to record the votes of all members present. It was quite significant that NCMP Lina Chiam and NMPs Laurence Lien, Faizah Jamal, and Janice Koh joined us to vote against the PAP's Population White Paper. NMP Eugene Tan abstained although his speech sounded as if he might have voted against. PAP MP Inderjit Singh was absent from the voting. He had given a scathing speech against the grow-at-all-cost economic model of the government earlier. He went as far as to say that the government had failed to deliver on its promise of the Swiss standard of living for Singaporeans.

The WP also voted against the temporary Public Order Bill, introduced in response to the Little India riot. The Little India riot took place in 2013 after a traffic accident had caused the death of an Indian migrant worker, resulting in hundreds taking part in acts of public violence. The Public Order Bill sought to give officers the right to search people in the area for alcohol and other prohibitive items, and limited the sale and consumption of alcohol as it was believed that alcohol escalated the unrest. While Singaporeans were shocked by the riots, there were strong sentiments that the powers given to law enforcement officers were too drastic, and a knee-jerk reaction to the riots, introduced even before the Committee of Inquiry's findings on the riots were completed.[7] Chiam and Tan also spoke against the bill. I found that recent cohorts of NMPs included some fairly independent-minded people. The participation of the NMPs who joined the opposition to vote against bills and motions was always welcomed. While our numbers are small, even including the NMPs, one has to remember that Parliament is a gladiator arena. The more NMPs voting against the PAP's papers meant that the PAP had failed to convince them. I got along well with some of the NMPs and

---

7 Tham Yuen-C, "Workers' Party opposes temporary public order law in Little India, The Straits Times, February 18, 2014, https://www.straitstimes.com/singapore/workers-party-opposes-temporary-public-order-law-in-little-india

we continued to keep in touch even after we had all left Parliament.

The most heated exchanges were over the Action Information Management (AIM) system, the Aljunied-Hougang-Punggol East Town Council (AHPETC), and, at the end of the mid-term President's Address, the issue of constructive politics.

### The Action Information Management system and Aljunied-Hougang-Punggol East Town Council saga

The sale of the Town Council information management system by the PAP Town Councils to the $2 paid-up capital company owned by the PAP prior to GE2011 sparked fierce exchanges in Parliament. For background, all the PAP Town Councils had been using a software developed and paid for from Town Council funds. In June 2010, the software was sold for $140,000 to the company Action Information Management Pte Ltd (AIM) owned by the PAP and with three of its former MPs as directors.

The discovery came to light when the WP won the Aljunied GRC. AIM's contract with Town Councils had stated that AIM had the right to a one-month termination of its services if there was a material change in the ownership of the Town Council.

The WP, led by then Town Council Chairman Sylvia Lim, made the issue public in December 2012. It created a furore online. For some, this was seen as a way to trip up opposition MPs who had won a constituency. Data is key to the proper running of Town Councils. A one-month notice was too short a time to develop any alternative information management system. The defence for the original transfer of the software to AIM was that the system was ageing, and it was bought by AIM from the Town Councils through an open tender. Also, AIM's argument was that the WP-led Town Council wanted to develop their own system and hence the use of the software was terminated by mutual agreement.

The Ministry of National Development (MND) launched a review of the 2010 transaction between the Town Councils and AIM. MND later released its findings in May 2013, reporting that the AIM deal was legally sound and had complied with the Town Councils Act and Town Council Financial Rules.

In response to the MND findings, Lim forced a debate on the issue by first filing an adjournment motion to talk about it. After Lim had filed the adjournment motion, Khaw Boon Wan, then Minister for National Development, scheduled a ministerial statement on the topic. Lim withdrew her adjournment motion, since the issue could then be debated in response to a ministerial statement.

What followed was a fiery debate, which you can read online, mostly involving Lim and Pritam Singh with Khaw. I could not resist joining in when listening to Khaw talk about how a Town Council management system was essentially a collection of different software such as a financial package, human resource package, and other standard software. He seemed to suggest that the Town Council information management system could be assembled within a month by going to Funan (a shopping centre specialising in technology products) and buying different packages off the shelf. I also happened to know a bit about the company that developed the very first Town Council management system.

I rose to question Khaw at the end of the AIM debate. The following is our short exchange:

> Mr Yee Jenn Jong: I have two questions for the Minister. One, the Minister said that the tender period was opened for three weeks and that the tenderers could seek clarifications. It was reported in *The New Paper* that one of the tenderers said that, 'After paying more than $200, we simply got a thin stack of documents and the Town Councils were unable to provide us

with more information.' So did MND interview the other four companies when they were doing the review?

The other clarification I have is that the Minister said that AIM is not an ordinary $2 paid-up capital company and it has helped to develop the TCMS[8] systems previously. Now, this does not gel with my own personal information.

From 2000 to 2003, I happened to work with Horizon and I am pretty aware that they have a town management technology company that claimed that in November 1994, it built the town management systems entirely for the 19 PAP Town Councils.

So I would like to seek the Minister's clarification on this part of the Report which says that AIM had built the systems. What manpower did AIM have at that point in time? What was AIM's role in the first-generation system?

And, finally, just to make a point. As a person who has been in the IT industry for the last 20 years, I find the Minister's suggestions that we can just buy an off-the-shelf solution for the Town Councils' operations to be impossible.

Mr Khaw Boon Wan: On the point about off-the-shelf software, we have noted his comment. But my key point is that AIM did not ask to terminate, so the one-month clause was built in, it is their legal right to do so; they never intended to do so; they were prepared to extend but they were not asked, no request and, therefore, nothing happened.

On the Horizon history, honestly, I am not familiar. We are just focused on this 2010 transaction and related issues. The past, I was not involved myself, so I cannot add value to this particular comment.

---

8 Town council management computer system

I share below a post I made on August 2, 2020 in response to a *The Straits Times*' interview with Emeritus Senior Minister (ESM) Goh Chok Tong after his retirement, titled "GE2020 showed Singapore at 'inflexion point': Goh Chok Tong". This post reflects my sentiments over what I deem as an unfair termination clause on the use of the information management software that can destabilise Town Council operations. I object to this the same way as the upgrading-for-votes irked me about the PAP's ways.

A Stable Singapore

(August 2, 2020)

ESM cited some 'stabilisers' for Singapore — namely GRC and town council system. He said that these were 'not aimed primarily at disadvantaging the opposition but to prevent disruptions to services.'

Getting opposition to run town council is fine with me. It is a way for them to show that they can run a town. It also allows elected MPs access to residents over their municipal needs. GRC was first created to ensure minority representation. Then GRCs got bigger and bigger and the justification was that you need economy of scale for town council management.

Gerrymandering aside, some scale is good. Anyway, the GRC system has come back to haunt the PAP. Once the opposition has anchored themselves in the GRC, it too can leave behind anchor members and renew with fresh blood at each GE. Then it becomes harder for the PAP to win it back. GRCs are no longer fortresses for the PAP when the opposition slate is stronger.

What upset me the most in my time in parliament was to find the AIM deal. The key engine to running a town council, the management information system, was transferred to a PAP company just before GE2011. I was not involved in the AHPETC as I was an NCMP. It affected my comrades but not me from an operational point. However, as a trained and previously practicing IT professional, I know how important an IT system is to any large operations.

Yesterday, I had tea with someone who is a trained accountant and now holds a very senior position in an international firm advising on merger and acquisition[9] deals. We happened to speak on the AIM arrangement. He said that in M&A, this is called a poison pill. The departing shareholders cannot plant time bombs or put land mines for the new shareholders. In M&A, they look out for such poison pills. Exiting stakeholders cannot have the right to press any button to trigger destruction in their old organisation! Whether the old stakeholders did push the button or not is irrelevant. They should never have the right to the button.

If we want to truly have stabilisers for Singapore, then any handover must be totally responsible. Anyway, AIM is behind us now. The AHTC[10] has developed their own system.

I did not begin my adult life as an alternative party supporter. I voted for the PAP in my first GE. Several things done by the PAP that I felt were not right moved me gradually away from them. The tipping point was upgrading for votes. This is using the people's money to hold them hostage. Philosophically, I could not accept any party that practices unfairness to this level.

Singapore belongs to Singaporeans, not to any one political party, no matter what they had achieved in the past. The decision

---

9  M&A

10 Aljunied-Hougang Town Council

as to who Singaporeans want is based on their choice at the ballot box. We need a stable Singapore. Thankfully, things have changed gradually and I hope that they will continue to change, for the better of Singapore.

## Aljunied-Hougang-Punggol East Town Council

After fending off our blows, the PAP got their revenge on the WP over the AHPETC. The handover was not smooth in 2011. The Town Council was hampered by the lack of a good management information system that could cope with an operation that is now six to seven times that of Hougang SMC. The use of FM Solution and Services (FMSS) as a managing agent was in the spotlight. Many audit issues cropped up. Soon, the powerful Auditor-General's Office was called in. That eventually resulted in a bad report and it was the PAP's turn to call a motion to censure the WP over the Town Council.

In February 2015, then Minister for National Development Khaw opened the attack, with other PAP MPs and then Minister for Law K. Shanmugam joining in the fray with sharp questionings. It was rounded off by then Minister for Education Heng Swee Keat's closing speech attacking the WP. The WP's defence was led mostly by Lim and Low, on the grounds that no corruption had been found, that contractors did not want to work for WP, that the handover in 2011 was not smooth, and that the WP was handicapped by the loss of the management information system.[11]

It was rather painful for me, watching the entire debate as the PAP rained one blow after another in this modern-day gladiator arena. It was early 2015 when this debate took place. The next general election might be called soon. It was time for the PAP to attack fiercely.

---

[11] "Parliament: Debate on AGO's audit report on Worker's Party-run AHPETC, Day 1", If Only Singaporeans Stopped to Think, February 13, 2015, https://ifonlysingaporeans.blogspot.com/2015/02/parliament-debate-on-agos-audit-report.html

I understood why the WP MPs took the route of appointing FMSS and the handicaps they faced running the operations. As NCMPs, Gerald Giam and I were not involved in Town Council operations, so there was not much we could add to the debate. I believe Low felt that in 2011, after the unprecedented win of Aljunied GRC, there was much to be done quickly. There was Parliament work, grassroots work, and Town Council management. The MPs and NCMPs had to do the parliamentary and grassroots work in person, so such roles cannot be outsourced. Only Low and Lim had parliamentary experience. The rest of us had to learn fast. Town Council work could be outsourced so that the MPs would be less burdened by these operations. FMSS was engaged to run the services.

Personally, I would have preferred for the Town Council to be self-managed. As I was not involved at all nor was my opinion asked, I did not wish to interfere with the decision. Having run start-ups, I would have preferred to do the operations ourselves if I were involved. Hence, in both GE2015 and GE2020 when I contested in Marine Parade GRC, we stated during the rally and political broadcast that we would manage the Town Council directly if we won.

Despite the fact that Giam and I were not in the Town Council operations, Heng tried to drag us into the debate with some side remarks about us. Our instructions were to stay out of the debate, so I resisted replying, much as I would have wanted to.

In 2019, in response to the court judgement on the case, the PAP called yet another motion to censure the WP over the Town Council again. However, in GE2020, the Town Council issue was totally absent from the PAP's campaign attack. I believe the massive response to the call for donations to fund the legal cost of the defence of the WP MPs and its town councillors must have shocked the PAP. More than a million dollars was raised in under three days. They must have also judged that the ground sentiments were not sweet to raise the issue for fear of an unnecessary backlash in voters' sentiments. Sentiments still rule the day when it comes to voting. Push too hard and it could backfire.

**A debate over constructive politics**

One of the fiercest one-on-one exchanges in the 12th Parliament was between Prime Minister (PM) Lee Hsien Loong and Low at the conclusion of the mid-term President's Address in May 2014, over the issue of constructive politics.

PM Lee wanted to paint the WP as tigers and heroes during the elections but mice in Parliament. Essentially, he wanted to tear apart our position of a First World Parliament with good opposition members. That had helped us score wins in 2011, 2012, and 2013. The next general election would be less than two years away. It would be the right time to attack the WP more intensely.

The exchange went back and forth for over 13 minutes. In all parliamentary debates, the PAP always wants the final say. Typically, we would figure at which point we should retreat if enough had already been said and there was little value in prolonging the debate. That time, Low rose to repeatedly rebut the PM, who became fiercer and fiercer as the debate continued.

In my opinion, I felt that Low handled the attacks and questioning confidently. He refused to let the WP be painted as incompetent and that we constantly made policy U-turns. The PM was equally relentless to keep at it with one challenge after another for Low. The PM showed his experience in understanding where he could try to pin the WP down.

In Parliament, Lim had to endure some of the attacks too as chairman, especially over the Town Council issue and during the 13th Parliament when she stood firm against several ministers' demand for her to apologise over the goods and services tax trial balloons comment.[12] When Pritam Singh took over as the secretary-general of the WP midway through the 13th Parliament, he had to lead the WP's attacks and marshal the defences. We all received our share of attacks, myself included. The fiercest attacks will always be reserved for the top leaders of the party. Anyone aspiring to lead the WP or any opposition in Parliament has to be prepared for these sorts of attacks. The Parliament is indeed like a gladiator arena, and words are the weapon. Perception is reality. You will be what the public perceives you to be and that perception is shaped by these battles.

## Farewell to Parliament

Following the loss of my team in GE2015, I bade farewell to the friendly staff of Parliament. Parliament had occupied much of my time over the four years, from 2011 to 2015. There were, on average, one to three Parliament sittings in a typical month, usually from 1.30 pm to 7 pm. There will be a break from Parliament in December. During the Budget debate seasons, sessions were long, often from 11 am till 8 pm, and stretching for around two weeks.

Being few in numbers, the WP MPs were expected to be present in the House unless we were overseas or had to attend to urgent matters. If we were expecting to be late or had to leave early, we had to inform the party's whip. During the Budget season, I was hardly in my office. My professional work would take a backseat. Fortunately for me, I ran my own businesses and could adjust my time to fit Parliament's demands.

I appreciated the discipline Low had insisted on. The general election for the 12th Parliament was when the WP made its breakthrough on the promise of a First World Parliament. I was recorded as having the joint highest speech count with PAP MP Lee Bee Wah — speaking in

---

12 Siau Ming En, "Sylvia Lim refuses to apologise for GST 'test balloons' allegation; Grace Fu slams 'deplorable' conduct", today, March 8, 2018, https://www.todayonline.com/singapore/no-apology-wp-chairman-sylvia-lim-over-gst-test-balloons-claims

87 out of a total of 115 sittings over the entire four years.[13] Lina Chiam and Gerald Giam followed closely behind with 83 and 80 times, respectively. Collectively, the WP parliamentarians had spoken on a wide range of topics. Although I felt that there were times where we could have pushed the PAP harder through more robust rebuttals and perhaps filed more adjournment motions, I thought it was a good enough start to be the rational, responsible, and respectable loyal opposition the WP wanted to be for Singapore. Future WP teams in Parliament can build on where we had left off.

Being active in Parliament had helped me better understand the process of law and policy-making. It also felt good when we do see policy changes in areas we had pushed for. Oftentimes, there would be instances when PAP backbenchers, NMPs, and WP MPs also pushed for similar changes.

Below is my blog post after clearing out my locker shortly after GE2015.

> Looking back at the past four years
> (September 14, 2015)
>
> Cleared my locker in parliament and gave chocolates to the nice staff in parliament who have been most helpful, whether in finding information in the library or helping with my filing of parliamentary questions and in other administrative things, as well as those looking after our welfare.

> I have enjoyed my 4 years in parliament. It has been an

---

13 "[TMG Exclusive] Speaking truth to Parliament", The Middle Ground, August 12, 2015, https://themiddleground.sg/2015/08/12/tmg-exclusive-speaking-truth-parliament/

enriching experience for me. Looking back, I am happy to see changes in the early childhood sector which I believe will lead to child care becoming a higher quality public good affordable to the masses. I am also glad that there is better recognition of the need to have more pathways for late bloomers in education and in their careers (although a lot more still can be done).

There are also changes which I had pushed for frequently which I hope can come soon. These include:

1. Pilot 10-year through-train schools from primary to secondary. I had spoken on this every year in parliament, as well as outside of parliament. I do hope that more will feel convicted to push for this as an option for those who do not wish to have their children being caught in an academic rat race of constant sorting by academic abilities.

2. School-based student care centres in all primary schools and greater government support to grow the student care industry. While MOE has pushed for more school-based centres in the last couple of years, we should not stop till every school has such facilities. In addition, I believe that better support by both MOE and MSF can be given to the industry so that student care can become a quality public good with private/VWO[14] partnership, and fees will stay affordable.

3. Grow our local industries and make winners out of them internationally. This can be in the form of better supporting infrastructure and schemes, and importantly to cultivate a mindset to support our local enterprises so that they can have a strong local base to move forward in the international scene. We will need to have the spirit of innovation, quality

---

14 Voluntary welfare organisation

and risk-taking in our next generation of local enterprises.

I congratulate all who have made it back into parliament. I also wish a fruitful journey to those who are coming in for the first time. Let's empower our future!

## Leader of the Opposition

Following GE2020, when the WP obtained 10 elected seats out of 93 in the 14th Parliament, the Prime Minister conferred Pritam Singh the title of the Leader of the Opposition (LO), with additional pay and allowances for three legislative assistants (LAs).

In case we get carried away with three LAs, the allowance for each LA is currently $1,300 per month. Three LAs mean $3,900 a month, just about what you need to pay for one good young graduate.

What do I make of this move by the PM? I believe the PAP is trying to throw the game back at Singh and at the WP. If we go back to the 2014 Parliament exchange between PM Lee and Low over constructive politics, this is a follow up from the challenge from the PM to the WP. The PM had asserted that to have a First World Parliament, the WP cannot be only about checks and balances. It cannot simply poke holes at the government and urge it to do better. The PAP wants to raise voters' expectations of the WP. This was reinforced at the opening of the 14th Parliament, during which President Halimah Yacob said that besides raising questions and criticisms of government policies, the opposition should put forth policy alternatives to be scrutinised and debated.[15]

---

15 Linette Lai, "S'poreans must learn to handle differences constructively, find consensus on issues core to survival: President Halimah", The Straits Times, August 24, 2020, straitstimes.com/politics/presidents-address-sporeans-must-learn-to-handle-differences-constructively-find-consensus

If the WP fails to live up to the expectations, then its progress will be checked.

In the past, the management of the Town Councils, especially those of GRCs, was the hurdle for the opposition to cross. When Town Councils and GRCs were first created, it was to set the bar very high for the opposition to convince voters that it could run the place without rubbish being piled three-storeys high. It required careful calculation of the political mood, capable team members, and boldness to make the GRC breakthrough in 2011.

Aljunied GRC is now running like any other town in Singapore. Its scorecard is good. A new Town Council information management system has been created. Data is no longer the handicap. Reports are delivered to MND on time. I feel very strongly that data was a terrible tool to weaponise. It is trading off the welfare of residents for the benefit of a political party.

The PAP is casting the expectation that the WP should function like a serious opposition in any democracy: to raise motions and even present bills. We need to put things into perspective. For all the gains that the WP made in 2020, it actually only added one parliamentarian from 2015 and 2011. We had seven elected MPs (including Lee Li Lian in 2013) and two NCMPs in the 12th Parliament (2011–2015). We had six elected MPs and three NCMPs in the 13th Parliament (2015–2020). NCMPs perform the same role as elected MPs in Parliament. I had to track and engage three large ministries when I was a NCMP. Even when the WP works with the two Progress Singapore Party's (PSP) NCMPs, there will be 12. The office-bearers of the PAP have the entire civil service working for them. Each MP only has an allowance of $1,300 per month for a part-time LA who usually support MPs in their constituency work as well. Data from the government side was not forthcoming to opposition parliamentarians previously. Going forward, will it be made available?

Despite the abovementioned handicaps, I am personally confident that Singh and the opposition MPs, including the PSP NCMPs, will do more than in the 12th or 13th Parliament. During my term in the 12th Parliament, it took a while for Low and the rest of us to figure out how to cope with the sudden increase from two to nine WP parliamentarians. Furthermore, the Town Council problems took a big toll on some of the MPs. Being audited over and over again was no easy task. It took precious time off from other needed work. Low was a cautious man. We went through the 12th Parliament decently. The 13th Parliament saw more aggressiveness from several newer WP MPs, notably Singh and Leon Perera.

It was not surprising that the PM and Singh had a very long exchange in the opening session of the 14th Parliament. It was expected that after a good general election outcome for the opposition in GE2020, it was time to cut the WP down to size again and the LO will take on the heavy responsibility of defending and attacking back at the same time. Singh did well to respond to the 'free riders' charge by the PM. The phrase was probably an off-the-cuff comment made by the PM in the heat of the debate to caution voters not to be complacent in future general elections by 'free riding' on voters in other constituencies to automatically bring the PAP back into government. Once again, it was to build on the fear of uncertainty that Singaporeans have. The PAP has been the only government Singapore had since self-governance in 1959. With the opposition still weak and inexperienced, the PM wanted to remind Singaporeans not to risk the economic progress that had been built over the decades.

However, I believe this 'free rider' term may come back to haunt the PAP in the future as it will not go down well with opposition supporters and the middle ground.

In the 14th Parliament, Sylvia Lim is into her fourth term in Parliament. Singh has shown confidence in Parliament debates. Leon Perera, Dennis Tan, Gerald Giam, and Muhamad Faisal Manap have good parliamentary experience and were very active in parliamentary debates. I believe the newly-elected MPs from the Sengkang team (He Ting Ru, Jamus Lim, Raeesah Khan, and Louis Chua) will be able to get up to speed quite fast with the guidance of many experienced hands. The PM had challenged the PAP MPs to debate vigorously with the WP MPs.

I expect the 14th Parliament to have more exchanges across the political divide and full motions initiated by the opposition. The opening session of Parliament in August 2020 and subsequent sittings already pointed to more attacks by PAP MPs and an increased willingness by the WP MPs to challenge back, both in Parliament and even outside. Jamus Lim's response via the forum page of the Chinese and English mainstream newspapers on various occasions on the issue of minimum wage and events such as the "Ask Me Anything" on Instagram Live by Lim, He Ting Ru, Raeesah Khan, and Louis Chua also point to more active engagement by the WP for mindshare going forward. The opponent and their supporters will be expected to hit back, especially at higher-profile WP MPs. Already, I see what I perceive as attempts to paint Lim as an elite academician, without real-world experience, proposing dangerous policies.

In my time in Parliament, Low made it quite clear to us that the WP parliamentarians had to be mindful not to raise issues that divide the country. I see that position being upheld firmly by Singh thus far. In the opening address of the 14th Parliament, the President also called for Singaporeans to learn to handle their differences constructively, and find common ground to build a broad consensus on issues core to the country's survival and future. Given the tone of constructive politics established and enforced by Low earlier, I am confident that the WP can play this role in Parliament under the current leadership, even as debates grow more vigorous due to bigger contestation for voters' mindshare.

Below is a repost of what I had shared in response to ESM Goh Chok Tong's comment about Singh being the LO:

### Having an Official Leader of the Opposition

In a recent Facebook post,[16] the retired ESM Goh Chok Tong called the official appointment of Pritam as Leader of the Opposition a "very significant move" by PM Lee. Mr Goh added: "Our opposition MPs and NCMPs will now have to go beyond merely serving as a check-and-balance. They can put forward their alternative policies and solutions so that Singaporeans would know the choices available, besides the Government's."

Mr Goh must have been in parliament when the WP proposed our alternative: A Dynamic Population For A Sustainable Singapore, or when we proposed our alternative model for ministerial salaries. I was deeply involved in those. I had also presented various proposals in education and early childhood during my time in parliament, amongst others. Most of what I had proposed for reforms to the early childhood sector[17] have now been adopted in one form or another. When I had proposed them early in my parliament term, the proposals were new at that time. Perhaps others had proposed similar policy transformation to the sector that I had called for, but not in parliament before I did, unless I am mistaken. I am not claiming credit for proposing these persistently. Just because the government does not acknowledge our contributions when changes were made does not mean that the opposition did not propose anything.

Similarly, I had persistently called for all primary schools to

---

16 Linette Lai, "Singapore GE2020: Opposition leader post a very significant move, says ESM Goh", The Straits Times, July 12, 2020, https://www.straitstimes.com/politics/opposition-leader-post-a-very-significant-move-says-esm-goh

17 Yee Jenn Jong, "Proposal for transforming the child care sector", September 10, 2012, https://yeejj.wordpress.com/2012/09/10/transforming-child-care-sector/

have Student Care[18] inside the school, and the proposal was brushed aside. I went through extensive effort on my own to even call many existing SC centres within schools to better understand the situation of urgent shortage of places. Some time later, MOE announced that all primary schools would eventually have SC centres. I was the first to propose in parliament that we could implement laws to punish companies outside of Singapore for transboundary haze. That was eventually done. There were many other proposals I had made which are not yet implemented but I hope will eventually be. These include through-train primary to secondary schools and smaller class sizes.

The WP had also made various significant proposals, done with extensive consultation with industry experts. These include Redundancy Insurance and alternatives to the HDB decaying lease issue. There are other policy ideas, proposed within parliament and outside (for those like myself who are now not in parliament).

Sure, the move to have an official Leader of the Opposition with government-funded staffing and resources is a significant first step. I hope data and the intent behind impending policy changes can be shared more openly with those in the opposition. In my time in parliament, I often had to probe and dig, and use various creative ways to file parliamentary questions because we sometimes get evasive answers. I cite my probe into scholarships for foreign students as one example. You can google for more details on this topic and judge for yourself by looking at the answers that I had been given.[19]

---

18 SC

19 Au Waipang, "Frustrating numbers: scholarships for foreign students", Yawning Bread, February 22, 2012, https://yawningbread.wordpress.com/2012/02/22/frustrating-numbers-scholarships-for-foreign-students/

I hope the 14th parliament will be a better experience for the opposition MPs. I am writing this to dispute that WP is just check and balance, that we just nudge the government to do a bit better here and there.

I think if there is to be a more significant change, it should be that elected opposition MPs must be allowed to use grassroots facilities, particularly the PA[20] resources and decide on use of Community Improvement Funds. There is absolutely no need for the PAP to appoint their grassroots advisor[21]. There is no need for WP elected MPs to have to get permission from GRAs for use of community funds from [taxpayers'] monies.[22] Contrary to what some try to portray that GRAs are doing the 'sai kang' or dirty work on behalf of residents, the Town Council where the real 'sai kang' are, is run by the elected MPs. GRAs basically just give the PAP a foothold in the constituency to launch their attack at the next election. There is no need for GRAs to have to write letters on behalf of residents when those by elected opposition MPs will suffice.

The road to a first world parliament continues. Let us continue to do more. A big 'thank you' to Singaporeans whose determination to see a fairer political system is now bearing some fruits.

---

20 People's Association

21 GRA

22 Pritam Singh, "COS 2015 Debate: MND – Community Improvement Projects Committee (CIPC) Funding (MP Pritam Singh)", The Workers' Party, March 11, 2015, https://www2.wp.sg/cos-2015-debate-mnd-community-improvement-projects-committee-cipc-funding-mp-pritam-singh/

# Chapter 5
# Engaging the Community

## Workers' Party on House Visits!

Post-2011 general election (GE2011), my sights were set on the next general election. Having come within one percent of success, I was raring to use the parliamentary position to show that I was capable of policy work and engaging with the People's Action Party (PAP). I had just six weeks to work through Joo Chiat Single Member Constituency (SMC) for the general election. From 2011, I would have four to five years to get ready for the next battle, if Joo Chiat were to remain an SMC.

I conducted one visit per week quite soon after the election was over. The visits were almost entirely in the neighbourhoods with landed properties as condominiums generally do not entertain campaigning visits outside of the election period. Accounts from some of the visits to the now-defunct Joo Chiat SMC can be found at the Joo Chiat Today blog website I had created in July 2011 to capture interesting stories from these activities.[1]

Some of the volunteers from GE2011 continued to help during these visits, including Dennis Tan. I also encouraged volunteers to help with the Aljunied Members of Parliament (MPs) as there was a lot more to do in elected areas. Several became regular volunteers with the elected MPs. Tan ended up speaking in the Punggol East by-election rally in 2013. He was co-opted into the Central Executive Committee (CEC), and became our candidate for Fengshan SMC in 2015.

I soon found that being a Non-constituency Member of Parliament

---

1   https://joochiattoday.wordpress.com/

(NCMP) was like a duckweed, as Low Thia Khiang described during the debate to have Daniel Goh take up the NCMP seat rejected by Lee Li Lian.

Government agencies do not recognise the letters written by NCMPs on behalf of residents. Since I was a Joo Chiat SMC resident, when I deemed certain issues raised by residents during house visits to be possible for me to act upon, I wrote in my own name as a resident. These were typically issues that were easier to handle, such as clogged drains, poorly maintained public playground, or other public facilities that needed to be fixed. I received responses and actions for these. There was no need to go through the elected MPs. Residents actually have the power to get authorities to act if facilities were not maintained as they should be. For these issues, MPs basically just act as letter writers for residents.

However, there were issues that residents sometimes raised that involved appeals to ministries or use of community funds. One example was a request by elderly residents of Opera Estate who needed to get from the estate to New Upper Changi Road. There were some flights of stairs near the bus stop which they could not manage if they were pushing their trolleys. Residents gave me their feedback. I considered the matter and channelled the request to Charles Chong, the MP for Joo Chiat SMC, by email, which he acknowledged. Some months later, I noticed sloped pathways were made at the location.

Often, house visits were just to keep in touch with residents. Few residents had issues to raise for me to solve. I set the target of visiting all landed households at least once before the next election, if not more.

For the Christmas of 2013, we wanted to hold an event at the Telok Kurau Park. I asked a volunteer to check with the police to obtain the usage permission. Needless to say, it was not approved. We decided to try something else. We found friendly residents in various parts of Telok Kurau, so our team went to these houses to sing Christmas carols. I even did some party magic tricks in those houses where there were children.

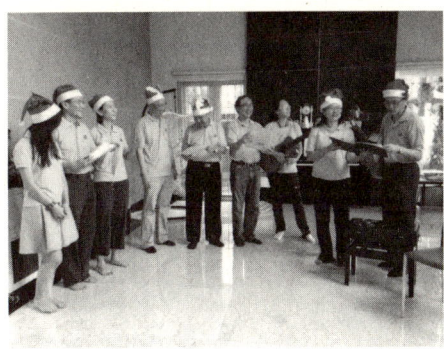

I came to know some residents better and was invited to parties. The most consistent and regular one is the annual Jalan Bintang Tiga Street Party, which has been billed as Singapore's friendliest street. Residents have been holding a street party every year for the past 20 years since the road was once closed off for massive drainage works. In 2011, I was invited to the street party for the first time. Chong was also there, and so were the reporters. The event was covered in the news. My blog post about the street party was also read by many. From 2012 onwards, the Singapore Kindness Movement and sponsors stepped in to support the annual event.

Landed houses were best to be visited on the weekends. On some weekday nights, I occasionally helped the East Coast team. Then somewhere around 2013 or 2014, I persuaded Low that we should explore Pasir Ris. The Group Representation Constituency (GRC) had six MPs. Sooner or later, a new GRC had to be carved out there, combined with perhaps Punggol East and Sengkang West. Seeing my enthusiasm, Low told me to proceed. So, on Thursday evenings, we visited different parts of the Pasir Ris-Punggol GRC. The Workers' Party (WP) was on a roll then, having won Aljunied GRC, and again in the next two by-elections. If there were to be some expansion, it was likely to be eastwards or north-eastwards from Aljunied.

With the general election approaching in 2015, I sensed that Joo Chiat SMC might be taken away. Hence, I expanded our visits to nearby Chai Chee and Kembangan occasionally. Then, in July 2015, it was announced that Joo Chiat SMC was absorbed into Marine Parade GRC.

This was essentially the challenge with being an NCMP. I had conducted so many house visits regularly in Joo Chiat SMC. It was difficult to represent residents as the authorities would not recognise any appeal or letters by me on behalf of residents nor could I write in for funds to get things done. I could not get permission to do events in public places. Worse, the constituencies where the WP did well tended to be absorbed and merged into other constituencies before the next general election — this happened to Joo Chiat SMC in 2015 and to Fengshan SMC, Sengkang West SMC, and Punggol East SMC in 2020.

I often hear people say that opposition candidates appear once every five years. In reply to Tan Chuan-Jin, when he made that remark to reporters in the 2020 general election (GE2020), I wrote the following post on the eve of cooling day. The post went viral. Three hours after making the post, at a coffeeshop in Kembangan, a resident whom I did not know showed me a viral circulation of my article in her WhatsApp group chat.

> Do Opposition Candidates Appear Once Every 5 Years?
>
> (July 8, 2020)
>
> I was told that our opponent said that we appear only once every 5 years and that they have covered the ground well in their term.
>
> I am sure they have to cover their ground. The voters elected them to be their representatives, for which they get the monthly MP allowance on top of their full-time pay if they are holding other jobs, which nearly all PAP MPs are. I am not so sure though, why some need to run from house to house during GE if they have covered the ground so well.
>
> My response:
>
> 1. From what I know of the WP MPs, they are full-time or

virtually full-time MPs. The reality is that to run an opposition ward with its town council duties, it does require full-time attention. How many in the PAP's Marine Parade team or other teams have been full-time MPs?

And yes, WP MPs do cover their grounds very well. All WP MPs work hard on the ground. I am 100% sure if elected for Marine Parade, my team members and I will dedicate ourselves more than 100% in our roles for town council management, community projects and parliament work.

2. When I was in parliament 2011–2015, the records will show that I was one of the most active, if not the most. I do not bother to count, but a major local newspaper did report the speaking tally.

After 2015, I continue to write on policies and contribute to my WP parliamentarians. WP MPs have to work harder. Some PAP backbenchers have zero or just 1–2 speeches in an entire 4–5 year term. Go check it out and see for yourself.

3. Some losing PAP candidates in past elections disappear after the GE. Some reappear elsewhere in easier wards on the coat-tail of ministers. Not all. Some stay on as Grassroots Advisors (GRAs), and they will get the support of the PA[2], funded to the tune of $1 billion a year. They also get access to certain spaces within the constituency to continue their work, with an army of people helping.

I lost in Joo Chiat SMC in 2011 by over 300 votes. I could not get any facilities to use. We once tried to use the Telok Kurau park but the use was rejected. We ended up going door to door singing carols for Christmas since our Christmas party could

---

2 People's Association

not be realised. Sorry for my bad singing and lousy guitar skills. The ministries cannot accept my appeals or letters for residents. It has to go through the PAP MP. GRAs, however, can.

4. Despite the challenges, I continued my twice-weekly visits from 2011–2015, only to find Joo Chiat SMC absorbed into Marine Parade GRC just weeks before the GE, with no reasonable explanation.

Just as one small proof, a lady came to me today in the Marine Terrace market to show me a picture taken with her son in her house in one of my many visits to Telok Kurau before 2015. Another showed me something similar too, yesterday at another market.

During this GE, I visited some parts of the now-defunct Joo Chiat SMC. A good number of people remembered my visit to their homes post-GE2011. One even thanked me for writing back in response to an email from her over an issue in her neighbourhood which I had tried to solve. I could not even quite remember it until she mentioned that she wrote to both the PAP MP and I, and only I had replied.

We did quarterly food distribution at Marine Terrace and later in a smaller way at Chai Chee after 2015. When Covid-19 Circuit Breaker came suddenly, all the RCs[3] and almost all social services had to cease operations on 7 April 2020. I volunteered immediately with an essential social service provider and we did daily cooked food distribution so that those who had been receiving could still get their food. Later, this expanded into Eunos in response to another request to help with distribution there.

---

3   Residents' Committees

Today, we give out some 400 packs of cook food daily, since 7 April 2020. It has grown to become a community project, by residents, for residents. No government funding at all. We just need to be more resourceful. We give them a run for their money. Competition is good.

I would like to see which high-flying PAP MPs can do any of the above when they lose in this GE? What happened to Ministers and those with Ministerial potential after they lose a GE? Go check out for yourself what happened to these high-fliers in the past. And try doing outreach work without the PA or an army to support you, or any space to do your work with. We did. Of course we can never be like the elected MPs. They are paid to do their work. Do they even do it full-time?

So, don't tell me that we just appear once every 5 years for 1 – 2 months before a GE. I find it ridiculous that an elected MP can compare the work we do versus the work for which they are paid to do.

## Aljunied-Hougang-Punggol East Grassroots Events and Outreach

When I was an NCMP and in the CEC, I attended many events at the grassroots level. These were held in Hougang SMC and Aljunied GRC, and later in Punggol East SMC after Lee Li Lian won in 2013. Such events could only be held in constituencies where the WP had won.

Some facilities in the community (e.g., basketball courts or open spaces) are allocated to the Town Council. These allow MPs to engage with residents through events. At the same time, the People's Association (PA) has control over another set of facilities, for which the grassroots advisers, who are typically PAP candidates who had lost in the last general election or potential future candidates, may use to engage residents. In 2011, after Aljunied GRC was lost by the PAP, 26 community facilities were transferred out of the management purview of the Aljunied-Hougang Town Council to the PA to manage, with the permission of the Housing and Development Board (HDB).

Typically, each constituency has at least four major dinners or celebrations — Chinese New Year, Hari Raya, Deepavali, and Christmas. The first three involve mass dinners and performances. Christmas is usually organised as a party, often with performances and games. There are also events like the mid-autumn festival. Events are typically ticketed, as there is a need to recover some costs. As tickets usually do not cover the full cost, the constituency grassroots committee, consisting of volunteers, needs to find sponsors.

There are annual overseas trips by MPs with residents. Most are to nearby areas in Malaysia for day trips or an overnight trip. Some are to further off places like China. I have accompanied residents on day trips to Malaysia before.

There are also temple dinners, especially during the Chinese seventh month. MPs are typically invited, as are grassroots advisers. I have attended a number of these. A table is usually given to the MP, who would invite grassroots volunteers to join his/her table. In return, the MP would sponsor an item for auction by the organisers to sell in the Seventh Month Festival to recover at least the cost of the table. I believe the Aljunied and Hougang MPs commissioned some silver coins by the Singapore Mint for such a purpose.

These engagements are necessary to root the MPs to the community. These are not the only way to engage with residents, but a necessary way. Hardworking MPs also need to pay constant visits to families of residents. I believe WP-elected MPs have to visit each house more than once per election cycle, perhaps as often as three times. During the non-election period, these are leisurely visits. During the general election, there is no time to be slow. The best time to understand and meet the needs of residents is during these casual visits. A hardworking MP would do visits about three times a week.

Elected MPs also frequent the market and eating places. I frequently participated in the weekly *Hammer* newspaper sale in the markets. MPs who are more established and known to the hawkers and residents are likely to receive strong support during an election. One can tell that Low and Chiam See Tong, the founder of the Singapore Democratic Party and leader of the Singapore People's Party, engaged in these sorts of deep engagement sessions with residents. Hence, they could not be easily dislodged from their SMCs. Low parked himself at coffeeshops often. I had observed a number of WP MPs also spending a significant amount of time in the community with residents.

The formula is easy, but the practice is hard. MPs who have busy full-time work can at best just pop into events organised by their grassroots as guest-of-honour and then leave. There would be no deep engagement.

I am the type who loves to engage with residents. I can build rapport quite quickly. Unfortunately, as NCMP from 2011–2015 and later as defeated candidate in Marine Parade GRC in 2015, it was difficult to build stronger engagement without the mandate and access to facilities and resources. Nevertheless, we still conduct outreach activities via house visits and a limited form of community projects. However, our scope is limited when compared to what an elected MP can do. Hence, I totally agree with Low when he used duckweed, which cannot sink roots into the ground, to describe the NCMP position. I would have loved to have been able to do more outreach actively in Joo Chiat SMC or Marine Parade GRC.

Grassroots engagement is important. The PA facilities and activities continue to be closed to the opposition MPs. The losing candidates or potential new candidates of the PAP continue to engage with residents through PA-organised grassroots activities.

## Meet-The-People Sessions

NCMPs do not have Meet-The-People Sessions (MPS). MPS was started by David Marshall when he was Chief Minister of Singapore in 1955.[4] The PAP found this practice useful for connecting with the ground and conducted such sessions as well. Soon, these sessions became something that all elected MPs would do.

Prior to 1991, all MPs were designated an office space, built by the HDB at void decks in their constituency, before this policy was changed. J. B. Jeyaratnam had his office built by the HDB in the Anson constituency. Prior to the completion of the office in Bukit Merah, Jeyaratnam conducted his MPS at a void deck. The office was demolished when Jeyaratnam was disqualified from Parliament.[5]

Soon after becoming the MP for Hougang, Low was served a notice from the HDB in September 1991 to move the Hougang Town Council out of the office at Block 810 Hougang Central. The HDB had said that the Hougang Town Council office was then located in Punggol SMC and was subsumed by Cheng San GRC in 1991, leaving Hougang SMC with no office. The HDB then gave approval that a new office could be built within Hougang SMC. As an experienced contractor himself, Low built the office at Block 701 Hougang Avenue 2 in 45 days. He then handed over the premises to the HDB which, as the owner, then rented the facilities back to the Town Council.[6]

MPS were not held in Town Council facilities as Low wanted to keep the Town Council and political matters separate. So, Low picked the void deck of Block 310 in Hougang for his MPS. That was also where

---

[4] "David Marshall and the Dawn of Meet-the-People Sessions in Singapore", The Workers' Party, https://www2.wp.sg/david-marshall-and-the-dawn-of-meet-the-people-sessions-in-singapore/

[5] Tan Kwong Moh, "WP achieved progress in spite of adverse political environment", The Online Citizen, November 14, 2017, https://www.onlinecitizenasia.com/2017/11/14/wp-achieved-progress-in-spite-of-adverse-political-environment/

[6] "Workers' Party will takeover current Aljunied Town Council offices", Yahoo! News, May 12, 2011, https://sg.news.yahoo.com/blogs/singaporescene/workers-party-mps-decide-wards-aljunied-085208182.html

my wife and I first met Low on March 2, 2011.

The logistics for the MPS were kept simple. A small storage room in the block is used to put away tables, chairs, and partitions. MPS take place once a week. Before each session, volunteers would set up the place, usually within 15 minutes. The MPS of WP MPs are conducted from 7.30 pm to 9.30 pm. Residents had to register before 9.30 pm. If there were many residents seeking help, MPS could drag on till past 11 pm to clear all cases. The sessions are held on a fixed day of each week. For MPs with wards that are more geographically spread out, such as Serangoon and Bedok Reservoir-Punggol, the MPS are conducted in two locations. Each location is opened once a fortnight.

After the last resident has been attended to, volunteers would pack up and store the tables, chairs, and partitions. MPS venues also double up as working outlets for the grassroots committees of the ward. A small mobile office is set up if necessary. These are to facilitate coordination for community events, such as the sale and collection of tickets for dinners and overseas trips with MPs.

The PAP holds its MPS mostly in the PAP Community Foundation preschools. As the sessions are held after 7 pm when the centres are closed, this arrangement is possible. The WP did not have any business operations nor office space within the constituencies they had won, so the WP had no such facilities available to them.

People have asked why the WP does not rent space from the HDB and establish our own offices; after all, rentals would be at below market rate as it is for non-profit use. First, the facilities would be used infrequently if the purpose is mainly for MPS. Secondly, the office set-up and facilities would cost a substantial sum. In the event that the WP loses the election in that constituency, it would cost money to reinstate the space to its original condition. There is also no budget from the government for building and operating such facilities.[7] Such an office for MPS use would likely have to come from the MP's own money. It would not make financial sense for the WP to fund these operations. The WP runs on a shoestring budget. Long-term recurring expenses would add to the need for more fund raising. Personally, I think holding the meetings in void decks with these mobile partitions and furniture is fine. It brings the WP closer to the ground.

It would have been interesting if I had won Joo Chiat SMC in 2011. The SMC only had the four small HDB blocks in Siglap. The four blocks of flats did not have any void deck space. I was focused on campaigning, so we did not plan too far ahead. If we had won, I reckon that I would have found ways to rent some unused facilities within the SMC for one evening a week to hold MPS. One supporter did suggest that he would happily loan an unused portion of the family's place in Telok Kurau for our weekly MPS, if required.

While I did not hold MPS as an NCMP, I kept in touch with residents through emails and our regular house visits. Earlier in this book, I had written on how I had tried to find ways to surface their needs to authorities. It was certainly more difficult as an NCMP compared to elected MPs who had the authority to represent the residents. NCMPs are constantly being reminded that we are 'non-constituency'. We have no constituents to look after.

Despite that, I was active in MPS. After GE2011, I volunteered to help as case writer in the Paya Lebar and Kaki Bukit wards. From 2011–2015, whenever MPs were busy on their scheduled MPS days, Gerald Giam or I were normally called to stand-in. I had covered MPS as stand-in MP in all the wards in Aljunied GRC, Hougang SMC, and Punggol East SMC.

I would function like the MP, listening to the requests from residents.

---

[7] "Media release on MPs' offices at void decks", The Workers' Party, July 21, 2011, https://www2.wp.sg/media-release-on-mps-offices-at-void-decks/

I would follow up within two days with the secretarial assistant or legislative assistant of the MP to vet the letters of case writers. If the MP was in Singapore, the MP would sign the letter. Often, we covered MPS because the MP was overseas. In such cases, as the covering person, I would sign the letters in my name on behalf of the MP.

MPs have their own style of handling MPS. In Paya Lebar and Kaki Bukit, case writers listen to residents and write out their requests in a draft form. Chen Show Mao would walk around to observe the cases and chat at the table with the resident and case writer from time to time. If the resident wanted to have a session with the MP, that would be arranged. Sometimes, residents just wanted some rather standard letters written, so they would not mind if they did not get to meet the MP, as long as the letter was written. Any resident who wished to see the MP would be granted the request. On the other hand, Muhamad Faisal Manap would see all residents with the case notes from the writers.

In other places, the MPS may be only between the MP and the resident. There would be no case writer in between. It would take more time and more work for the MP, and the MPS may drag on longer past the scheduled closing time. Some MPs prefer this format as it brings them closer to residents.

Whatever the preference of the MPs, whenever I stood in for their MPS, I would adapt my style to theirs. If I had to run my own MPS, I would prefer having case writers to first interview residents, but I would still talk to each resident. Case writing is an important skill for volunteers to have. From case writing, one could tell if a volunteer had good abilities to interact with residents and write their issues down concisely. Many of the candidates in our general elections have had much experience in case writing.

One of the fulfilling aspects about MPS was to be able to address residents' needs. My most memorable case was when I was a case writer helping at Chen's Paya Lebar ward.

## Journey in Blue

It was July 2011. The time was already 9.30 pm when I had finished meeting all residents assigned to me and had written the case notes. I saw that the queue had cleared, and I was about to pass my notes to the person-in-charge. I had planned to leave for home since all residents had already been attended to. Then, I saw a young lady who had just arrived at the registration desk. I overheard her describe her situation that she was about to be kicked out of her school because of non-payment of school fees at an art college.

I happened to know people in that College, so I asked to take the case.

It turned out that Miss S. had been unable to pay school fees as she was from a single-parent family and her mother was doing odd low-wage jobs. Although Miss S. also did some part-time work, her income was insufficient to pay for school fees. She had borrowed money from relatives previously, but they were not willing to lend to the family anymore at that point in time.

She was due to start her final year in the College. However, because her school fee was long overdue, the College had refused to release her examination results to her. The next day would be the deadline to register for the final-year modules. Without her examination results, she could not register for the modules, and according to the rules, she would be kicked out of the school. She was in tears.

This was not a typical case. The usual response would be for the MP to write to the College to seek leniency and help for her. As she said that the matter had to be resolved by the next day, I called my friend, a department manager in the College. The next morning, he arranged for an urgent meeting with the finance manager. I accompanied Miss S. to the College. They informed her that she had passed her examinations and they would allow her to register for the next semester. They also arranged for a bursary interview and she was awarded a bursary for her final year of studies.

The administrators of the College were really nice and prompt. I am sure that if they had known of her financial situation earlier, they would have helped, even without an MP's letter. I asked Miss S. why she did not apply for a bursary. She was unaware that she could qualify. In fact, she was at her church prayer meeting that evening in Paya Lebar when she had shared her plight, and someone had suggested that she find her MP. Chen's MPS happened to be on the same evening. She immediately came to the MPS, which was why she arrived only at 9.30 pm, the closing time.

As she was in an art college and I ran an art education company, I offered her a part-time teaching position with my company. She taught occasionally for us for a year. She graduated and found a good job with a multinational firm and has been working there even until today, at the time of writing this book.

In 2011, I also wrote an appeal for a lady in the Kaki Bukit ward for her husband to have a heavy vehicle parking lot near their flat. She had been trying for over a year. Despite the previous PAP MP appealing for them, they still could not get the parking lot. Her husband had to park quite a distance from where they lived. As he finished work late at night, he would only be able to park at the designated parking area past midnight and there was no public transport home. He often slept in the vehicle for the night to save on the expensive private transport back.

A few weeks later, she came to the MPS elated, and had brought food for our volunteers. They had been allocated a parking lot. She went around telling people that was why they should vote for the opposition! Of course, I believed it was probably because a season parking lot near her flat happened to become available then. Nevertheless, it was nice to see the family so happy. My observation is that government agencies had been fair in reviewing letters from all MPs, whether these were from the PAP MPs or from elected opposition MPs. If a case merited action, it would be attended to fairly by the agency, according to the policies and available resources of the government at that time, regardless of who wrote the appeal.

The MPS show how each MP interacted with the residents. Faisal connects well with his residents and with the hawkers in the markets. Chen ran his MPS in an organised manner. He brightened up the place with extra lighting. Early after being elected, he set up a mobile computer, printer cum copier, and a computerised registration system. After about a year, there were enough case writers so I kept my involvement with MPS to when MPs needed me to stand in for them. I was active during 2011–2015. From 2015–2020, the then NCMPs did their fair share of standing in for MPs. I continued to be called, but less frequently.

David Marshall pioneered the MPS. It is indeed a good way to interact with residents and to meet their needs.

## Bricks in Blue

Around 2012, Low initiated the Building Fund project. The rented premises at Syed Alwi Road was not an ideal facility. The place was small. As a tenant, it would not make sense to invest in major renovation works. We wanted a key project to start off the public phase of the fundraising. Privately, we were already canvassing for donations from supportive individuals. We created separate accounts to capture donations and revenues related to acquiring a property as our office.

The public phase would start with a concert. We termed it Bricks in Blue. The Jubilee Hall of Raffles Hotel was booked for our shows. Each parliamentarian had to do his or her own item. We could get helpers, but it could not be with another parliamentarian.

I was in trouble. I could neither sing nor dance. I am tone deaf. I decided to try performing some magic tricks even though the little bit of magic that I knew then was only suitable for small parties with friends. The post below is reproduced from my blog summarising the magical experience I had that allowed me to put up a rather professional magic act. Only when the social media publicity for the actual concert was launched a month before the concert, an Aljunied GRC resident trained in magic contacted me and loaned me proper big stage magic props and taught me some tricks. I practiced daily. Thankfully, my children and I were fast learners. Two of my children performed with me. We pulled off a decent magic show worthy of the occasion.

The party eventually raised sufficient funds by 2018 to buy a small leasehold office in Geylang. After the concert, I became an in-house magician for the party in some of our grassroots events.

A Magical Journey
(January 8, 2013)

At the recently concluded WP Bricks In Blue variety show, I had thanked the audience for their wonderful support. I shared that I had personally experienced the magic of the support of everyone during my two years in politics. It is the magic of their support that has carried the Party so far, and it is this magic that makes dreams come alive. Whether the help is small or big, when many come together to help, we can make dreams come true. With that, I turned a piece of wet tissue paper into a snow storm lasting nearly a minute.

I meant every word of what was said. For this show, I was brought on a magical journey. It was magical not because I had put up a magic performance, but for what I had experienced in the process.

When the idea to put up a variety show to thank our supporters became serious, each MP had to put up an item individually. Singing was never my forte. I needed an alternative, and soon.

Being fascinated with magic from young, I toyed with the idea of performing magic. A WP member, Michael heard about it and offered to teach some tricks to me. So I picked up a few tricks and acquired some small props. Still, I was not confident how the tricks would work on the big stage, and how to script the sequence of acts. For lack of a better alternative, I committed myself to doing magic for Bricks In Blue, despite having never performed for anyone before.

A month before Bricks In Blue, the publicity went online. That same evening, I received a Facebook message from Eugene, a young man living in Aljunied GRC. He is a full-time student living overseas and is back on holiday. He had worked full-time for a professional magic team and had performed on the big stage. He had some professional props which he could loan me as well. He was [a] godsend.

I loaned his props, including a crate with which I was to be handcuffed and locked in. I would have just a few seconds to unlock myself, escape, and change position with my assistant. He warned it would take a month of practice to get the act perfect. The assistant would be my eldest daughter, Faith. The practice required both of us to be fast and coordinated.

Eugene also helped to sequence the routines, polished our script and introduced a few more tricks. Then, we tested some of the effects in five of the Christmas parties held in Aljunied GRC and in Hougang. When Faith could not attend two of the sessions, I recruited my son, Harel to stand in. He loved it so much that we decided to add him into the big show. He would turn a burning torch into a rose.

For Bricks In Blue, we had three full-dress rehearsals and two other combined practices for the singing items in a studio. It was at these sessions that I saw how the many volunteers from

### Engaging the Community

all the divisions in Aljunied and Hougang put in so much sacrifice to make the show a good one. In the 56 years of WP history, the Party had never put up a variety show before. Everyone was determined to put up a good show. Many of the volunteers have a demanding day job. By day, they are lawyers, accountants, businessmen, office executives, hardworking workers and many more. Many have their families to take care of. Some are students and some even had school tests in between the rehearsals. Yet they would practice hard to make things as perfect as they could.

None of us are professional entertainers. Most do not have performing experience. The back stage crew worked tirelessly too, ensuring that the setup, sound system, backdrop and lighting worked according to plan. There seemed so much to do in the short two weeks that preparation for the show went intense.

As I watched how these volunteers piled in the hours after work and after school, I wondered what drove them. I also thought about all the hours they piled in at the weekly Meet-The-People sessions and in organising all the constituency events. I recalled the energies they burned during GE2011 and during Hougang BE[8]. I remembered how empty fields and stadiums were transformed into huge rally sites. The logistics were immense. Setting up within hours and dismantling immediately thereafter, repeating that night after night. Combing houses tirelessly to meet as many residents as possible. All these were executed by the determination of hundreds of volunteers, many of whom have day jobs.

These volunteers are the engine behind what keeps the Workers' Party going when the going gets tough on the ground. They

---
8   By-election

are the volunteers who do not get to go to National Day receptions at the Istana which are for official grassroots members recognised by the government. They will never get any awards by the government. No PBM[9], no BBM[10]. They will not get any priority for registering their children into their preferred primary school. They will not get parking privileges. Yet they work on tirelessly.

I too had experienced how many would come up to offer help to us. I experienced that during GE2011 as a newbie in the political scene. People I had never met before would magically [come] forward to help in all sorts of things just when I needed help. Even for this show, I took up the challenge without any idea how I would learn my magic or how to handle the performance. Yet, everything happened magically, with people who came along the way.

This is the real magic which I had experienced. It is the magic that had carried the Party through difficult times and will continue to carry the Party forward. The magic is in all of you. Thank you, wonderful volunteers. Thank you, wonderful supporters.

---

9   Pingat Bakti Masyarakat, the public service medal

10  Bintang Bakti Masyarakat, the public service star

# Chapter 6
# The Battle for Marine Parade GRC

## A Disappointing Electoral Boundaries Review Committee Report

With the passing of Lee Kuan Yew, Singapore's first Prime Minister, there was a massive outpouring of emotions. Soon, it became quite obvious that the general election would be held early. I had suspected that it would be held just after National Day, because it was also the SG50 year (Singapore's 50th year since independence in 1965) and a big celebration was planned. Furthermore, there had been a long series of events throughout the year highlighting the 50 years of the People's Action Party's (PAP) achievements as government. My friends who were in the civil service had also been called up for election training duties.

There is no Parliament sitting in June each year. So, at the July 2015 Parliament sitting, I filed a question about the formation of the Electoral Boundaries Review Committee (EBRC). I suspected that it was already formed. Unfortunately, the formation of such committees is not known to the public. So, I used my parliamentary rights to file it as a question using my best guess of when the committee might have been formed. The committee would usually take two to three months to deliberate and then issue the report. From historical experience, once the report was out, the general election would follow very soon.

After I had filed my question, PAP's backbencher Arthur Fong also filed a similar question the next day. Our questions were answered by the prime minister at the first Parliament sitting of July 2015. Yes, the EBRC had been formed in May 2015. That meant the report could be released in July itself!

Indeed, it was, on July 24. I was on my way to lunch. I received a call

## Journey in Blue

from a reporter asking if I had read the report. I had not as I was on the road. She broke the bad news to me. Joo Chiat Single Member Constituency (SMC) was no more.

At the LTN coffeeshop in Siglap, I read the report on my phone. It was a very depressing lunch. I had hoped to give Joo Chiat SMC a second shot. It was tough. The massive outpouring of emotions on the death of the late Lee indicated this would be a tough general election for the opposition.

I cannot remember if I was the one who contacted Low Thia Khiang or if he was the one who contacted me. I wanted to meet him immediately to work out the strategy. Joo Chiat was now part of Marine Parade Group Representation Constituency (GRC), a frightening stronghold of the PAP anchored by Emeritus Senior Minister (ESM) and former Prime Minister Goh Chok Tong and with a relatively strong PAP team there. It would be Goh's 10th general election.

After lunch, I drove to Low's house. On the way there, I spoke with Gerald Giam and Dennis Tan on the phone. Both had been on the East Coast GRC team for some years and were slated to be key members there. Now, Fengshan had been taken out of the GRC to be an SMC.

I recall telling Giam my preference. I would like to be in Fengshan, followed by East Coast, then Marine Parade. It was obvious. I knew I could fight in an SMC with my style of campaigning and retail politics. Fengshan was earlier helmed by then PAP Member of Parliament (MP) Raymond Lim who was in his final term; he had also become a backbencher MP. He had not made a single speech during the entire 12th Parliament term.[1] It was obvious that he would not be contesting again. A new candidate might open up opportunities as the PAP candidate would also be new to residents.

---

1  "[TMG Exclusive] Speaking truth to Parliament", The Middle Ground, August 12, 2015, https://themiddleground.sg/2015/08/12/tmg-exclusive-speaking-truth-parliament/

Furthermore, I was familiar with Fengshan. The church which I have attended for 25 years was in the SMC. My in-laws stayed there. The only problem with being in an SMC was that if I had lost but done well enough, I would be offered the Non-constituency Member of Parliament (NCMP) position again. Both Giam and I decided some time ago that we did not want the NCMP position. You only need one term to prove that you can do Parliament work, and we believed that we could. In an SMC, you cannot automatically pass the NCMP position down to the next highest losing candidate. The NCMP is a tough post. It was difficult to connect with the ground. And despite trying hard, I was disappointed that Joo Chiat SMC was taken away completely.

I did not mind contesting in East Coast either. My home in Joo Chiat SMC borders East Coast. The College which I attended, of which I became the president of the alumni and was serving on the College Advisory Board, was located there. East Coast GRC traditionally would be Team B for the Workers' Party (WP), with Aljunied GRC being Team A.

When I met Low, I indicated that same order of preference to him, too. We did not have a conclusion. He wanted time to plan and to talk with the East Coast GRC team. I needed time to think as well.

If I were to be in Marine Parade GRC, I needed a team. I never planned to be in Marine Parade nor in a GRC, so I had no teammates. I had been engaging as the sole candidate-to-be in Joo Chiat SMC since 2011. My first choice would be Terence Tan, who had helped in some of my house visits at the SMC prior to 2015. He would be a strong candidate too given his legal and business experience. He had spoken at the 2013 Punggol East by-election.

I called Tan to gauge his interest. He had not quite decided then if he would want to be a candidate, but it did not take long to persuade him. I needed three more members to form the team. All the permutations went through my head that night. I had very little sleep. Then, I decided that I should take Marine Parade. I hate bullies. I felt I was being bullied out of my turf with the EBRC report. I had disliked the way the PAP played their politics in the past, which was one of the key reasons why I chose to be in the alternative camp. Now, it was my turn to be pushed around.

The next morning, Low called me. We both had reached the same conclusion after one day. He wanted me to be in Marine Parade. I had independently decided that I should be there. Secretly, I would still have preferred Fengshan. I would not have rejected Fengshan or East Coast GRC if they had been offered to me. Low decided to put Giam in East Coast and Dennis Tan in Fengshan, and I did not want to protest his decision. I knew Marine Parade was the toughest of the three. It was nearly impossible to win. I knew Tan well. He had helped me a lot during the 2011 general election (GE2011) and was very active in the party thereafter. He was younger than me and he might end up with a NCMP post, which would be just as well for him and the party.

I am not sure if the PAP expected the WP to take on Marine Parade GRC, given that ESM Goh was an extremely strong anchor. Shortly after the EBRC report was released, I recall meeting ESM Goh three times in three days in Marine Parade while I was doing house visits. At the third meeting, when I met him as he got out of his car at Marine Crescent for his Meet-The-People Session, he asked why I kept going there. I think I replied cheekily with something along the lines of, "Well, I live nearby." ESM Goh replied, "Why are you wasting your time here!"

At the final Parliament sitting in August 2015, I met PAP MP Inderjit Singh in the tearoom. He had already announced his retirement on Facebook. We were alone, taking a short break from a long sitting. Singh wanted to know where I would be contesting. I replied Marine Parade. He was surprised and remarked, "But we want you to go somewhere else!"

## Assembling the Team

Since the battleground had been decided, I would need the strongest possible team. East Coast GRC had their team configuration planned long ago, quite soon after GE2011. A consistent team of potential candidates had been doing house visits there weekly. No one was slated for Marine Parade GRC. It was not a battlefield we had wanted.

I told Low that I wanted Terence Tan to be in the team, which he agreed. Next, I wanted a lady. Low suggested He Ting Ru, whom I was very happy to have. I had interacted with her before. She is intelligent and has excellent education and work credentials. I also needed a minority candidate. I was given two to choose from. I had conducted house visits with both before. I chose Firuz Khan. I wanted the team to have people with experience working things from ground up. I was an entrepreneur. Tan had good legal and business experience. Khan had a chocolate business which he started when he lived in Europe several years ago. He had great credentials. I knew Town Council management would be on the mind of residents following all the issues with the Aljunied-Hougang-Punggol East Town Council (AHPETC) saga. I wanted to be able to pitch to the residents that our team could run the Town Council directly, that we have people unafraid to take on unknowns because we have done that before and succeeded in our businesses.

Of course, I still needed to independently speak with them to find out if they were interested to be in the Marine Parade team. I had only cleared with Tan. So, I contacted He Ting Ru and Khan and they agreed.

The final member took more time. I cannot remember exactly when Low offered me the choices for the last slot. He asked me to choose between Koh Choong Yong and another person. I had worked with Koh before and was comfortable with him. However, I looked at the profile of our team and felt that we may need someone with a finance background. Koh was a computer science graduate like myself. I wanted finance experience because finance appeared to have been one major issue in the AHPETC, or at least that was how it was being made out to be. I felt someone from the financial industry might give Marine Parade residents more assurance that we would be able to run the Town Council more smoothly. I asked to try this new member out for a while as I did not know him.

We had to move fast. The team went into action with immediate house visits. We had formed the team within two days of the release of the EBRC report. However, things did not go so smoothly with the last member as we tried to engage with him. Tan was already made the deputy team leader. I was the team leader. After several days, we both felt that we should ask for a change.

I went back to Low asking for Koh, but Low said no. Koh had already been deployed to return to Sengkang West where he had contested in 2011. I asked for Leon Perera. I had heard that he was in the Yishun team, which I thought would be an even tougher battle than Marine Parade. I had interacted with Perera, who was an active policy team member, and was very impressed with his analytical abilities and professional credentials. Low informed me that Perera was redeployed to East Coast GRC. I was happy that Giam had gotten such a gem, but remained concerned about our lack of a candidate to complete the team.

I told Low that I still preferred someone from the finance industry. He said there was one — Dylan Ng, who was then working for a foreign bank in Singapore. However, Ng was still deliberating very hard because in the finance industry, some of the big companies might be worried about their employees going into opposition politics. Some may think that government scrutiny of their operations would increase. Ng was not sure if his career prospects might be affected as a result of being our candidate. I asked to meet him anyway.

I arranged a meeting. I recall it was at Funan Centre before it was redeveloped. We probably met at the McDonalds there. We had a good and long conversation. I was very comfortable with Ng as his answers

*Family portrait, 1972. (Yee Jenn Jong, leftmost)*

*Family outing at the Old Nantah University. Nantah University was merged with the University of Singapore in 1980, angering many of the Chinese educated. (Yee Jenn Jong, leftmost)*

*Yee Jenn Jong (right) visiting Japan for research as a teaching staff of the National University of Singapore, 1992. During the visit, he met and debated with an American over freedom of choice in Singapore's political system.*

*Yee Jenn Jong and other party members were introduced to the public for the first time in Yishun, April 3, 2011.*

*Yee Jenn Jong visiting houses in Telok Kuaru in early April 2011 before his candidacy was announced.*

*Candidates, election agents, assentors, and supporters gathered at Hougang Town Council on the morning of nomination day, GE2011, before departing to their respective nomination centres by chartered buses.*

*Yee Jenn Jong stopping to speak with the press outside Tao Nan School, one of the nomination centres, on nomination day, GE2011.*

*Supporters at Tao Nan School, one of the nomination centres, GE2011.*

*View from the balcony of Tao Nan School, one of the nomination centres, shortly before speaking on the podium.*

*Yee Jenn Jong bumped into his extended family at a coffee shop in Siglap while campaigning during GE2011. Visits to coffee shops were an almost daily affair in the few weeks before polling day.*

*At coffee shops, pamphlets are given out, which provide more details about candidates and the party.*

*Yee Jenn Jong meeting with Channel News Asia reporters in Jalan Jamal during a planned media outreach, GE2011.*

*View from the balcony of Tao Nan School, one of the nomination centres, shortly before speaking on the podium.*

*Yee Jenn Jong bumped into his extended family at a coffee shop in Siglap while campaigning during GE2011. Visits to coffee shops were an almost daily affair in the few weeks before polling day.*

*At coffee shops, pamphlets are given out, which provide more details about candidates and the party.*

*Yee Jenn Jong meeting with Channel News Asia reporters in Jalan Jamal during a planned media outreach, GE2011.*

*When campaigning, even bus drivers and commuters on the road are not missed out.*

*Yee Jenn Jong visiting houses in Opera Estate in GE2011 with his father.*

*Yee Jenn Jong's first rally speech at Bedok Stadium in GE2011.*

*Rally crowd at Bedok Stadium, GE2011.*

*Rally crowd at Serangoon Stadium, GE2011.*

*During the final rally of GE2011, all candidates gathered on stage.*

*Yee Jenn Jong after a rally speech, GE2011. Candidates often receive flower garlands from supporters at each rally.*

*Perambulating vehicle in Yee Jenn Jong's home estate during GE2011. The vehicle carried a ladder so that any election poster that had fallen off or needed fixing could be attended to by the crew.*

*Yee Jenn Jong and his team drove through Joo Chiat SMC to thank voters the day after polling day.*

*Yee Jenn Jong cycling around Joo Chiat SMC while visiting houses after GE2011 with Dennis Tan and other volunteers.*

*Yee Jenn Jong speaking to graduating students of Temasek Junior College at its Farewell Assembly, October 2011.*

*Yee Jenn Jong and Charles Chong at the Jalan Bintang Tiga street party in September 2011. This is the longest-running street party in Singapore.*

*Poster of Bricks in Blue. An Aljunied GRC resident contacted Yee Jenn Jong, taught him magic tricks, and loaned him professional magic props for the show.*

*Yee Jenn Jong having a drink with then newly-elected Prime Minister of Bhutan Tshering Tobgay in Thimphu, 2013. Bhutan's democracy began in 2007.*

*One of the many Sunday Hammer visits. This took place in 2014 at one of the coffee shops in then Joo Chiat SMC.*

*Yee Jenn Jong inspecting a poorly maintained drain during a weekly estate visit between 2011 and 2015.*

*Yee Jenn Jong and other WP parliamentarians on National Day, 2015.*

*Nomination Day Speech, GE2015. Left to right: Firuz Khan, Dylan Ng, He Ting Ru, Yee Jenn Jong, and Terence Tan.*

*Supporters waiting patiently for WP candidates to emerge from Kong Hwa School, one of the nomination centres, GE2015.*

*Terence Tan, He Ting Ru, Dylan Ng, and volunteers bumped into the WP perambulating vehicle crew during the GE2015 campaigning.*

*Hard at work to get posters ready to be hung up after nomination is accepted.*

*A chance meeting between Yee Jenn Jong and Tan Chuan-Jin and Fatimah Lateef while campaigning in Marine Parade GRC, GE2015.*

*WP supporters brought inflatable hammers to the rallies. This was captured during the GE2015 WP rally at Simei.*

*An illuminated hammer brought to the WP GE2015 rally at Simei.*

*Some residents from nearby HDB flats watched the rally from the corridors, which provided a birds-eye view of the event.*

*WP and PAP representatives attending Iftar, the breaking of fast, at Darul Arqam in Joo Chiat. Yee Jenn Jong has attended Iftar here yearly from 2011–2019.*

*Members of the GE2015 Marine Parade GRC team at a National Day flag distribution event in 2017.*

*Yee Jenn Jong with other WP MPs during a visit to Armenia for a political conference, 2018.*

*(L-R) Low Thia Khiang, Yee Jenn Jong, and Png Eng Huat on a visit to the Democratic Republic of Korea on the 70th anniversary of its founding, 2018. They are pictured at the Arc of Reunification.*

*Two boys ran out of their house after taking their bath when they saw Yee Jenn Jong knocking on their doors during a quarterly food distribution to Marine Terrace in January 2018. They greeted him with a hug, having known him from earlier distributions.*

*After an evening of house visits in Kembangan before the COVID-19 circuit breaker started, early 2020.*

*A visit to Telok Kurau Park in GE2020, where Yee Jenn Jong coincidentally met Dennis Tan (left), who was leaving his house to campaign in Hougang.*

*The WP Marine Parade GRC team arriving at Kong Hwa School on nomination day, GE2020. Only the press, election personnel, assentors, and other key individuals involved in the nomination process were permitted to be present in the centre in light of the COVID-19 pandemic.*

*The WP Marine Parade GE2020 team posing for a photograph after a media outreach in Marine Terrace market.*

*Yee Jenn Jong going about campaigning in GE2020 during a drizzle. Rain or shine, campaigning goes on.*

PAP and WP counting agents at St Stephen's School after counting at the centre was completed.

WP candidates are issued a badge with a hammer logo for each general election. Notice the different shades of red and gold of the badges from different general elections.

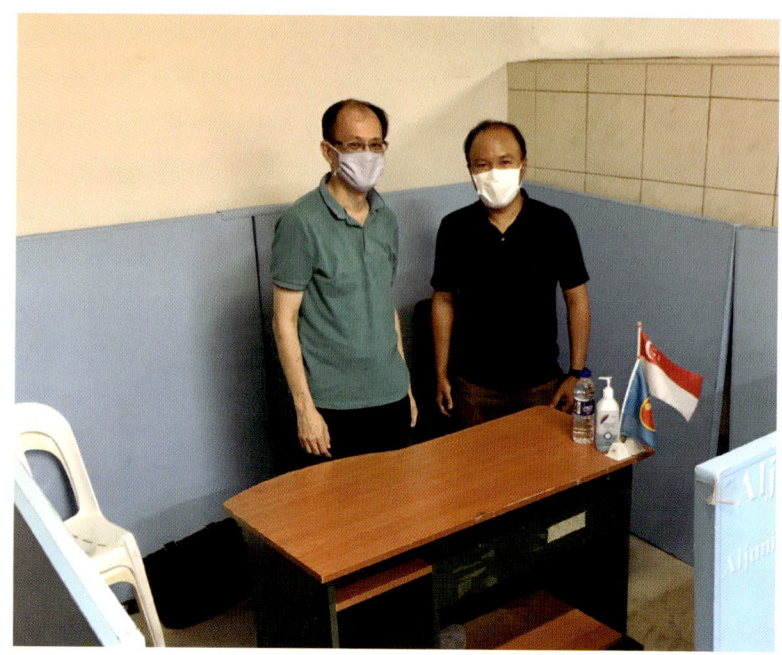
*Yee Jenn Jong with WP MP Muhamad Faisal Manap at his Meet-The-People Session, October 2020.*

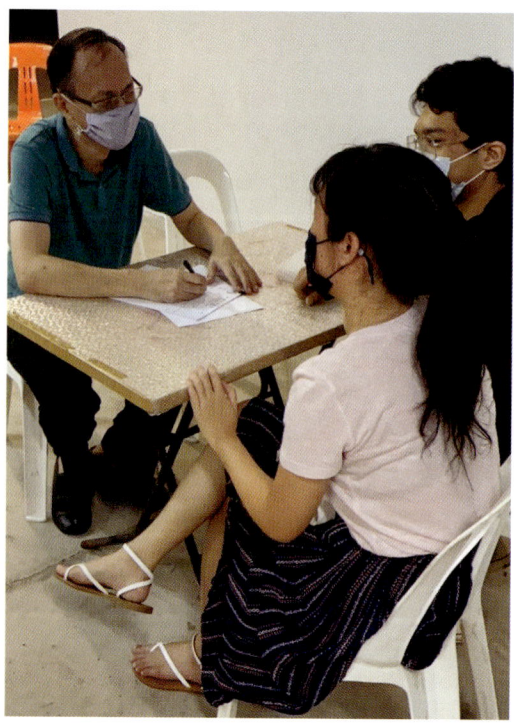
*Yee Jenn Jong chatting with WP volunteers at the Kaki Bukit Meet-The-People Session, October 2020.*

*Food distribution at Eunos Crescent after GE2020. Some 190 packets of food and other items were being given out daily since April 2020. A volunteer donated home-baked cookies after reading about our food distribution on social media.*

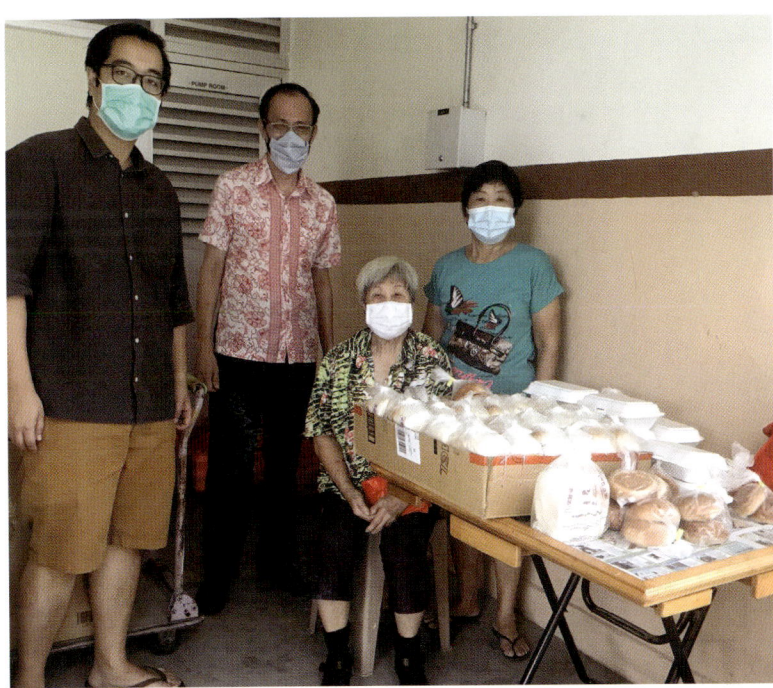

*Food distribution at Eunos Crescent. While we continue to help at the distribution points in Marine Terrace and Eunos Crescent, local residents have since taken over and fronted all daily distributions.*

*Donated sacks of rice, 25 kilograms each, stored at a volunteer's house. These were later repackaged into five-kilogram packets for distribution to residents who required assistance in Marine Parade GRC.*

*Yee Jenn Jong delivering food packets to households in Eunos Crescent.*

*Journey in Blue — Abstract mixed-media painting by Yee Jenn Jong, painted September 2020.*

*Journey in Blue — Digital doodle art by Grace Yee, September 2020.*

*Self-portrait in oil by Yee Jenn Jong, based on the GE2011 official photograph. Yee Jenn Jong had learnt art at a young age from artist Wee Beng Chong, but had stopped at 15 years old. He started painting again in 2013.*

*Yee Jenn Jong with abstract mixed media painting of Hammer by artist Chen Yi Quan.*

*Little Guilin — Bukit Batok Nature Park, painted by Yee Jenn Jong in 2015 for a SG50 charity art exhibition.*

*Painting of the National Day celebrations at Marine Bay by Yee Jenn Jong for an art charity in 2015, modified in 2020. The National Day Parade is attended by parliamentarians every year.*

*Standing Its Ground — Surrealism painting of an elephant defending its turf with a Hammer trunk. Its melting clock ear depicts time running out for the environment given climate change and rapid urbanisation taking place. This was first painted in 2013 for a charity art for Zambia, and later modified in 2020.*

came across as authentic. He did not try to hide anything, even when I asked difficult questions. Ng reminded me of my own journey in 2011, very interested but fearful of many things. I shared my journey with him. I did not find doors closed to me after I had become an opposition politician. In fact, I was conferred the Distinguished Alumnus Award by my alma mater in 2013. I separated work and politics.

I told him how my family went through that journey with me. Ng's two children were young then. While we were at it, I asked him for character referees too. Politics can be a dirty business. I was roping others into the team and I wanted to give as much assurance as I could that we would not run into some nasty situations later if our opponents managed to dig out something unpleasant about one of us and used that to sink the team. None of us in the team had worked with Ng before, so I felt that I should check him more thoroughly. Ng readily provided me with two contacts.

I reached out to Ng's character referees on the same day. Both came back with excellent comments about him. Several days later, Ng got back to me that he was ready to join in. He was still uncertain if his job would be affected, but he agreed anyway. To him, the worst that could happen was that he would be asked to leave, and he would then have to find another job. He had definitely passed our team's selection test!

Our team was complete. I felt that it was a good team, one that was able to match that of the East Coast GRC team, which was expected to be the WP's Team B. Team A was the Aljunied GRC team. East Coast had a great team, with Giam, an NCMP like me; Daniel Goh; Leon Perera; and Mohamed Fairoz Shariff. I was happy that it was possible to squeeze out another excellent team for an unexpected battleground. It showed that there were more good candidates in the party than before. The overall quality of the WP slate had definitely come a long way since Low took over as secretary-general in 2001. In 2001, the WP could only contest in two SMCs.

### Journey in Blue

As you can tell from my experience, team selection was two ways. First, candidates must make it past the general election committee, which would be formed nearing each general election. The committee consisted of the secretary-general and a subset of key people in the Central Executive Committee (CEC). It was a powerful committee that would directly control how the election would be run and where the candidates would be deployed. I was not in the committee. As a team leader, I could negotiate for those who had been cleared. I could also nominate someone whom I strongly felt would be a good candidate for our team. The election committee would still need to clear the person. I did not have anyone to nominate and I was happy with how our team formation went.

In general, where do our candidates come from? Most would have served for some time in the WP grassroots, constituency work, or in policy work. After GE2011, many signed up to be volunteers. Many, in particular, were attracted to serve in the Paya Lebar ward. The star power of Chen Show Mao had attracted many, including high-flyers. After a while, when there were too many volunteers in one area, some flowed to other wards. When Daniel Goh started organising the policy groups from 2012, those with suitable professional and education experience for policy work were roped in.

Volunteer activities are strong recruitment grounds for new candidates. Tan, He Ting Ru, and Ng had been serving in various aspects of the WP's work since 2011 and Khan even before me. He moved to Europe and returned to Singapore a couple of years before 2015. I first met Jamus Lim in 2019 at a regular money-counting session for our *Hammer* sales collection. *Hammer* outreach is a way for the WP to engage with supporters as well as to raise funds to support our operations. It is also an effective way to enable members to walk the ground. No matter what our positions in the party were or our professional background, during *Hammer* outreach, we had to walk around the markets and shops to interact with residents to sell our newspaper for a dollar a copy.

I was a regular in money-counting ever since I was the treasurer of the party. I continued to help with some of these finance-related matters even after stepping down from the post. There I was, counting money and chatting with an unassuming member I had not met before. I found, to my pleasant surprise, that Lim had a doctorate degree, was an economics professor, and was formerly an economist with the World Bank. I next met him at a *Hammer* outreach in a market. I was hoping he would eventually contest in the next general election, as we sometimes have high-flyers who opt not to contest elections. Of course, Lim did, and won in the 2020 general election.

Today, the WP has become more systematic in the recruitment of candidates, even though the process can still be improved. It was not the case earlier. Once in a meeting, Low shared the experience of his first general election in 1988. He only knew on the morning of nomination day who the last member in his Tiong Bahru GRC team would be. In 2001, only two SMCs were contested by the WP.

Improvements to the process can include putting committed volunteers with the potential to be a good MP through a more systematic structure to help in the spectrum of activities vital to gauging the person's performance on the ground and in policy work. The very large base of volunteers coming through as helpers during each general election is actually a good place to start. Unfortunately, people who are not sufficiently engaged will drop off from our radar very soon.

Talent scouting was rather ad-hoc and left to the initiative of the individual senior leaders of the party. Some were more organised in looking out for good people to be roped into the party. I was told that Yaw Shin Leong was a strong ground activist and constantly on the lookout to recruit people. Some of those he had brought into the party included Gerald Giam and Frieda Chan. Leon Perera is also quite active in attracting new blood. The secretary-general has the opportunity to meet more people and the greatest burden of ensuring a constant flow of good candidates. I tried to assist in that way, too, and I am glad that among those I had recruited included Dennis Tan. There were several others I had brought in, but some declined to be candidates even though the party had found them suitable. Some fizzled out after a while. Politics, especially in the alternative camp, is not for everyone.

## The WP's Way

The first four members of the team had been decided upon quite quickly. We each picked our election agent (EA) too. I took Shaun Lee, my EA from 2011, again as my EA. He also became the principal election agent (PEA), which was the lead EA for a GRC. Each candidate can appoint an EA, and one of the EAs will function as PEA. He had continued to help in some of my visits after GE2011. My ex-National University of Singapore (NUS) computing student, Yap Keng Ann, who had helped in 2011, also became one of our EAs. Each candidate was to find their own EA, but if they could not, we would find one for them.

We hit the streets within two days of the release of the EBRC report. General election campaigning does not start when Parliament is dissolved. Any serious party will start campaigning as soon as the EBRC report is released. If we waited until Parliament was dissolved and polling date announced, there would be just about two weeks to campaign, an impossible time to make an impact.

We had good responses from the ground from our outreach. Ng joined us about two weeks later. The difficulty with campaigning was that candidates will never know when elections would be called. Most candidates still need to work. Khan and I were more fortunate that we ran our own businesses and our time was within our control. The rest had to juggle with work and to also keep their annual leave for the actual campaign. Hence, some could only do campaigning during weekends and weekday evenings.

I was sent as the lead representative for the WP to the traditional "pow-wow" meeting among opposition parties after the EBRC report was out. The meeting was to iron out constituencies that the alternative parties would contest in. Muhamad Faisal Manap and Daniel Goh also accompanied me for the meeting. I was selected as the lead representative because the main negotiation was for Marine Parade GRC, which had been contested by the National Solidarity Party (NSP) in the previous general election.

We insisted on Marine Parade GRC. The other parties were trying to persuade me to go to an SMC or to another GRC. I held my ground. We offered not to contest in MacPherson SMC. The NSP was rather upset with us. They would not take MacPherson SMC either, since we forced them out of Marine Parade GRC. After the meeting, the WP publicly announced that we would take both Marine Parade GRC and MacPherson SMC. The next day, Low deployed Bernard Chen to the ground in MacPherson SMC. Several days later, the NSP wanted MacPherson SMC back. The matter was already out of my hands. We had already announced our decision to the public, so there was no turning back.

When the press reported that the WP would take Marine Parade GRC and that I would likely be leading it, I received an email from Nicole Seah, the star candidate for the NSP in GE2011. She was working in Bangkok then. I had represented the WP in a public forum after GE2011. Seah was also a speaker on the same panel. We had a casual conversation after the forum and exchanged contact details. Some months later, I read about her resignation from the NSP. I arranged for a lunch meeting between Seah and Sylvia Lim. Not long after the lunch meeting, Seah went overseas for long-term work. I thought the chance to attract her to join the WP was gone. Female candidates are still hard to come by in Singapore politics, and I thought that she could fit an expanding WP well.

In our correspondence, Seah offered to help with our 2015 general election (GE2015) campaign. She had already planned to leave her overseas job and move back to Singapore to settle down. She was not interested to contest in 2015 but wanted to help us do well since it was the GRC where she had previously contested.

I discussed with the team and they were happy to have Seah too. Before nomination day, she was back in Singapore. We met to discuss her experience in the various parts of the GRC at the last general election. We were planning a day when she would come along wearing a WP volunteer blue T-shirt and visit the markets with us. I organised a lunch to formally introduce Seah to the rest of the candidates.

Shortly before we were to execute the plan to involve Seah in public visits, I received a text from Lim asking if it was true that Seah would be campaigning with us. I confirmed it. Lim said that we should not do it. I protested and indicated that we still wished to. That same day, Low contacted me over the same matter. I cannot remember if it was by phone or by text. He insisted that we must call it off. I still refused, so he asked to meet me.

We met at the Housing and Development Board void deck beside Damai Secondary School in Low's ward in Aljunied GRC. I had earlier discussed with the team whether I should insist on proceeding or if we should back down. The consensus was that if I could not persuade Low, then we should preserve the harmony of the WP team.

We spoke for some 45 minutes. I was fairly insistent. Low was visibly exasperated. I recall him saying, "Of all people, I expected you to have better political judgement. We are WP. We must fight as WP." To him, Seah was no ordinary volunteer. The attention would be on her and it would distract the WP's campaign. I was focused on trying to find any way to get a few percentage points more in votes. I was not totally convinced then, but I agreed to back down.

I was also concerned about the promise I had made to Seah, which led to her promise on her social media that she would be back in Singapore to help with an opposition party during the general election. I did not like to break my promise, and I did not want to make her break her promise.

To fulfil both our promises, I asked Seah if she could help in a low-key manner in Opera Estate, where she had grown up in with her grandparents. She was not to wear WP blue. I sent my wife and our two daughters in WP blue to distribute flyers with her. My daughters went in their roller blades and the four of them covered Opera Estate.

Seah was obviously not happy. It seemed so hard just to help with the WP. Besides hoping to win more votes for ourselves in the general election, I had hoped that Seah would join the WP in our future general elections. Getting her involved was a way to get it started. We agreed to keep her help low-key. I chose not to inform anyone, not even the other candidates nor our EAs. I did not join in the flyer distribution that day as well. The only photograph I posted online was that of my two daughters in their roller blades with our flyers. While distributing, the group ran into some volunteers for Edwin Tong, a PAP candidate also contesting in Marine Parade GRC. They remarked to my wife that roller blading was a novel and productive way to do the pamphleteering.

Looking back after the general election, I agree with the position by Low and Lim. I had then not yet realised even after five years with the WP, how jealously Low guarded the WP's brand. Win or lose, we had to fight our own fight. It was not that the WP did not welcome stars. They must first come in to the WP, work as a team with the WP, and do it the WP's way.

I was a little embarrassed to face Seah after my backdown. The good thing that came out of this was that she got along well with He Ting Ru and Terence Tan after my introduction. I knew they continued to keep in touch after the general election. Then, I heard she started helping in some small ways. When the WP60 (the WP's 60th anniversary) book was published and Seah's name was listed inside as one of those on the editorial team, I knew she had assimilated into the WP. She was now one of our team players and not just an individual star. She was ready for the WP's way.

## The Campaign

Marine Parade GRC was immensely bigger and more challenging than Joo Chiat SMC. We could not quite play the local boy card, even though Khan had grown up in Geylang Serai, Tan was then living in the Joo Chiat area, and I was still living where I had been, in the defunct Joo Chiat SMC. Marine Parade was too big and diverse to have any local boy effect.

Shaun Lee was quite good at amassing volunteers, perhaps too good as we ended up with many and could have better managed their deployment. We started with more help in this regard than I did in Joo Chiat SMC in GE2011, when I had only one helper, Lee himself. We decided to split by locations and let each candidate handle different areas. Given the short campaigning period and the fact that some of the candidates were still struggling to ease off their professional work, I offered to cover both Joo Chiat and Marine Parade wards of the GRC. Khan, who had more flexibility of time to visit more frequently, covered the areas managed by PAP MP, Fatimah Lateef. The remaining two wards were assigned to Tan, He Ting Ru, and Ng.

Ground sentiments were actually quite good. Even the reporters who trailed us on our campaign felt so. Many residents had told us we had a good team and they were very happy to have such an alternative selection.

During my first rally speech, we played to our plan to convince voters that we had carefully selected a team capable of taking over and running the Town Council. Here is an extract from my rally speech:

Yee Jenn Jong Rally Speech — September 20, 2015

(Earlier parts omitted)

The EBRC report also made me reflect on why I had joined the Workers Party in the first place. I had wanted to see a fairer democratic system, where rules are clear and contests are fair, and Singaporeans can choose the leaders without fear of repercussions. I had wanted to see a stronger alternative being developed, because I think it is dangerous to leave it only to one 'A' team. I had strongly believed that Singaporeans are talented. We are more talented than the PAP thinks we are. There is enough for more than one 'A' team and that we can benefit from a contest of ideas.

So, my mind became very clear. The next morning after the EBRC report was out, I requested for the Party's leadership to let me lead a committed team into Marine Parade GRC.

I didn't have to look far for the passionate team members whom I had wanted. They have been right in our midst, serving alongside with our many volunteers.

Let me first introduce you to Terence Tan, lawyer. Many would know that he fought the cases for AHPETC with NEA[2] and with MND[3], pro-bono, without charging us any fees. He also does pro-bono work for capital offences cases and others requiring legal aid. He is not just a lawyer, but was an entrepreneur who started a popular bar and restaurant establishment early in his career. He had stints overseas that included being the Managing Director of a multinational hotel group with operations from Spain to South-East Asia.

---

2  National Environment Agency

3  Ministry of National Development

Terence joined WP after GE2011 and has been walking the ground with me for over 2 years. He's also a local boy of Marine Parade GRC, a Peranakan who lives in the traditional part of Joo Chiat.

Terence has served faithfully in our grassroots and [meet-the-people sessions]. Today, he's your candidate for the Marine Parade GRC.

Next, we have He Ting Ru, just 32 years old and already a successful corporate lawyer heading up the legal department in a public listed company. She volunteered as a helper in our [meet-the-people sessions] right after GE2011. She came on her own, seeking to find ways to contribute to Singapore. From there, she expanded her work into our community events and diligently [assisted] in the policy work of our parliamentarians. You may find it hard to believe that a bright, successful and busy lawyer would spend so much of her free time to volunteer week in, week out with us, but here we have the living proof. Ms He Ting Ru, your candidate for Marine Parade GRC.

And right in the Malay heartland of Singapore, is your local boy, Mr Firuz Khan from Haig Road. He has been in the Party longer than I had, since 2006. His service was disrupted when he went with his family to UK for several years, where he started a successful chocolate factory. Then he came back to Singapore in 2010 and continued his service with the Workers' Party serving Singaporeans.

Firuz's heart is in the right place. He took a pay cut from his banking career in 1999 to be the principal for the Pertapis Children's Home, where he had learnt first-hand the issues of those that have fallen through the cracks in the Malay-Muslim community. He is also a hands-on guy, who started and grew the Royce' Chocolate business for the Japanese company in

Singapore and in the region, before starting his own chocolate factory in Wales, UK. Mr Firuz Khan, a hands-on person with commitment to help the vulnerable and needy in the community, your candidate for Marine Parade GRC.

Last but not least, Mr Ng Foo Eng, Dylan. Foo Eng came from a humble family background, studied in neighbourhood schools, [and] worked his way through university. He found success in his banking career, working in both local and foreign banks. He has built up the wealth management business for the bank from scratch.

Foo Eng is passionate about serving the community, and has served as a volunteer in WP's grassroots and in the [meet-the-people sessions]. Mr Ng Foo Eng, your candidate for Marine Parade GRC.

This is a team that's part of the renewal story in the Workers' Party. This is a team that's willing to take on the difficult task in what the PAP considers as one of its strongholds, to give you a credible alternative to choose from. We know the challenges are not just in fighting this election. We know there will be lots of start-up issues. This is a team with a good range of complementary strengths and operational expertise that can see this through. You will hear more from this team in the coming days.

This is team Marine Blue, because Marine should be blue, not white! Come September 11, vote the Workers' Party. Empower your future!

Of the candidates, He Ting Ru became the most popular on social media. Her speeches were sharp and clear. Everyone in our team in general did well.

We saw many fake bookies' odds. They were definitely false. We thought we had put up a good campaign and had a good team. We might push the PAP to the wire but there was no way that we would win Marine Parade GRC or East Coast GRC by the landslide margins in those fake bookies' odds. The massive turnout at our rallies might have frightened some voters who felt the WP was going to put many ministers out. The WP had also taken on 28 seats, up from the 21 seats in the last election. We had the momentum going for us with the wins in the 2011, 2012, and 2013 general election and by-elections.

There were also false viral messages claiming that the WP was pushing a lesbian, gay, bisexual, and transgender (LGBT) agenda. The messages could have been calculated by those who began spreading them to cause the WP to lose votes from conservative Singaporeans. Coming close to the end of the general election campaigning, the party was caught off-guard and did not respond to them. Some years later in 2019, when Pritam Singh took over as secretary-general, he decided to address this issue at a NUS forum because if we did not, such messages would be repeated at every general election. Section 377A, which criminalises sex between men, is, as presented by Singh, "a divisive issue that splits Singaporeans". The party would not be calling for the repeal of 377A because there was no consensus within the party's CEC on the issue.

We had a warm reception and good supporters in every area that we visited. Polling night, however, was something else.

## Analysis of the GE2015 Results

The results on polling night were devastating. For my first counting station, I had chosen to check on the polling district that sank me in GE2011. There had been only one area where we did very badly for GE2011. I had thought that if we could pull the votes up at that hard ground, we might still have a chance.

## The Battle for Marine Parade GRC

I was shocked. I was in the counting centre for voters in the Joo Chiat ward. Instead of improving, our votes sank badly. The night was over in 15 minutes. Every counting station painted a massive swing away from us. It became just one depressing drive after another, from one counting centre to another to see the obvious. Still, we had to hold our heads up high and encourage our counting agents.

Even the PAP was shocked. I could see great delight and disbelief among our opponents. I did not think that they had expected themselves to do that well. If they did, a minister would have been put into Aljunied GRC and it would have been won by the PAP.

The reporters were shocked too. Reporters whom I had chatted with post-GE2015 told me that after we had visited residents, they had checked with those willing to speak with the press on how they had planned to vote. The reporters felt it was closer to 50-50. The feedback was nothing like what they saw from the results.

I was devastated. I had worked hard on the ground since GE2011. It amounted to nothing.

Many analysts came up with explanations post-GE2015. I doubt any analyst expected the almost 10 percent swing. My own observation from talking to voters post-GE2015 was the Lee Kuan Yew (LKY) effect. The general election was a reminder of what Singapore had achieved under the late Lee.

Of course, it was the SG50 year, with a whole year of celebrations and reminder of what the PAP had done for the country. Combined with the passing of Lee, it was powerful. The two went hand-in-hand.

I had thought that the WP would do better with first-time voters. We also lost with this group. The pioneer generation (individuals born before 1949) appeared to have swung back to the PAP in a big way too. Furthermore, there had been a generous package of goodies given to them in the 50th year of Singapore's independence.

There was also political instability in neighbouring countries. That served to play up the fear in voters of potential instability in Singapore, especially seeing the massive crowds at our rallies. Some older voters did tell me that they switched away from voting for us after seeing our crowds and seeing the fake bookies' odds. They thought that it would be too destabilising for Singapore if the PAP lost too many seats at one go.

The swing in private estates and large flat-types was quite obvious too. There was a big swing in Joo Chiat. The PAP had implemented several social policies since their poor showing in GE2011, such as the pioneer generation package, lowering the purchase cost of Build-to-Order public flats for new buyers, investments in early childhood, and more. These social reforms, coupled with the LKY effect, could have made a good number of middle-ground voters swing back to the PAP.

On polling day, I had gone early to my polling station at St Patrick's School. In the queue behind me, the voter recognised me. I told him that I had contested here in Joo Chiat SMC in 2011 too. He outrightly told me, "If this is an SMC, I will vote differently. In a GRC, there are other things to consider." He was brutally honest. I knew what he meant. He was not going to vote for the WP. He probably voted for the WP in 2011.

Before polling day, *The Straits Times* had interviewed residents of Marine Parade GRC.[4] It reported that one resident, a regional controller in a finance company who voted in Joo Chiat SMC in 2011, said that it would be harder to decide his vote now that Joo Chiat was absorbed under Marine Parade GRC. He had reportedly said, "I am not voting for only one person but a team that includes a minister… The question

---

4   Jermyn Chow and Chong Zi Liang, "PAP, WP gear up for stiff contest", The Straits Times, September 8, 2015, https://www.straitstimes.com/politics/singapolitics/pap-wp-gear-up-for-stiff-contest

is whether we have people who can make laws or whether we want to give a chance to those who tell us they are willing to speak up."

Post-GE2015, my wife met the owner of a shop which she frequented. The elder gentleman, a voter in Marine Parade GRC, had by then known that I was the candidate. He told my wife in Mandarin, "The old one is still around. I must give him face." He was, of course, referring to the most senior member of our opponent. In a GRC, it could be a single person drawing in the votes. The mountain we had to climb proved to be too tall an order.

**Responding to an Attack by *The Straits Times***

A month after the general election, I was surprised to read a bad report by *The Straits Times* about the GE2015 Marine Parade WP team. I felt that I had to respond. Running a general election under the difficult circumstances and short notice was tough enough for all of us. I found it unacceptable that the members were attacked and portrayed as fighting among ourselves. It was the furthest thing from the truth. None of the leaders of the WP had told me nor any of us that they were displeased with us, as reported in the newspaper. It was also not true, as reported, that none from our team was offered to be co-opted into the CEC. One was, but, for various reasons, declined. It would have damaged the former candidates of the team if I did not speak up. I thought that all of them did well and deserved to be in future general elections again, if they wished to.

Furthermore, I was upset that Chong Zi Liang, who was the first to feature me in GE2011 as the likely candidate for the WP in Joo Chiat SMC, was the author of the article. I texted him to ask for an explanation on how he had arrived at the conclusion. Chong was in Europe then, attending an official conference. He replied that he had indeed written the article before he flew off, but the offending statement was put in by another person based on information from "insiders" and he did not know about it. Oh, those "insiders" again. We get this quite often in news reports about the WP — from "Secret Squirrel" to "long-time party insiders" and "sources which did not wish to be named".

I replied Chong that even if one or two unhappy "insiders" said so did not mean that it must be true. He agreed that *The Straits Times* could have at least asked me for my response before publishing the article. Political desk reporters covering the WP all have my mobile phone number. Anyway, after the incident died down and I had responded with a post on my social media channels, I met Chong for lunch at a chicken rice shop in Katong. It was still necessary to mend things even if I had been unhappy over the incident.

Below is my response via my social media channels to *The Straits Times*.

> A response to Straits Times: My wonderful Team Marine Blue
>
> (October 11, 2015)
>
> I read to my great surprise this feature by The Straits Times today, "Workers' Party trying to move forward".[5] The report stated, "It is also, perhaps, trying to send a signal about the importance of party discipline, insiders say. They point to how its Marine Parade team was also made up of highly-qualified candidates — including crowd favourite, legal counsel He Ting Ru, 32 — none of whom were brought into the CEC. The team was apparently plagued by simmering discord among members, which displeased party leaders, who have always prized tight discipline and frowned upon power play."
>
> As leader of the WP team for Marine Parade GRC for GE2015 (or Team Marine Blue as we call ourselves), I am shocked by

---

5  Chong Zi Liang, Workers' Party trying to move forward", The Straits Times, October 11, 2015, http://www.straitstimes.com/politics/workers-party-trying-to-move-forward

## The Battle for Marine Parade GRC

what was reported of "simmering discord" and "displeased party leaders".

During my first rally speech on 2 Sep 2015,[6] I had introduced Team Marine Blue proudly. Allow me to put on record that I have become even prouder of the team since delivering that speech. Marine Parade GRC was never going to be an easy contest. We were thrust into that battle because of a small but powerful Electoral Boundaries Review Committee.

We had just 6 weeks to campaign in one of the biggest GRCs that is a stronghold of the PAP. The team had signed up for the contest knowing very well of the challenges and of our chances. Yet, they pressed on diligently to visit almost all of the public housing units and a good number of homes in the private estates. We had many volunteers to manage, many of whom were signed up only during the campaigning period. Keeping volunteers trained, organised and motivated in such a short time was challenging. Yes, it was stressful for all of us and things could always have been done better in hindsight. I am proud of how each of them managed their group of volunteers as we divided up our roles and areas to cover as much ground as we could. Except for me, all were first time candidates. They also had to prepare for and deliver their own rally speeches, often a formidable task for new candidates.

None of us are aware of any "power play" or "discord" amongst ourselves. The team had cheered and encouraged each other along the way as we kept ourselves posted of each other's campaign activities. In her interview with Yahoo Singapore last

---

6   Yee Jenn Jong, "YJJ Rally Speech — 2 Sep 2015", September 3, 2015, https://yeejj.wordpress.com/2015/09/03/yjj-rally-speech-2-sep-2015/

week,[7] He Ting Ru shared about a group hug with the fellow candidates at one of the counting centre when it was evident that we had lost. She had recalled that "at that moment, I really felt that we were part of a team. That, to me, was something that was quite striking for the night itself, that we were in this together." We were also given encouraging words by the party leaders during the campaign and even after the results were known.

Today, a month after polling day, I am pleased to say that all candidates of Team Marine Blue remain committed to the party, with some taking on additional responsibilities within the party. My respect for each of them has increased throughout the campaigning and thereafter. They are all good team players, completely dedicated to the tasks they had been entrusted with, no matter how difficult the tasks were. Never mind the difficult circumstances and short time that were given to us to put the team and campaign together. I could not have asked for better fellow candidates.

I am deeply disappointed that the Straits Times had run the report on the Marine Parade Team without checking the facts with me or any of the candidates. How many 'insiders' did they speak to and what evidences do these 'insiders' have of 'discord' and 'power play'. The article did, however, allow me this chance to publicly say "Thank You" once more to my wonderful Marine Blue team members and our many volunteers.

---

7   Nicholas Yong, "Post-GE2015: Business as usual for WP's He Ting Ru", Yahoo! News, October 6, 2015, https://sg.news.yahoo.com/post-ge2015--business-as-usual-for-he-ting-ru-080540361.html

# Chapter 7
# The Second Battle for Marine Parade GRC

## After the 2015 General Election

I was uncertain about my plans after the devastating results. General elections come once every five years. Each time, the next general election seemed so far away once you have failed to win.

I told the team that I preferred someone else to be the team leader to continue the groundwork in Marine Parade. I was the team leader for the 2015 general election (GE2015) and the oldest member. Now that the election was over, I had hoped someone else could lead the ground engagement going forward.

I opted not to contest in the Central Executive Committee (CEC) in 2016. I felt that it was time for younger blood to be given the space to prove themselves in the CEC. We had then just concluded GE2015 with a number of first-time candidates; it would be good for younger ones to rise up.

Finding a successor as team leader to continue work in Marine Parade Group Representation Constituency (GRC) proved hard. We continued with occasional house visits and provided manpower for quarterly food distributions. As with all election cycles, volunteers were enthusiastic just after the general election. After months, it again became a struggle to muster a decent number of volunteers to do house visits and to have enough manpower for food distribution. We continued anyway.

After a while, the party also decided to redeploy talents. I knew quite early that the key members of the GE2015 East Coast GRC team would be moved out to Aljunied and Hougang. Daniel Goh started to shadow Low Thia Khiang quite early. Then Dennis Tan started to shadow Png

Eng Huat. Later, Leon Perera shadowed Sylvia Lim. The plan to retire three in the next general election was already set in place progressively from 2016 onwards. East Coast GRC had been the Workers' Party's (WP) next big battleground after Aljunied. Positions in East Coast GRC were opened up to some of the former Marine Parade GRC team members. I did not object. They had performed well in GE2015 despite the depressing results. It was good for them. But I asked for others to be sent to Marine Parade GRC.

The party did send a couple of new talents. But later, there were plans to open up a new front in the north-east. Punggol East Single Member Constituency (SMC) was certain to disappear, as Joo Chiat SMC did in the last general election. The whole north-east of Singapore was growing more populated. A GRC had to come out from there. The Pasir Ris-Punggol GRC was too big. We were already waiting for a new GRC in the north-east to be formed in GE2015 but it did not happen. With Punggol East SMC back to the People's Action Party (PAP), it was a certainty. We just did not know where the boundaries would be.

Talents got moved again. Only Firuz Khan and I remained in Marine Parade till early 2020.

I tried to bring in new talents on my own and got them involved to help with the party's activities. But after a while, their involvement died down for various reasons. It was quite a pity. I was eyeing two very strong candidates for their command of Mandarin. One had a very strong background in Chinese education and culture, and had obtained a PhD from a leading United States university. He was very articulate and spoke fluently in several languages. I arranged for him to meet with Pritam Singh, who had cleared his candidacy. However, he decided not to contest. The other was a lady who had received bilingual education from a young age, and had worked extensively in the Chinese media. She was also an excellent bilingual translator. However, she, too, declined to be fielded. I knew Low had planned to step down. We needed new people who were very strong in Chinese culture, but they were the hardest to find.

I was also unsure of the party's plans for Marine Parade GRC. It was an unexpected battlefield for us in 2015. I was closely associated with the GRC because Joo Chiat SMC became absorbed into it. I then led the team in the WP's first contest there. Marine Parade Town itself, helmed by Emeritus Senior Minister (ESM) Goh Chok Tong for the past 10 terms, was definitely hard ground. Even when the National Solidarity Party (NSP) did well in the 2011 general election (GE2011), inspired by their then-rising young star Nicole Seah, their results in Marine Parade Town itself were really bad. The NSP did not do well in this area, but did well in all other areas. Our only consolation in GE2015 was that we matched the NSP's results in Marine Parade Town but fell badly elsewhere with the huge national middle ground shift.

Marine Parade GRC shares extensive borders with Aljunied and East Coast GRCs, two areas where the WP has a strong presence. The WP's strategy has been obvious to all — grow from its base in Hougang and Aljunied into adjacent areas. The PAP had used Ang Mo Kio, Marine Parade, and Pasir-Ris Punggol GRCs to box in the WP. If the WP no longer contests in Marine Parade GRC, it will be easy for the PAP to gerrymander to strengthen East Coast GRC in future.

By early 2020, I was not quite confident that there would be a team for Marine Parade GRC. Since I could not manage to form a team as I had in 2015, I left the decision to the party. I offered to go elsewhere if the party had any slots. Actually, I preferred an SMC. I believed that I could fight an SMC better. In a GRC, there would be many factors beyond my control. And Marine Parade GRC would not become easier even though we had anticipated that ESM Goh would surely retire. I offered to go to a totally new SMC if necessary. The problem remained that if I did well enough but did not win, I would be offered the Non-constituency Member of Parliament (NCMP) position again, which I would not be keen on.

I had a meeting with Singh. I was aware that the party had been conducting house visits in Tampines GRC for some two years and was keeping its options open. Singh asked for my views on contesting there. The prime minister (PM)-designate Heng Swee Keat was a Member of Parliament (MP) there. There was a pandemic sweeping the world. The general election might be called soon. A young team to take on the PM-designate in his home turf where the WP had not previously contested was going to be a challenge. But the WP had pulled strategic surprises before. In 2006, the party fielded a team in PM Lee Hsien Loong's constituency, Ang Mo Kio GRC, after he took over as PM. And the WP team performed credibly. COVID-19, however, complicated calculations. In my view, in a pandemic general election, it was better to take a lower profile, fight fewer battles, and not be portrayed as trying to disrupt the fourth-generation succession in a crisis situation.

The WP decided to take Marine Parade GRC again for the 2020 general election (GE2020). I had earlier told Singh that if I were to contest in the GRC, I definitely did not want to be the team leader and I would not take up the NCMP post if the team qualified for it. The new leader had to be someone younger with more runway and more years ahead of him or her to continue the work there. He agreed. I knew, and had worked with, most of the new Marine Parade team members before — Ron Tan, Muhammad Fadli Bin Mohammed Fawzi, and Nathaniel Koh, who were previously part of the team planned for Tampines GRC. They are good and hard-working members, mostly working without complaints behind the scenes. I privately met with Muhammad Azhar Bin Abdul Latip to get to know him better.

I let the team decide on the leader. Ron Tan was selected. I was back to Marine Parade GRC once more.

## A COVID-19 General Election

The PAP knows very well that a crisis situation is the best time to hold

# The Second Battle for Marine Parade GRC

a general election for the results to be in their favour. However, the general election has to be held early in the crisis or when Singapore is about to enter a crisis. Once caught in the middle of a crisis that drags on, the incumbent will lose all advantages. People will grow tired. Jobs will be lost. Faults will be exposed. The incumbent will be shown as not being able to do its magic.

My guess is that the PAP had wanted the general election early. Singh filed a parliamentary question on the formation of the Electoral Boundaries Review Committee (EBRC) in July 2019. It had not yet been formed then. If the PM did not choose to disclose its formation, the WP would surely find creative ways to keep asking every other month in Parliament. The PM, and later Minister for Trade and Industry Chan Chun Sing, then disclosed in September that the EBRC was formed on August 1, 2019. The general election could have been held at the end of 2019, but I suspect that the PAP itself was not fully prepared. This is purely my speculation.

The COVID-19 crisis emerged in China in December 2019 and exploded in late January 2020. It was too close to Budget season. The general election could still be called and the Budget would have to be delayed till the new Parliament was formed. It might not look responsible to do so, though. It was likely that the PAP would have wanted to call the general election in April, after passing the Budget. Leaked photographs had circulated online with PAP election posters ready. If the COVID-19 cases had not exploded necessitating the circuit breaker (lockdown) in early April, the PAP would have won big time with a snap general election.

As it turned out, the circuit breaker lasted more than two months. Even the reopening was phased out and careful. The shine on the PAP was lost. Despite the provision of massive funding and support, jobs were still being lost. The number of COVID-19 cases in the foreign employees dormitories continued to explode. Singapore was no longer the shining global gold-standard for COVID-19 management.

Beyond party branding, I believe the most important factor for success or failure in a general election is the general sentiment among the people. The ruling party decides the timing. The PAP caught the timing really well in 2001 and in 2015, holding the general election when there were heightened fears following the September 11, 2001 attacks on the World Trade Centre Twin Towers in the United States, and when Singaporeans were reminded of the achievements of the founding leaders of the PAP after the death of Lee Kuan Yew in 2015, respectively. They had misread the huge economic rebound in 2010 to be positive for the general election. It turned out to be the opposite. In Singapore, the fear factor plays perhaps a stronger effect than in other countries. We have grown up with a risk-averse culture. Fear of crisis and chaos is far more powerful than feel-good. Again, these are my personal opinions formed by my observations.

The problem with a pandemic election is the lack of campaigning opportunities. No one has experience in conducting such a campaign. The ruling party, with its control of government and media, obviously has the advantage of using political office-bearers to be featured in the media during the circuit breaker.

Even though the EBRC report was published in March 2020, the circuit breaker came soon after in April. When the country was partially reopened and only for selected forms of activities and small group gatherings, the general election was called. Effectively, ground campaigning was limited. With limited ground campaigning, the teams that did better in social media and mainstream media campaigning would perform better.

## Making the Most of Limited Ground Campaigning

As soon as a limited form of campaigning was permitted, our team went out daily. Ron Tan was the team leader who directed operations. I would advise based on my previous experience and also familiarity with the

GRC. As with our GE2015 strategy, we split the team and volunteers to cover more areas. With restrictions due to COVID-19 still in place, it was also better to split the group to conduct our engagements in smaller numbers.

I covered Marine Parade and Joo Chiat with Azhar, who was new to campaigning in a general election. The rest had experience either as a candidate, election agent (EA), or volunteer in past general elections. Tan lived in the Braddell area, so he volunteered to take that area. Nathaniel Koh took Kembangan-Chai Chee while Fadli covered Geylang Serai. We planned for certain days when we would be together as a team, especially when the media were invited to come along. We let the party allocate the EAs. We had an entirely new EA team from our previous general election. They were passionate people who worked well together despite most of them not having previous EA experience.

We had a surprisingly large number of people signing up to be volunteers. Our team had young doctors, young lawyers, business owners, highly-educated professionals, as well as high-flying corporate executives. I had never seen such an overwhelming quantity and quality of volunteers. It was unfortunate that we had too short a time to deploy them effectively on the ground given the circuit breaker. We had slightly over two weeks of campaigning. Furthermore, campaigning was subjected to many restrictions.

In this election, our team had four candidates below 40 years old. I was the most senior at 55. We discussed how to pitch ourselves to residents and decided to play up the ground experience the team had at Aljunied GRC in Town Council and grassroots management. Tan was the last legislative assistant to Low Thia Khiang before his retirement from Parliament. He had helped in constituency work for several years. Koh served as secretarial assistant to Singh for several years. Fadli had been town councillor at Aljunied-Hougang Town Council for six years. Azhar had been helping Muhamad Faisal Manap at the Kaki Bukit ward of Aljunied GRC. I had parliamentary and start-up business experience.

We wanted to sell the message that we would be able to hit the ground running.

We also preferred not to make any firm plans for estate upgrading. To make such plans, one will first need to be elected and assess the financial situation of the Town Council, negotiate for the use of community improvement projects funds, as well as work with the Ministry of National Development on the upgrading plans and budget. Our plans would also have to be generated from residents. Hence, we would do monthly townhall meetings with interested residents in different parts of the GRC to evolve our plans.

The next best thing was to commit only to what we would definitely be able to deliver. Hence, we highlighted the earlier food distribution initiatives conducted by the WP in Marine Parade GRC since 2015, especially the daily cooked food distribution since the start of the COVID-19 circuit breaker. It would demonstrate that the WP was a serious party that did not make an appearance only during the general election. I also genuinely believed in building community involvement and the neighbourliness spirit, which I had also focused on during the GE2011 campaign for Joo Chiat SMC.

These strategies were translated into our political broadcast on television. The first three speakers Tan, Koh, and Azhar spoke in Mandarin, English, and Malay, respectively, using the same content. Our speeches focused on our desire to build the GRC together with the residents. Fadli, with his significant Town Council experience, was tasked to go deeper into this topic. I anchored the presentation, first drawing on the WP's persistence to stay in this area since first contesting in Joo Chiat SMC in 2006 and 2011 and then in Marine Parade GRC in 2015. As we did in GE2015, this time I also presented the best characteristics of each of the team members. We also adhered to the party's call to not give the PAP a blank cheque. Here is an extract of this portion of the speech.

# The Second Battle for Marine Parade GRC

The Workers' Party Marine Parade Team — Constituency Political Broadcast July 5, 2020

(other parts omitted)

The PAP does not have a monopoly of wisdom. Our team members are passionate, hardworking and resilient.

Ron has many years of experience serving in the grassroots in Aljunied. He served under Mr Low Thia Khiang for the past 3 years.

Nathaniel, an IT professional, has been with the Party for 11 years and is actively assisting Mr Pritam Singh.

Azhar had to take a year's break from university to earn money for his school fees. He graduated from NUS[1], had a stable career. Then he lost a leg and his job after a nasty road accident. These did not kill his desire to want to be a voice for ordinary Singaporeans.

Fadli is driven by his passion to help the less fortunate. He switched to being a lawyer because he wants to be better equipped to champion for ordinary Singaporeans. He has been a Town Councillor in Aljunied-Hougang for 6 years.

Singapore needs MPs who can connect with the people, who [care] deeply for them. We have the right team to be your voice in parliament and to manage this town.

The PAP wants 100% dominance of parliament. They tell you that you can have 12 NCMPs because they want to win it all. They want all 93 seats.

---

1  National University of Singapore

As a former NCMP, I tell you that this will not be the effective check against the PAP. They only fear when their vote share is low. Do not give the PAP a blank cheque.

Make your vote count. Vote The Workers' Party.

## Analysis of the GE2020 Results

I was slightly disappointed with our results in Marine Parade GRC. I was under no illusion regarding our chances. It was hard ground even with ESM Goh retiring. Marine Parade Town was still warm to ESM Goh and the PAP after his 10 terms there. I had felt that we might end up with 45 percent and have an outside chance to be offered the NCMP seats. I had earlier told the team that it would be among them to choose the NCMP representatives as I would decline. To win would be extremely hard. Our team did not have any natural media star. Having been through two general elections and two by-elections, I have developed a reasonable sensing of who might end up as the stars.

When the team was formed, I had told them to expect that we would be low-key compared to East Coast or Sengkang. It was not necessarily a bad thing. I remember Low once shared with me years ago about his experience at Hougang. In 1991, there were hot seats elsewhere. The media attention was not on Hougang. He felt the low media profile was good as it was not used against him. If the PAP had sensed that he would win, he would have the media coming down so hard that it would have distracted the public from his campaign.

However, I was less optimistic for my third campaign. In 1991, there was no pandemic. It was a regular campaign. Low used his command of Teochew very effectively at rallies. He was also very natural at engaging with people on the ground. The then PAP incumbent Tang Guan Seng only had one term as an MP in the SMC, which had housed many resettled farmers. Marine Parade GRC in 2020 was different. Our campaign period was short. Our opponents were quite established and

## The Second Battle for Marine Parade GRC

with relatively high profiles. ESM Goh, though retired, was still campaigning with the team. With a short campaign time, social and mainstream media would be needed for us to make a breakthrough.

The party supported with social media outreach and also helped to arrange for a few doorstop interviews with the media. Singh and Sylvia Lim came for one of these events. All the candidates were involved in our internally produced Hammer Show. Each show featured a broad topic. We were either speaker, panellist, or both on shows that we each took part in. These Hammer Shows were to substitute for the lack of night rallies. The candidates from various constituencies were split up and featured in different shows. Each of us participated in about three shows.

I took part in the "Economy" show as panellist and speaker, in the "Workers" show as speaker, and in the "Seniors" show as panellist. I believe all the WP candidates did reasonably well in these shows. However, the videos were long and did not go as viral as we had hoped for. I met many people during campaigning unaware of our Hammer Shows. The media did not report much of what we had discussed in each of the shows.

Online Hammer Shows were different from physical rallies. In the past, we had 20,000 to 40,000 people in attendance at rallies. The atmosphere was charged. The media picked up more stories from these. Rallies also allowed some to shine. I recall that in GE2015, He Ting Ru and Cheryl Loh were well-received in the rallies and their social media "likes" shot up. In GE2020, I had the most social media attention among my team, and even so, I considered my social media outreach as moderate. My views and shares came from my writings and not from my speeches. Some of my writings were reported by the mainstream media. My teammates, however, did not receive much attention from the media.

I knew from the start that Nicole Seah would be able to draw in social media attention for the East Coast GRC campaign. Key leaders like

Singh and Sylvia Lim would of course be well-covered. I was confident that among the candidates, Jamus Lim and perhaps He Ting Ru might do well on social media from what I knew of them. Prior to the general election, I had spoken to Jamus Lim on a few occasions. He was natural, quick, and witty with his replies. He had been interviewed in the past by Channel News Asia on television and on radio, discussing economic matters. He had conducted these well. In the general election, he exceeded everybody's expectations with his stellar debate on television.

Our media coverage was also helped by Minister for Foreign Affairs Vivian Balakrishnan calling the WP the "PAP-lite" and suggesting that the PAP could have written our manifesto. I was shocked to hear that. I immediately knew that it would help the WP. The people do want PAP-lite. They want someone to be able to run the constituency and eventually the country. Being risk-averse, many also want a party that can carry on the essential parts of the PAP's policies. There were aspects of the PAP that people did not like, so being lite was actually good. I suppose in the debate, Balakrishnan might have wanted to use the WP to contrast against the Singapore Democratic Party (SDP). That statement benefitted more than harmed us. The PM tried to neutralise this later by saying that the people should not go for a PAP-lite because they could have the real thing. From my reading of sentiments on social media, I doubt that sank into the people's mind, especially the middle-ground voters. Not many shared posts about what the PM had said compared to the viral posts on Lim's performance at the debate.

I felt our team had decent candidates — young, hardworking, and all with good educational qualifications. I expect most may feature again in future general elections. However, without high-profile WP candidates in Marine Parade GRC and with limited time to do ground visits, the best card that we could play was to try to assure residents that we had the experience to run the town well and that we would invest in building the community together. Actually, community spirit is difficult to cultivate across a GRC because every neighbourhood is different. It is easier to do this for SMCs.

# The Second Battle for Marine Parade GRC

We eventually swung less than seven percent back to the WP from the tough GE2015 campaign, 2.76 percent less than the 45 percent result which I had hoped for. The result was decent enough to build upon for future campaigns. The team is young. They have more elections ahead of them, whether back in Marine Parade GRC or elsewhere. Fadli drew in some social media attention thanks to his witty pantuns, which are short Malay poems that connected well with the Malays. His Juris Doctor law degree, Master's degree, and good work profiles also contributed to the positive responses. Tan's Facebook profile was already established from his previous general election in Nee Soon GRC. After GE2020, he became the legislative assistant to He Ting Ru in Sengkang GRC. The new candidates created their public Facebook pages and other social media sites as they deemed fit. Past candidates can build upon these social media channels as building blocks for their next campaign. The party had also arranged for various media channels to feature Koh and Azhar.

My main consolation from our Marine Parade GRC contest was that we managed to swing the votes back in the Joo Chiat and Marine Parade wards. The results in the Joo Chiat ward in GE2015 had been hugely disappointing, especially for me. However, voters in this ward swung back to us the most this time in GE2020. The Marine Parade ward is also no longer the impossible hard ground. Although still solidly backing the PAP, our share of votes there was a lot better than in GE2015 and GE2011. The gap between Marine Parade Town and the rest of the GRC had narrowed. Since GE2015, we had spent the most time in Marine Parade Town with the quarterly food distributions. Nearing GE2020, we did daily cooked food distributions. These efforts did reap some appreciation from local residents.

At the start of GE2020, I was fairly certain that the opposition would do better than in GE2015. I had explained to various people, including political desk journalists whom I had met after GE2015, that Singapore's voting pattern will follow a pendulum swing. We had one extreme in 2011 and another in 2015. In 2011, there were many issues the people were angry with the PAP over, but the opposition slate then was too weak to make bigger inroads. In 2015, the PAP did well for a number of reasons, and other factors including the passing away of Lee Kuan Yew, political instability in neighbouring countries, and the fear that the PAP might lose a significant number of seats. With the successive losses by the PAP in elections and by-elections in 2011, 2012, and 2013, people were calling it the "new normal" and feared big losses for the ruling party in a time of greater uncertainty.

The flight to safety swung the pendulum back. The PAP was highly unlikely to repeat its success of 2015. With the delay in holding the general election and perceived missteps in the government's handling of COVID-19, I expected the opposition to receive better support this time. Had the general election been called in early April and there was no large COVID-19 spread in Singapore, it might have been quite different. The Progress Singapore Party (PSP) and SDP also attracted some well-qualified candidates. The PM's brother was now on the side of the opposition, although he did not contest, while the PM's sister still remained critical of the PM. The LKY effect could not be used.

Overall, support for the alternative camp was strong. Early in the campaign, I read that some political analysts predicted that the PAP would win 70–75 percent. I knew that it was impossible. Perhaps the PAP knew it themselves. They did not even attempt to send a stronger team to Aljunied GRC to try to win it back. At the start of the campaign, I told a former political desk journalist that I had expected the outcome to be around 65 percent. I was happy that the press was reporting the predictions for a strong win for the PAP. Low, Chen Show Mao, and Png Eng Huat were retiring from parliamentary contests. This was back to the GE2011 situation when it was possible that there could be an opposition wipe-out when the incumbent opposition MPs left their strongholds. It would be better for the opposition whenever people could vote without fear of a freak result against the PAP.

# The Second Battle for Marine Parade GRC

After nomination was done, I thought that Sengkang GRC was the most vulnerable for the PAP. It was dangerous to have three changes of candidates in a GRC of four, and in a new GRC to top it all. For incumbents, and even if political office-bearers were put in, every replacement of a former MP carries some risks. In the past, the PAP could use this playbook. Times have changed. The PAP was being challenged all over the island. Many areas had higher-quality opposition candidates than before. East Coast GRC would have been more vulnerable if not for putting Deputy Prime Minister (DPM) Heng Swee Keat in. Even so, it was DPM Heng's first time in the constituency. Hence, the result was not good for the PAP. Voters have not warmed up to the person and might feel less obliged to vote for the PAP. Political office-bearers mean nothing to today's voters unless it is a super heavyweight or popular minister. There are few real heavyweights these days who can draw votes in any new constituency simply by their presence.

One of the significant outcomes of the general election is that the stronger alternative parties have pulled apart from the pack. It had to happen. In business, I have seen that too often, especially in start-up situations. Eventually, those that pitched better to the customers and have better products will grow while the competition fizzles out.

In politics, the products offered by political parties are their candidates, packaged along with the values that the parties communicate. Good candidates will only join when the party is moving along in a sensible direction. Talent is attracted to political parties by what they stand for. Low understood all these well. As a strict disciplinarian, he weeded out negative influences and gradually shaped the party in the direction he wanted. It was a tough journey from 2001 when he took control. It did not make him popular in some quarters of the party. I would not have joined if the party had been antagonistic towards the government all the time. I would not have joined if I did not think I would find fellow candidates who were able to share my vision for Singapore. The good candidates in recent general elections were not by accident. Every successful general election and decent performance in Parliament brings in fresh new talent for the next general election. New talent joining a party helps to redefine the party, whether for better or for worse.

It is easy to start a political party, just like it is easy to start new companies in Singapore. Making it relevant to the electorate is a different matter. The PSP, led by long-time and popular former PAP MP, Tan Cheng Bock, appealed quite successfully to moderate candidates, some with good academic and professional qualifications. I read about some ongoing disunity when the PSP grew rapidly. My own two-time election agent, Shaun Lee, had also joined the PSP. I had told friends earlier on that the party was bound to face some problems because it grew so fast. The WP's growth had been more gradual. We had the luxury of more time. Tan did not have that luxury. The PSP, as a new party, had to make its impact quickly or risk becoming irrelevant in future general elections.

Lee later left the PSP. Some others did, too, including a few potential candidates. I thought the PSP handled these departures fairly well. It had grown rapidly by absorbing many people from different parties and diverse backgrounds. There would be some clash of political philosophy and also jostling for positions, as with any organisation in a fast expansion mode. It was best to let members go when they no longer could see eye to eye with the party. I wish the PSP well in the 14th Parliament and as they attempt to retain the people who have joined.

Compared to previous general elections, and despite bearing a lot of attacks from the PAP, I felt that the SDP held on quite well and improved on their showings. The SDP's efforts at rebranding, coupled with more new young voters who were more accepting of them, likely contributed to the improvements.

I shared earlier about my pendulum swinging analogy. The voting shares did swing wildly from 2011 to 2015, and back again in 2020. It is too early for the alternative camp to feel elated. The pendulum might yet swing back again. The PAP is a seasoned fighting machine. It can bounce back. How the PAP will perform next depends very much on the fourth-generation leadership handover. The handover has so far not proceeded as well as the PAP might have hoped for. Unlike in 2011, the PAP had not signalled that it would make big changes in the aftermath of the general election. Instead, it had said that the results reflected the aspirations of Singaporeans for more diverse voices.[2] The electorate has also rejected the bullying tactics of the PAP. The PAP needs to calibrate its use of unfair tactics or risk further alienation by an increasingly more educated and informed citizenry. Another important factor in the opposition's performance in the next general election will also depend on Sengkang GRC, where the WP team had won. If it is perceived to be well-run and the new WP MPs do well in Parliament, it will further break the PAP's narrative that only they have the A team. Alternative parties that can continue to attract and hold on to good candidates will continue to have relevance in the Singapore political landscape.

---

2  "GE2020: GE results reflect broad support for PAP, desire for diverse voices", The Straits Times, July 11, 2020, https://www.straitstimes.com/singapore/ge-results-reflect-broad-support-for-pap-desire-for-diverse-voices

# Chapter 8
# A Peek into the Workers' Party

## Leadership and Structure

The highest decision-making body of the Workers' Party (WP) is the Central Executive Committee (CEC). The Constitution provides for 14 CEC members. If there is a tie in voting for the final position, there can be more members. The CEC can also co-opt new members as it deems fit, up to a total of four more. In 2011, after the general election, Chen Show Mao, Pritam Singh, and I were co-opted as Low Thia Khiang felt that those who had made it to Parliament should be on the CEC. Prominent members who had been co-opted prior to them becoming parliamentarians include Dennis Tan, Daniel Goh, and Leon Perera. By co-opting into the CEC, the leadership team becomes strengthened. The co-opted member also has the opportunity to show leadership ability and thereby stands a better chance to be elected in future CEC elections.

A CEC term is for two years. Only organising members (also termed as cadre members) can vote for the CEC. This method is similar to that of the People's Action Party (PAP). The PAP had themselves adopted this system in the early 1960s to block the socialist faction from filling the party with members sympathetic to them, and then voting their faction in. The PAP had learnt this from the Catholic system whereby only a select group of cardinals can choose the pope and the pope also chooses the cardinals.[1]

How does one become a cadre member? The CEC must vote to accept new cadre members. Prior to my joining, past general election candidates would automatically be cadre members. That was not the case with candidates from the 2011 general election (GE2011) onwards. Members

---

1  Koh Buck Song, "The PAP cadre system", The Straits Times, April 4, 1998.

must have served for quite a long time and shown themselves to be loyal to the party's cause. During my time in the CEC, two members of the CEC were required to endorse the application for a member to be nominated as a cadre. Such nominations usually take place several months before the biannual Organising Members' Conference (OMC).

At the CEC meeting, the supporting CEC members must present the case for why the nominated member should become a cadre by listing the member's past contributions. When all nominations have been presented, there is a voting by all CEC members in attendance. Members with 50 percent or more votes in the voting exercise will become a cadre. Once a cadre, the member will stay a cadre unless the CEC votes to demote or expel the member. During each nomination cycle, I had proposed or seconded the nomination of several members with whom I had worked actively. To stand a better chance of success, I would sometimes lobby other CEC members to help support those I was nominating.

The only tangible benefit of being a cadre is the ability to vote for the CEC. This voting happens during the OMC. The first position to be voted upon will be for the chairperson, then the secretary-general (SG), and lastly for the remaining 12 CEC members. A cadre interested to be in the CEC must first be nominated by another cadre and also have another as seconder, both of whom must be in the meeting. The person being nominated can turn down the nomination. I turned down my nomination in 2016.

After all positions have been voted in, the SG will decide the positions within the CEC. The SG will contact the elected CEC members individually to work out the positions. Before the first meeting of the new CEC, Low would call to see if I was comfortable with the position he had in mind. And when there was the reshuffle which he did in 2014, he discussed various roles with me before we finally settled on me being the webmaster. I had suggested to him that those holding a finance-related position should be rotated out after a few years, consistent with the practices of various organisations I had been a committee member in.

Not all CEC members will hold positions. These positions are to allocate specific areas of work. Important positions include the treasurer and organising secretary. I was deputy treasurer when I was co-opted in and was moved to be the treasurer when Yaw Shin Leong left the party. Frieda Chan filled my deputy treasurer position. I remained treasurer for about three years, during which the WP started our Building Fund campaign. Reshuffling of appointments takes place once in a while as deemed necessary by the top leaders, usually at the start of a new CEC term. Chen Show Mao took over the treasurer position from me and I became the webmaster around the end of 2014.

Increasingly, the chair of the media team is also becoming an important position. In the past, the media chair was to mainly create press releases and guide candidates during general elections. With social media becoming increasingly important, the WP has become very active online. Daniel Goh was in charge of media while concurrently one of the organising secretaries from 2016 before stepping down from these positions in early 2020.

The organising secretary role is important because a political party must have regular ground activities. The role is even more important closer to a general election. The organising secretary is supported by a deputy organising secretary. Sometimes, there can even be two organising secretaries and a deputy organising secretary. This is especially so if it is an "election year" CEC — if it was expected that within the duration of the two-year CEC term, a general election might be called. Ground activities are stepped up especially in the one to two years before an expected general election. In the CEC of 2018–2020, Dennis Tan and Daniel Goh were organising secretaries, and Terence Tan was the deputy organising secretary.[2]

Cadre membership is for life, but some become inactive over time or cease to be member of the party, in which case the cadreship is automatically cancelled. About 100 or more usually attend each OMC. Attendance had been increasing over the several OMCs that I have attended — in 2012, 2014, 2016, and 2018. The 2020 OMC had been postponed due to the 2020 general election (GE2020), and is now scheduled to be held in December 2020. Between meetings, there would be an addition of some 20–30 cadres. However, there is natural attrition as some cadre members might have passed away, left the party, or moved to live abroad.

For CEC voting, there may be around 20 or more competing for the 12 CEC member positions. Each cadre member can vote for up to 12 from those nominated. To be elected, a candidate requires roughly about 40 percent of the vote. Votes exceeding 50 percent would be a good result. The best scorers would be above 60 percent.

It does not take much to guess that if one is eager to be in the CEC, the cadre can lobby other cadres. I had been approached before each meeting by those keen to be voted in. I was not interested to canvass for votes for myself nor ask others to nominate me. Neither did many of those who were in Parliament. It is almost a given that a sitting WP parliamentarian would be voted in because in the CEC voting from 2012–2018, there were only eight to nine parliamentarians to fill 14 CEC positions. Those still serving as a parliamentarian have always been voted into the CEC. Indeed, as a parliamentarian, you were expected not to decline nomination to the CEC. There is a lot of work to do, especially for those holding positions in the CEC.

On the PAP side, there are many political office-bearers (37 appointed

---

2 "Workers' Party appoints new office bearers after Central Executive Committee meeting", CNA, September 26, 2019, https://www.channelnewsasia.com/news/singapore/workers-party-cec-meeting-new-office-bearers-10132544

after GE2020). Many do not make it into their CEC, which is structured almost like that of the WP. Even ministers sometimes did not get voted into the CEC, though they can be co-opted later.[3]

Unlike most other political parties, the WP does not actively seek out new members. In fact, it has become increasingly harder to become a member. In the past, all potential members had to be personally interviewed by Low. The person must have a track record of serving in some of the volunteering activities. I was an exception, mainly because I appeared just before a general election and was deemed to be suitable as a candidate. The WP is actually powered by volunteers more than by members. We have thousands of volunteers who work very hard in many of our activities, but most are not members. Volunteers are more than welcome to serve.

Volunteers who have served for some time can be nominated to become a member of the WP. They have to be supported by a WP parliamentarian. This system was instituted by Low after GE2011 when he decided that he should not be the only person deciding on membership. He also wanted to make sure that the volunteer had been active on the ground. There must also be a seconder in the CEC to support the nomination. From time to time, the CEC would consider applications for membership. All applications are put to the vote.

I understand Low's reasons for instituting a strict process for accepting new members. People may join the WP for different reasons. And once a member, the person remains a member unless there are some disciplinary issues that necessitates expulsion, or the member resigns or passes away. Members do resign if they are unhappy over some matters or if they are joining another political party, as they cannot be a member of two political parties at the same time. All expulsions must be voted upon at a CEC meeting and must have majority support. Hence, Low

---

3   Chan Chung Sing, "PAP's 35th Central Executive Committee", People's Action Party, November 28, 2018, https://www.pap.org.sg/news/paps-35th-cec/

did not want people with wrong motivations or beliefs misaligned with the WP's to join. It would be drastic to expel anyone. During my time in the CEC, we had to go through some unpleasant expulsions. Sometimes, the CEC decided to simply issue written warnings regarding disciplinary matters.

If a WP member creates trouble on social media or is in trouble with the law, sometimes the press might report that the person is a WP member. Since a volunteer can do almost anything to support the WP that a member can do, there is no need to have a large membership. Also, volunteers tend to fizzle out after helping for a while. The waiting period of a couple of years is to ensure that the volunteer is willing to be active in the party for a long time, during both good and bad times.

Candidates must, however, be members. I had to be accelerated as a member when I was shortlisted for consideration as a candidate in 2011. In 2015, Dylan Ng had already been an active volunteer with Low in the Bedok Reservoir-Punggol ward for about two years. When we decided to field him, I nominated him as member and Low was the seconder. Ng became a member together with a few other volunteers who also became candidates in the 2015 general election (GE2015). Membership or being a cadre are not the determining factors to be a candidate. Volunteers who are outstanding and who fit the WP's expectations for Parliament and grassroots work will be accelerated to become members in time for general elections.

## Powered by Volunteers and Members

The WP is powered by a large number of passionate volunteers. Many do eventually become members, cadre members, and even candidates. We need volunteers for our many grassroots events. Each WP constituency has a grassroots committee that organises events with the help of volunteers. Volunteers also assist at Meet-the-People sessions that are organised by the secretarial or legislative assistant of the Member of Parliament (MP).

During a general election, the support of volunteers is even more critical. There is a massive number of houses to visit. There are the logistics for rallies (except for the 2020 pandemic general election which did not have rallies) and the sale of merchandise.

However, there are two events that non-member volunteers cannot attend: the *Hammer* outreach and the annual Members' Seminar. Only members are allowed.

*Hammer* outreach is conducted weekly on Sundays in the markets and crowded public areas whenever we have publications to distribute. The WP generally produces two to three publications a year, with each issue being sold over a period of around 10 weeks. Members wear the party polo T-shirt bearing our logo. As the WP's image will be on public display, it is easier to manage with only members being allowed to participate. The *Hammer* newsletter is also useful to feature members whom the party wishes to have a higher public profile. Closer to a general election, potential new candidates are urged to write articles for the *Hammer* such as those by Jamus Lim and Nicole Seah before GE2020. I was a regular writer for the newsletter from 2011–2019.

The annual Members' Seminar is a half-day event that is usually held at the beginning of each year. It serves to update members of key developments of the party. Prior to a general election, it sometimes also serves to feature potential new candidates so that members can know them better. I understand that Chen Show Mao and Pritam Singh spoke at the Members' Seminar in 2011 before I joined the party. In 2020, Nathaniel Koh and Muhammad Fadli Bin Mohammed Fawzi spoke at the Members' Seminar. They eventually joined the Marine Parade GRC team.

Some long-time members played an important role in sustaining the party through its difficult times. I share the following blog post which I had written after a member whom I was familiar with had passed away. Ng Ah Chwee had lived through the times when it was difficult, even dangerous, to be an active WP member. It took commitment and dedication. The WP of today is so different from that in the days of Ng. People like him had held the party together so that we could build upon the base for today's breakthroughs. What impressed me about Ng was that although he had done so much during his younger days as an active member, he recognised that times had changed. To him, the change was good even though it meant that older members like him had less of a role to play in the party.

Farewell to a veteran warrior

(September 5, 2013)

Yesterday, I attended the wake of long-time WP member, Mr Ng Ah Chwee. He had passed away on Tuesday at the age of 66 from heart failure due to complications from various ailments.

I first met Ah Chwee a few weeks after I had started ground campaign in Joo Chiat for GE2011. I was then a newbie in the Party. Everyone in the Party was busy with their own campaigning. Ah Chwee had volunteered to help in my campaign. He had been the elections manager for Dr Tan Bin Seng in 2006, who had also contested in Joo Chiat SMC.

Ah Chwee was already in poor health when I met him, having been diagnosed with diabetes and kidney problems not long before then. Yet he insisted on helping whenever he could, when he was less unwell. Along the way, I found out that Ah Chwee had been a long-time member of the Barisan Sosialis, which he joined after leaving secondary school in the 1960s. He would have worked alongside Lim Chin Siong and company. I later heard he helped as a volunteer for Mr. JBJ[4] in the 1980s. When

---

4   J. B. Jeyaretnam

the Barisan Sosialis merged with The Workers' Party, Ah Chwee became a WP member. He became the Organising Secretary of WP from 1992 to 2006, during what would have been difficult years for the Party. The Organising Secretary plays a key role in a political party, often directing campaigning activities and logistics before and during elections. He stepped down from the Party's Central Executive Committee in 2006 in an exercise that saw many young members take over the Party's leadership.

What struck me about Ah Chwee was his keen desire to help despite his failing health. He had decades of political experience yet he did not impose any of his views on me. He would share with me what he had done during the 2006 GE campaign when he was Elections Manager for Joo Chiat SMC. I would listen and decide what I could use, but I would run the campaign the way I was comfortable with. Ah Chwee was happy just to come along, introduce me to residents and then step aside for me to interact with them.

Once, on a gruelling campaign visit at Villa Marina in Siglap, we had to cover 28 blocks of walk-up apartments on a hot Saturday afternoon. Ah Chwee insisted on coming along. After completing a few blocks, he struggled to keep pace. He slipped and fell and we arranged for him to take a cab home. A few days later, he would come back again to join on the campaign trail.

Post GE, I met Ah Chwee often at the Party's events, at by-election rallies and at the weekly Hammer Sales. Sometimes he would show up at various Meet-the-People sessions. He came whenever his health permitted him to. He came not to interfere in [any way]. He would offer help and assisted when help was needed. When help was not needed, he would cheer the rest on.

I recall at a Members' event, some veteran Party members said that they felt left out by the changes that have been taking place. Ah Chwee stepped forward and told them that they should just come for events and make themselves useful; and if they were not needed, they can be happy that the Party is progressing. Ah Chwee certainly lived by example, doing as he had said. He made himself useful during my GE campaign despite his poor health and did not try to impose his views on anyone. He was happy to let me do what I thought was best.

Whenever I look at veteran opposition warriors like Ah Chwee, I try to imagine what politics was like in their times; the turbulent 1960s, the barren 1970s, the moments of breakthrough and struggles in the 1980s, the ups and downs of the 1990s and the renewal from the 2000s. Ah Chwee lived through all that. He once used a Chinese proverb, "长江后浪推前浪" to tell me why it was necessary that new people like us came forward. The phrase translated means that from the back, the new waves of the mighty Yangtze river pushes the earlier waves forward. It means that the new will come forward to take over from the old. That's the only way progress can be made. One day in the future, like Ah Chwee, I hope I will be able to use this phrase on a new batch of younger people who can continue on the progress that have been made.

Farewell my friend and comrade. Rest in peace.

## Retail Politics

Joo Chiat SMC comprises many private housing estates. The needs in private estates are different from those of Housing and Development Board (HDB) estates. Even among HDB estates, needs differ greatly by housing type.

From 2011–2015, we found no need to organise food distribution in Joo Chiat SMC. However, when I took part in the contest for Marine Parade GRC in 2015, it opened up a different world. A few weeks before polling day of GE2015, I had befriended a long-time Marine Parade resident, Judy Zhou, who had been very active for the previous 15 years donating cooked food and dry rations to residents. She invited us to be part of the already-scheduled food distribution in August 2015. We did so in our WP uniform.

Post-general election, we became a regular feature in Zhou's quarterly food distribution. Initially, she raised the money for all the items and purchased them herself. She would get some friends to contribute and she would chip in with her own money. She is a generous person who allocated a good sum of money to these charitable acts. The WP supplemented with manpower.

After GE2011, Low felt that with a much bigger area to look after, there would be many areas with needs served by charities. The WP Community Fund (WPCF) was registered as a charity organisation in January 2014.

The WPCF gradually built up its sources of donations. Soon, we had periodic supplies of dry rations, and even fruits and vegetables, to distribute to needy residents. Some of the WP MPs used these supplies, besides other earlier established sources of charity, for their distribution programmes. I too added items through WPCF to Zhou's quarterly distribution. The WP East Coast and Fengshan teams were also very regular in organising food distribution to residents, led by Leon Perera, Dennis Tan, and Gerald Giam. These three spent a lot of time on the ground, covering the areas where they had previously contested as well as in Aljunied GRC and Hougang SMC. While these supplies were useful, former candidates and volunteers often chipped in additional items for the distribution programmes with their own monies. With an expanding scope of coverage by the WP in areas which we had won or had contested in, there is a constant need to look for more sponsors in cash and in kind.

With more sources of donated items, we boldly set out to visit residents of the rental flats in Chai Chee as well, but on a smaller scale compared to Marine Terrace. During our house visits there, we obtained the names of needy residents and occasionally visited them with donated food items.

The back-breaking part of these distributions was collecting items, sorting them, and then having to deliver to the recipients. Very often, rice came in 25-kilogram sacks. We would collect about a tonne of rice each time and then repack it into five-kilogram bags. I frequently had to use my car, a multi-purpose vehicle, to transport the items. My office near Marine Parade served as the storeroom as we would have to collect when donors were ready to give and keep the items until our quarterly distribution schedule. My car's suspensions had to be changed far more frequently than usual.

Volunteers' availability was also difficult to forecast. Sometimes there were far too few and it really stretched those doing the distribution. Initially, all five GE2015 Marine Parade GRC candidates were involved. Later, some were redeployed elsewhere by the party. Only Firuz Khan and I remained till early 2020.

When COVID-19 hit Singapore and the lockdown was announced, I was presented with an interesting opportunity. Through our earlier quarterly food distribution programme, I got to know the people in Willing Hearts. I received a call from Willing Hearts in the afternoon on April 6, 2020, before the circuit breaker (lockdown during the early stages of COVID-19) was to kick in. The entire daily cooked food distribution programme in Marine Parade Town was to stop on April 7 as the distribution organisations were classified as non-essential social service providers. However, Willing Hearts was classified as an essential social service provider. I was asked if I could get the food distribution programme started with Judy Zhou the very next morning.

Zhou was keen and I knew she loved to do such charity work for her neighbourhood. I agreed without hesitation. Zhou and I immediately registered ourselves as card-carrying volunteers of Willing Hearts so that we would not infringe the circuit breaker rules.

The next morning, we took 80 packets of cooked food and waited at the void deck of Block 54 of Marine Terrace where residents usually collect their food. Many did not turn up because they had been told the day before that food distribution would stop immediately. Undaunted, Zhou and I took the remaining 40 packets of undistributed food door-to-door among the rental flats. Whenever doors were opened, we would ask if they needed the food. We shifted to Block 20 the next day because that was where Zhou stayed, and it was easier for logistics.

That began my daily involvement in food distribution during the circuit breaker. We managed the distribution quite well. As no other places in Marine Parade Town were providing free food initially, word got around that we were giving and many more came. We rapidly increased our food order from 80 initially to some 250 packets per day at one stage. Sometimes when there were uncollected packets by the end of our distribution time, I would visit the rental flats of the nearby Blocks 15 and 16 and engage with residents whose doors were opened. Many later became regulars and came down to collect on their own.

The nearby Residents' Committees (RCs) started to take cooked food from Willing Hearts again within a week after we started. We continued to give many packets, even when the circuit breaker was over and when the regular welfare providers could resume their normal distribution. Zhou was resourceful enough to find additional items to add to the cooked food. To supplement, she would often bake her own cake or bread, or cook her own food. Occasionally, I sought out sponsors to give some special items. Some residents preferred to come to us, even when the RC was distributing right at their doorsteps.

About three weeks into the distribution at Marine Terrace, I received the news that another regular food distribution had suddenly stopped.

## A Peek into the Workers' Party

A couple had been distributing food at Block 1 of Eunos Crescent for the past two years. However, the lady was hospitalised. I took up their challenge to start another distribution point as there were three rental blocks in that vicinity with needs.

It was far more challenging than our operations at Marine Terrace. Zhou was very experienced and organised in food distribution. By 2020, she had been doing this for some 20 years. The residents knew her. We could scale up the number of recipients quickly. She lived right above the distribution location, so she could be on standby each morning for the food to be delivered.

I did not live in Eunos. I did not know anyone living in the distribution point. I simply had faith that if we start and it was a good thing, the residents themselves would come forward to take over. I started with a volunteer who already had some experience with our distribution at Marine Terrace. She could only help for the weekdays till 8.30 am as she had to work from home from 9 am.

The first day, we had 80 packets delivered to us. We only managed to give out 40 packets. As usual, I went door-to-door at the rental flats to see who wanted the extra food. From there, I got to know some residents and I also learnt about the dynamics of the neighbourhood. It was very different from that in Marine Terrace. Some of the long-time residents had issues with one another. For various reasons, some had stopped collecting cooked food from the previous couple distributing the food. We managed to get most of them back onto the programme.

We gradually increased our daily cooked food supply. I also enlisted new volunteers who were available during the circuit breaker. They did not live in the area. Their help could only be short term. We needed to find a way to make this programme sustainable.

Thankfully, within two weeks, we found ringleaders in the community. I first initiated them as helpers. Once they were familiar with our processes, I persuaded them to take over. I would support by coordinating the food supply. I would also source for new donors to give items so that it would not be just the cooked food daily. Social media was a useful tool. Each time I posted about our distribution programme, I would receive responses. People were willing to buy items to give. We had eggs, bean curd, biscuits, instant noodles, soap powder, and all sort of items given to us to be donated to the needy.

Collectively, at both distribution points, the number of packets given out daily exceeded 400.

When operations at Marine Terrace and Eunos had stabilised, I ventured to start at the rental flats in Chai Chee, where I was told that the cooked food distribution that used to run in the morning had also stopped due to the circuit breaker.

I started small. Soon, I found two residents willing to help with the distribution as well and was giving up to 30 packets at one stage. However, it was getting close to the scheduled lifting of circuit breaker regulations. A charity organisation in Chai Chee resumed their food distribution about two weeks after we started ours. Since the local charity group had restarted their programme, I decided to stop our distribution there. GE2020 had already been called by then. Our distribution at Chai Chee was still in its infancy. It was impossible for me to continue with the distribution as I had the GE2020 campaign to run.

At the time of writing this book, the distribution still continues at Marine Terrace and Eunos Crescent. It has been continuous on a daily basis since April 7, 2020, through every single public holiday, every weekend, and even during the general election and polling day. I am pleased that these could continue because the residents took over. It took some faith to get started. It also took being thick-skinned to get down to speak with residents, to go door-to-door when we had uncollected food. We visited residents until every single packet was given out. From working on the ground and identifying ringleaders, we created a sustainable programme. Regularly, I still visit the distribution points to encourage the key persons there and to see if there were other things I could do to support.

Why am I sharing these?

In the aftermath of GE2020, in an online lecture, Ambassador-at-Large Chan Heng Chee said that the younger generation of voters prefer "personal narratives and 'I feel your pain' connectivity, approachability and authenticity". She called it the "new retail politics — up close and personal".[5] The WP's style of retail politics did not start in GE2020. It has been in the culture of the WP to be on the ground and personal with residents for a long time. With social media, it was amplified.

I observed how Low established himself in Hougang. He got down to the ground quickly. He visited every single funeral wake. He found people willing to start sustainable programmes. He supported them with resources, perhaps often with his own money. The WP's own version of grassroots sprung up in many blocks, even without any government funding and support. There were several informal groups of residents who would use void deck spaces as gathering points and they organised regular events for the neighbourhood. The ground interactions were not only during election periods or occasional big events. They were sometimes on a daily basis.

When I was actively helping during the Hougang by-election in 2012, I interacted with many residents. I realised why Hougang was so firmly supportive of WP. Low had cemented the ties between the WP and the residents with retail politics. It required investment of time and took hard work. Low built up friendships by spending time seeing to the needs of residents without ever asking them to vote for him in return. I had the chance to see the works of the WP MPs in different parts of

---

5  Wong Pei Ting, "PAP has to better understand millennials to win back votes, says Ambassador-at-Large Chan Heng Chee", Today, July 15, 2020, https://www.todayonline.com/singapore/pap-have-better-understand-millennials-win-back-votes-says-ambassador-large-chan-heng-chee

Aljunied GRC. Retail politics is very important in the WP ethos. It was, too, in the early days of the PAP. The late Ngiam Tong Dow remarked in an interview in 2013 that the PAP had become "too elitist", unlike "the first generation of PAP (that) was purely grassroots".[6]

I subscribe to this philosophy. I was not elected. If I had been, I would have become a full-time MP. I have said this publicly before. Since joining the WP, I was involved in retail politics in areas that had needs, as did some of the teams in other areas the WP had contested in but did not win in earlier general elections. These were done on top of my regular work and without access to government-funded resources and facilities. I shared our community projects with the rest of the GE2020 Marine Parade GRC team when they joined me. These are important things which we can try to do to get ourselves quickly connected with the ground. I am sure that if we had won, we would learn from and carry on the retail politics exemplified by Low.

## The By-elections of Hougang and Punggol East

In 2012 and 2013, I was intensely involved in the by-election campaigns for Hougang and Punggol East. It was expected that all our parliamentarians had to help as these were critical battles. For each by-election, I recall having to work very hard daily during the nine days of campaigning. I led a team of volunteers each day to cover different flats and engage with residents. I also spoke at the rallies several times. I had, by then, become better at writing speeches for such occasions.

In February 2012, it became apparent that Yaw Shin Leong would have to vacate his seat and force a by-election in Hougang SMC. His expulsion remained the most painful moment for me in my journey with the WP. Being Non-constituency Members of Parliament (NCMPs), Gerald Giam and I were considered as candidates. I recommended Png Eng

---

6   Natasha Meah, "Ngiam Tong Dow, former top civil servant turned outspoken critic, dies aged 83", today, August 20, 2020, https://www.todayonline.com/singapore/former-top-civil-servant-ngiam-tong-dow-dies-aged-83

Huat when I met with Sylvia Lim over another matter during the time for selection. I felt that Png was closer in profile to Low. Given the unfortunate circumstances necessitating the by-election, it was better to have a more mature candidate who could speak dialects well to match the profile of Hougang residents. I was also quite impressed with Png's speeches during GE2011. During the by-elections of 2012 and 2013 and GE2015, Png's speeches were also full of sting. Later, when he was elected into Parliament, he also dared to take on some sensitive issues, such as the accusation by the PAP in GE2015 of a 'missing' $22.5 million from the Punggol East SMC accounts, a matter that Png pursued relentlessly, and which today remains unanswered. Png also played a key role in the development of the new management information system that is now used by our Town Councils.

In 2013, Lee Li Lian was selected by the party as the candidate for the Punggol East SMC by-election. Despite Giam and myself being NCMPs, the leadership felt that if Lee was good enough to be selected in 2011, then she should be good enough to go back to the same constituency. I supported that decision. It was a brave decision by the party considering that the secretaries-general of the Reform Party and the Singapore Democratic Alliance both announced that they would also contest, making it a four-cornered fight. The contest proved the strength of the WP's branding and campaign machinery. Lee became a great addition to our Parliament team in 2013. Unfortunately, her time to cement relationships with the residents was too short and the WP lost in the tough election of 2015.

Below are two blog pieces I had written after each of the campaigns.

> A personal journey through Hougang
>
> (May 29, 2012)
>
> Hougang first captured my imagination in 1991 when it unexpectedly rejected the incumbent MP, Tang Guan Seng and

voted in Low Thia Khiang. I was watching the results on television and had not anticipated anything to come out of the Hougang contest as there were other more publicised fights. I was then fresh out of university and beginning my long journey of political awakening.

Hougang returned Low Thia Khiang as MP again in 1997 and 2001, despite the now infamous strategy of linking votes to PAP with estate upgrading. The upgrading carrot grew bigger in 2006. Even as a politically neutral Singaporean then, I could not stand such unfair behaviour and wrote a critical piece to The Straits Times Forum. I was relieved when both Hougang and Potong Pasir rejected the upgrading carrot. I detest unfair fights.

Such bravery was abstract to me then, as I did not live in either constituencies. I cheered them [on] from a distance. I shared emotional links with these two constituencies, pride that there were defiant groups that dared stand up to the mighty ruling party and pride that Singapore had people-centred opposition MPs that held the hearts of the residents despite intense and unfair competition. It was hard then to feel as Hougangers do, because I did not live there nor participated in the hustling.

Going through GE2011 as a newcomer, I was caught up with my own campaign in Joo Chiat SMC. It wasn't until By-Election 2012 that I felt the Hougang spirit strongly. The crowd [was] fantastic at the rallies, vociferously cheering [for] us in our speeches as they did in GE2011. The people were very friendly during our house visits. However, it was the heavy downpour during the rally night of 22 May that made me realised the sterner stuff they were made of. Those who had no umbrella stayed on, even the old and the frail would not move. People were sharing umbrellas, plastic sheets, newspapers and cardboards with one another, even with strangers to use these to shield off the relentless rain.

The celebrations in Hougang were spontaneous when the result was announced at around 10:30 pm. Hundreds or even a thousand had gathered around each of the popular coffeeshops in Hougang. The people celebrated the announcement as if we had just won the World Cup.

The Thank You Parade was yet a different and immersive experience. We started off in the cluster of flats around block 701. A good crowd had already gathered and chatted with us before we set off. At each block, people would come out to the windows and corridors and waved to us. Some waved blue flags, blue umbrellas, inflatable hammers and even real hammers.

*A fervent supporter*[1]

---

1 Photo from: https://www.facebook.com/#!/limzhilikyle

**Journey in Blue**

*Mourner shaking hands with us while the others cheered for us*

Some shouted "Workers' Party" or "Huat ah!"[7] from the windows. A primary 5 boy from Punggol Primary who had earlier had his photo taken with each of the MP / NCMPs followed our pick-up to all the different blocks to cheer us at every turn. He must have trailed us for at least 30 minutes.

At every traffic junction, there were loud horning, waving from wound down car windows and the occasional cheer. At one traffic junction, a man pulled beside us and chatted with Low Thia Khiang like old friends. A [procession] of cars sometimes followed us, happily honking away.

The mourners at a wake along Avenue 7 were amazing. They heard us from afar, rushed out and started cheering for us. As our pick-up drove past, one came forward and shook hands with us. I could not imagine that even in their mourning, they would pause to cheer for us.

At several clusters, people had heard we were coming and had

---

7 A Hokkien phrase used to welcome prosperity.

A Peek into the Workers' Party

gathered. The first major crowd was at Block 309/310 where several hundred people came forward, shook hands, cheered and several asked for autographs on umbrellas and flags.

*Crowd at Block 309 and 310*

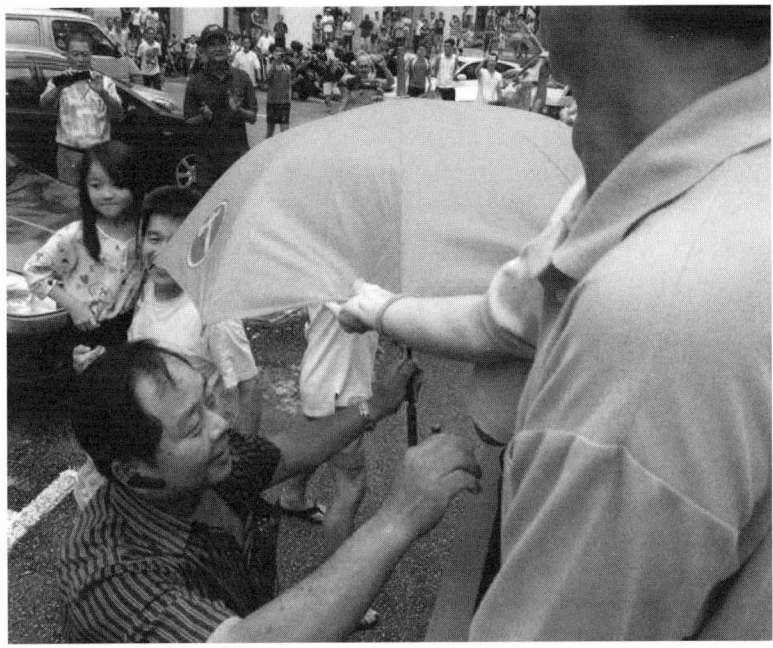

*Autographing umbrellas and flags*

The most unforgettable moment was along Avenue 5, outside block 322. A crowd of several hundreds, maybe a thousand had gathered, waiting patiently for us. As we approached, they poured onto the road, oblivious of traffic around them. We stopped and celebrated with them. The people were so reluctant to leave. Volunteers had to steer them out of the traffic's harm while we inched our way out of the area.

We continued through to every turn and corner in Hougang SMC, into dead end lanes and tiny carparks, and into every public and private housing area. At every turn, residents would come out to greet us. Low Thia Khiang would occasionally call out a resident by name. By 3:30 pm, we were done for the day.

The Thank You parade left me with lasting memories. The type of warm and spontaneous support was simply unimaginable. The cheering, clapping, singing and even dancing came from their hearts. The parade completed my journey through Hougang. What started for me in 1991 as a distant spectator of the fight for democracy has now become a part of me. I had experienced first-hand their long and determined fight to keep alight the fragile flame for a fairer democracy despite huge disadvantages stacked against them. I am now an active participant in this fight. It's a surreal feeling as I stood on the pick-up, soaking in what this long journey since 1991 had meant for me.

After the WP victory, The Straits Times commented, "Hougang speaks, but for itself". Does Hougang speak only for itself? In 1991, perhaps so, then along with 3 other constituencies. The crowd at the rally did not come from just Hougang. It could not be. The crowd on the last rally night would have equalled the total number of voters in Hougang. No, they came from afar to cheer Hougang voters on.

Hougang perhaps spoke ahead of its time. It was so in 1991. Then, it spoke to me to plant the seed of political awakening in me. Its flame eventually spread to Aljunied GRC in 2011. In 2011, I witnessed an outpouring of support for the opposition that I could not have imagined in 1991. From the man in the streets, to vocal voices in the cyberworld, to professionals, businessmen and even civil servants, the fear factor and political apathy [appeared] to have been broken. Perhaps in 2012, Hougang is again speaking, ahead of its time for all [of] Singapore. It is perhaps speaking ahead of its time for a more inclusive political landscape and a more inclusive society. Thank you, Hougang.

What kind of politics do we want in Singapore?

(January 26, 2013)

It is now just past 8 pm. Polling for Punggol East By-Election has closed. I wish Li Lian well.

While this by-election is relatively mild in terms of the hustling, it has nevertheless generated some negative incidents.

Former NMP[8] Calvin Cheng FB[9] messaged me in the afternoon today to let me know that he had just made a police report. Someone had threatened to kill him and burn him over his article published in Yahoo criticising the performance of WP in parliament. Earlier, Reform Party's candidate Kenneth Jeyaretnam had filed a police report over online threats to his family in London. An arrest had since been made. Reporter Kor Kian Beng had written about the Boo boys of the

---

8   Nominated Member of Parliament

9   Facebook

opposition, referring to the booing that took place during nomination day, mainly by supporters of WP.

I was not spared either. Last Saturday, I was campaigning in the flats next to Rivervale Mall for Li Lian. My car was vandalised. I had just gotten out of my car in the HDB multi-storey carpark and was walking towards the block where a group of WP volunteers [was] waiting for me. I received a call from a WP party member. A Zaobao[10] reporter friend of his was in the carpark, his car parked right next to mine. The reporter had seen someone come towards my car shortly after I had left and looked at my parking coupons. The person then walked to the side of the car away from the reporter and took out his phone, seemingly to call HDB to come and summon my car. Out of concern, the reporter who had recognised me, called the WP member to inform me to check if my coupons were valid.

I was sure they were but I went back to my car anyway. No one was around my car when I reached. There was sufficient time left on my parking coupons, so I went back to join my group to canvass for votes. It was only when I drove home that I realised the left door at the back of my car was rather badly scratched. Apparently, the person had taken a sharp object and while pretending to call on one hand, he made a number of scratch marks on my door with the other hand. He would have known I was a WP member. I was in my WP uniform and my car had Li Lian's calling cards exposed in the back seat.

I called the reporter. Unfortunately, he did not take any photograph of the vandal and the vandal was not dressed in any obvious party colours. The candidates of two other political parties, with their entourage of volunteers were campaigning in the same cluster of flats as I was that afternoon. I could not

---

10 Chinese-language newspaper in Singapore

be certain who would have done that to me. I deliberated for a while and decided not to make a police report.

Emotions run high during elections. Politics get people high. PAP MP Seng Han Thong was once even set on fire by someone in a community centre. That action simply cannot be tolerated.

I do not like to see such behaviours. During nomination, I was in the midst of the crowd. We had made announcements to the crowd not to jeer the other candidates. That was to no avail. Perhaps it did get them to be milder than they would otherwise have been. The jeering came anyway. A few of us tried to "Shhh" the crowd when the booing got too loud. It got quieter for a while but it came back again shortly afterwards.

I can understand why they are angry. Many Singaporeans had spoken to me about politics in the 2 years that I had stepped onto this arena. Many felt helpless at their situation. They were angry at the ruling party but could do little to bring the PAP down, or get them to change tracks. Elections offer them the chance to vent their frustrations.

The PAP is not helping in the situation. Some of their practices simply turn people off. Long before I harboured any interest to participate in politics, I was already turned off by the way the PAP used upgrading to buy votes. I was turned off by what I considered as overly harsh tactics on people who disagreed with them. I wrote in to the Straits Times forum during GE2006[11] to criticise the use of upgrading carrots. To me, linking votes to public funds was simply incorrect. Whatever respect I had for their earlier economic achievements was negated by these practices. Now that I have formally entered this arena, finding out that there are contracts such as the

---

11 2006 general election

software arrangement with AIM[12] strengthened my conviction that such practices are wrong.

The Prime Minister had said in his party seminar in November last year that Singapore can't have a blue constituency and a red constituency. His party has been trying to make sure Singapore's constituencies are about the same colour, because all constituencies should share the same interest. He was referring to the Democrat versus Republican politics of the USA, where there are often policy gridlocks due to party politics.

Being the one party that had overwhelmingly dominated Singapore's politics since independence, one could also interpret that to mean that the PAP hopes to see Singapore as all white. While we can criticise the Democrats and the Republicans for forcing policy gridlocks due to party's interests, I also respect the way power is handed over smoothly whenever there's change of power effected by the results of balloting. The losing party will simply hand over control of the office and come back to fight another day. The president would even appoint members of the opposite camp to become his office bearers. This is a level of maturity which Singapore politics has yet to reach. And I believe the days of a monotone colour for our constituencies map is gone. For the sake of Singaporeans, we need to get to the stage to have a smooth handover of control when constituencies change hand. And that should include grassroots organisations funded by public monies.

Perhaps it is because people are turned off by Singapore's brand of politics that they vent out their frustrations at election time. However, this is no excuse for some of the behaviours we had seen. All parties should work together to educate people to eradicate such actions. But understanding what lies beneath

---

12 Action Information Management Pte Ltd

their frustrations will be useful towards stemming the behaviours.

Now, back to my car. My wife told me to leave the ugly scratches alone. Now that I had chosen to walk the path of politics, she said the marks on the car will serve as a reminder to me of what politics can be like. It is the ugly side of politics that we should be reminded of, an ugly side that everyone should work together to eradicate. So, if you see a Honda Odyssey on the road with ugly scratches on its left side, you may also wish to ask yourself what you want Singapore's politics to be like.

## Leadership Renewal

During the Organising Members' Conference (OMC) of 2016, Chen Show Mao challenged Low Thia Khiang for the position of secretary-general (SG). It made big news in Singapore. The SG position had not been challenged for many years. It was vacated by J. B. Jeyaratnam in 2001. Low had never been challenged.

Was I surprised at the challenge? Not really. But I was also not sure if it would come to pass until it happened.

There were warning signs before that. At each OMC, cadre members would be approached for votes. I was approached as usual and it was to vote for the cadre interested to contest as a CEC member. It was nothing abnormal.

Then I received an invitation by a friend for lunch. He said that he would bring another friend along, someone interested in politics. I meet new people all the time. We talked about Singapore politics and other matters of a general nature. Then they opined that the WP had been too conservative and posed the question as to whether the WP was ready for a change of leadership. Chen Show Mao's name was suggested as the possible new leader. I was surprised. I was with two non-party members. People in the WP knew that I would likely be supportive of Low. I was not fixated on Low having to be the leader. I did not consider anyone else suitable at that time. I told them that I was not able to discuss matters of the party and changed the topic. Obviously, there were those interested enough to mount a campaign to even lobby people outside of the party to check out my allegiance.

Soon, the lobbying became obvious. Different cadre members started sharing that they were being approached. I did not exactly go around canvassing support for Low. I did not think he needed it from me, nor was I asked by anyone to canvass support. However, any cadre that came to me asking for my opinion, I expressed why I would not support a change of SG at that time.

## A Peek into the Workers' Party

Yes, we had a bad GE2015. In any democracy, after a general election, leaders of parties which did not do as well as expected will become vulnerable. There were always some members who felt that the WP should challenge every seat since we were the opposition party with by far the highest number of Parliament seats. After the successes in the 2011 election and the 2012 and 2013 by-elections, people got carried away with unrealistic expectations. For whatever successes we had, it was not even 10 percent of the Parliament seats. I definitely did not agree that we should overstretch ourselves. Challenging for all seats before we were ready for it would bring a swift and certain death to the WP.

In 2015, we contested too many seats. I was guilty of misjudging the situation myself. Prior to GE2015, Low once asked how many candidates I thought we should field. I cited a third of all seats to show our ambition to deny the PAP their two-third majority. I wanted exposure for younger candidates who could use 2015 as a base to contest in future general elections. Low told me that would be overstretching the party's resources. He said that there will not be enough volunteers to support so many candidates and not enough rally exposure for them. We need solid candidates. Having weak candidates will leave us vulnerable to attacks. Having too many weak candidates would deter good ones from joining the party to gear up for future general elections.

Other than that, there were also older members who felt ignored and unappreciated. Some were not happy with Low because he was a strict disciplinarian and had weeded out members in the past as he went about rebuilding the party. Some also felt that certain WP MPs had mishandled the Town Council matters. There was always a segment unhappy with Low, but they needed a leader with a chance to overthrow him. Their camp was too small in numbers. They needed at least an MP level candidate to root from behind to win others over.

To me, anyone wishing to be SG must be able to withstand fierce attacks by the PAP and must be able to counter-attack when needed. I had observed some fierce verbal sparring in Parliament. The SG must first pass this test. The WP will be finished off very quickly if we keep losing in the gladiator arena of verbal sparring with the PAP. Politics is a constant fight for the mindshare of the electorate. I did not see anyone then capable to be the new SG who could come close to what Low had achieved.

So, we waited to see what would happen on that OMC of May 29, 2016. We wondered if Sylvia Lim would be challenged for the chairperson position. She was not. Then the challenge was made when it came to the SG position.

As reported in the press, the vote was 61 to Low and 45 to Chen. Each vote pulled out of the ballot box was immediately added to the spreadsheet tabulating the live score and projected onto the big screen. Initially, the count was close and the mood tense. Then, Low's votes started to pull apart midway through the counting. There were 107 cadres present that day. Low himself did not vote. He held up his unused ballot paper at the end of the counting for all to see and explained that he left it to others to decide if he had done enough to remain as SG.

After the 2016 CEC election, at the first CEC meeting, Pritam Singh was appointed as assistant SG, a post that had been left vacant for many years since it was last held by Poh Li Guan in 2006. Low had at that time said that there was no need for the position as the CEC then was relatively young and needed time to develop. The CEC in 2006 indeed consisted of mostly young people, many who later became candidates in 2011. The assistant SG post carried with it some expectation that the person may succeed the SG. Low must have felt that none was suitable in 2006 and for many years to come. Ten years later, Low was ready to move Singh to a bigger role with higher expectations.

At the WP's 60th year celebration dinner in 2017, Low announced that he would not contest the SG post in the next CEC. It was a surprise to many members and the public. All eyes looked to Singh, the assistant

SG. After the leadership challenge of 2016, we wondered if a fresh challenge for the SG title would be mounted in the OMC of 2018. It was better not to be left to chance. Those of us who were more concerned about the leadership plans checked around to see who would be interested. Sylvia Lim was not interested. Many who supported Low supported Singh as he was seen to be shadowing Low in the party's leadership role, and he had also taken on more of the attacks by the PAP in Parliament.

Were we concerned that the leadership would move from a Chinese-educated leader to an English-speaking Indian/Sikh? Not for me, nor for many of the senior members in the party. Those with Parliament experience especially felt that our biggest selection criteria would be how the person could stand up to attacks by the PAP. We are, after all, a political party with a very powerful opponent. There would also be the need for the person to be able to connect with and inspire confidence in members. In fact, for several of us, Leon Perera also featured high on our list of possible successors, given his good Parliament performance. The disadvantage that Perera would face was that he was an NCMP at that time. With elected MPs in the WP, the SG should preferably be an elected MP who could have a ground to be rooted in. Since Singh was able to take the role and was the best fit, many of us decided to put our support behind him. Race never came into our consideration. Two of our preferred candidates for the SG post were non-Chinese.

We went into the 2018 CEC election waiting to see if there would be any fireworks. There were none. The chairperson and SG positions went to Lim and Singh uncontested, respectively. The transition was almost complete. After Low had stepped down as SG, people wondered if Low would contest in the next general election. I knew that there was a very high chance that he would not. Around the end of 2016 after the leadership challenge, Low invited me for lunch. He had met with a few of us individually to hear our views about leadership change. He was already planning his retirement from Parliament. He wanted my opinion of him not contesting at the next general election.

Low would just be in his early 60s at the next general election, which I felt was still quite young to retire from Parliament. But I understood his thought process. He wanted to force leadership renewal and make way for more new talent. He did not say so himself, but his retirement would send another fear of an opposition wipe-out. By not contesting, he would help clear the way for more to come in. For someone so respected as an opposition politician, he was also quite forthright. He said that he should let the newer generation do things differently, that he did not even want to do his own social media channels.

I did not try to discourage him from his plans. It might be risky but not necessarily a bad thing for the WP. It had also been a super tough job for him. As I write this book, the lawsuit from the Aljunied-Hougang Town Council is still ongoing. It can potentially bankrupt Low and Lim, as well as the other defendants.

For the next three years, when I followed all that was happening, including Low's announcement in 2017 that he would step down as SG in 2018 and Singh's successful accession to the SG post in 2018, I viewed them with the privileged information from that lunch meeting. Low's unfortunate serious injury after a fall in 2020 had nothing to do with him not contesting in GE2020. He had already been formulating a plan to do so since 2016. He just needed to see if the leadership transfer would be smooth and if Singh would be able to step up. The SG position is a hot seat. Low would be leaving behind big shoes to be filled. In 2020, Low was convinced that his mission to hand over leadership was successful and that he was not needed to contest for Parliament anymore. Singh went on to pass his first major test with flying colours as the SG in GE2020 after the WP won the new Sengkang GRC, as well as the seats it had held in 2015.

## Myths, Perceptions, and Questions about the Opposition

Through this unexpected journey, I had developed my personal insights into the political process in the WP and about politics in Singapore. I will share my views on common myths, perceptions, and questions about opposition politics in Singapore.

### 1. The opposition is here to disrupt the work of the government. They are disloyal to Singapore.

The WP that I was involved in sought to find ways to contribute to better policy making and to give alternative sources of feedback to the government. The WP did vote against some government bills and motions, but had supported the majority of bills and policies. Even in the process of supporting, we often suggested areas to improve on and how enforcement could be more effective. I credit this to Low taking a conscious decision to take such a stance and to guide WP parliamentarians along the same line too. Singh has since carried the party forward in a similar approach. As a parliamentarian, I had to often remind myself, and we sometimes get reminded too, how we would have executed a policy if we were to be in government. This principle had guided us in how we had engaged with the ruling party.

I am certain that the WP which I was involved in is loyal to Singapore. I am proudly a Singaporean and will do my part to defend Singapore, as I know those around me will too.

Each opposition party is different in how it engages with the ruling party. The engagement may also change over time as new leaders and key members emerge in a party. I continue to believe in the positive role a loyal opposition can play in developing a more resilient Singapore.

### 2. Opposition members appear once every five years during general elections.

It depends on how much a party or a candidate wants to win in the next general election after having contested in one earlier. Some do spend a lot of time on the ground and some do indeed appear every five years. The main challenge remains the uncertain electoral boundaries and the short time between changes to electoral boundaries and general elections. That makes it difficult for serious candidates to cover the ground when boundaries have changed. Also, the mainstream media generally do not report activities of those not in Parliament so there is less visibility for candidates who did not win elections but remain active in working on the ground. Nevertheless, you will find serious parties spending more effort in areas they had previously contested in.

**3. Opposition candidates contest to earn the relative well-paying MP salary. It does not cost them to contest.**

While the cost for contesting in a general election in Singapore is lower than in many other democratic countries, the expenses to contest in a serious manner is also not cheap. While a party may fund part of its candidates' campaign costs, most candidates have to raise their own funds to cover many other items. The bulk of the costs in a general election are in the rallies (in the absence of rallies such as during the COVID-19 pandemic general election in 2020, the cost was in production of media content), printing and postage of candidates' information to voters, and putting up and subsequently removal of election banners and posters. The odds are stacked heavily against opposition candidates in a general election, so opposition candidates have to invest in campaigns with almost no chance of any returns. For new candidates without wide public exposure, donations for the candidates are often insufficient to cover the full cost. In GE2011, when I was a new candidate, I spent around $20,000 on my campaign on top of shared costs covered by the party. I received less than half of the amount I had spent in donations. The party mostly covered the cost for the rallies, but candidates were expected to also raise their own donations. The PAP candidates spend, on average, two to three times that of their WP counterparts.[13]

---

13 Chew Hui Min, "GE2020 expenses: PAP candidates spent nearly S$7 million, while opposition candidates used S$2.2 million", CNA, August 21, 2020, https://www.channelnewsasia.com/news/singapore/ge2020-expenses-pap-wp-candidates-voters-general-election-13042388

### 4. The WP is PAP-lite.

The WP did not set out to be PAP-lite. The political stance of a party stems mainly from the core beliefs of the key leaders and that evolves whenever there is a significant change of leadership. The WP had taken a left-of-centre approach under the leadership of Low and this has been continued by Singh. By having a clear stance, it attracted members who share similar beliefs. As shared earlier, in my time in Parliament, a core principle behind our engagement with the PAP was how we would run Singapore if we were in government. Some of our positions may end up quite similar to that of the PAP. The PAP themselves had taken a move to the left following the poor results of GE2011, moving towards the WP left-of-centre position. One can also argue that the PAP has become WP-lite to regain lost political grounds.

### 5. The WP also has its own whip and party discipline for its parliamentarians. That is no different from the PAP which does not allow MPs to vote against its own bills and motions unless the whip is lifted.

Without a party whip and discipline, it will be hard for a party to function properly in Parliament. Public disagreements between parliamentarians from the same party could become damaging for the image of the party. Hence, I agree with the strict manner in which Low enforced discipline within our ranks. He had seen from past experiences how much damage could be caused when opposition MPs publicly disagree with one another. Low had shared his view with us that the problems faced by the opposition after the electoral successes of the 1991 general election had set the opposition movement back by some 20 years.

In my time in Parliament, I did not have any major disagreement with the positions of the party. The positions of the party had also been made known publicly, which I had read before joining. Being deeply involved in policy and Parliament work, the WP parliamentarians also end up shaping future policies of the party. There could be areas which one may end up philosophically disagreeing with the party, but such matters did not surface during my term in Parliament.

## Journey in Blue

Being not part of the PAP, opposition MPs are not subjected to the PAP's whip and hence we had, on various occasions, voted against bills and motions initiated by the PAP. This allows the opposition to play an important role to check against policies which we believe will not be good for Singapore.

### 6. NCMPs now have full Parliament and voting rights as elected MPs. That makes them the same.

This is far from the truth and it is something that the PAP will continue to try to make people believe. In theory, NCMPs can now do what elected MPs can do in Parliament. In reality, the NCMP does not represent any constituents. The PAP is also not afraid of those who enter Parliament via NCMPs or as NMPs positions because they had not cost the PAP any elected seats. Electoral boundaries can be changed, as they frequently had been, to disadvantage NCMPs in future electoral contests.

Under the current constitution, there will only be NCMPs if there are less than 12 elected opposition MPs. Voting rights make no difference as all the NCMPs and NMPs combined together will not even form a third of the Parliament votes to block any change in constitution.

The NCMP position does offer a public profile, which can be useful for someone wanting to press on in the political scene. People have asked why the WP and other opposition parties still take up NCMP positions despite objecting to the scheme. It is akin to asking why the WP contests in GRCs even though we object to the way GRCs are used to manipulate the electoral system. Boycotting elections because we object to the GRC system will hand the elections to the PAP on a silver platter, like how the Barisan Socialis opposition handed absolute control to the PAP in 1968 with its boycott of the general election. Since such schemes are part of the electoral process, the best way to change the system is to beat the PAP in its own game. The GRC is now no longer the feared fortress that it was earlier. And the best thing that can happen to the NCMP scheme is to make it redundant by having 12 or more elected opposition members in Parliament.

## 7. Singapore will collapse when the PAP loses power or when the PAP loses a large number of seats.

I hear this quite often, especially during general elections. It is a fear that the PAP has successfully planted in many people over the years. This was reinforced when the opposition became very weak after the PAP took absolute control of Parliament. I strongly believe that Singapore has more than enough for just the so-called 'A-team' of the PAP. The problem had been that capable people in the alternative camp in the early years of Singapore politics had been exiled, imprisoned, bankrupted, or dealt with in a harsh manner that many became deterred.

In his book *Governing: A Singapore Perspective* launched in November 2020, former Senior Minister S. Jayakumar had issued a warning, "As I see it, the camel (the WP) has gotten its nose into the PAP tent. It will want to occupy the whole tent in 2, 3 or 4 elections down the road." Jayakumar warned in his book that a "revolving door" system, in which one party constantly competes against an opposition party, or a coalition of such parties, would be a weak and populist government, and urged Singaporeans to reflect on what they want for the future.

".. the camel has gotten its nose into the PAP tent. It will want to occupy the whole tent in 2, 3 or 4 elections down the road." Former PAP Senior Minister S. Jayakumar

Credits: Camel and faces from 360 Education's doodle library

Whether the WP or another party will eventually take over from the PAP is up to Singaporeans. The tent that Jayakumar referred to does not belong to the PAP but to Singaporeans. The PAP has to constantly demonstrate its competency for the right to occupy the tent. My purpose for joining the WP, and I believe it is the same for many others I know of, is to build up an alternative credible enough to one day take over the government without Singapore failing. It is better to build up a good alternative when Singapore is still functioning. All governments in history had to eventually decline and be replaced, no matter how powerful and pure they had started off initially. The PAP had also planted the fear in people that their flats would lose their value and that rubbish would be piled up three storeys high if the opposition won in their constituency. So far, this has not happened. The civil service and other institutions of the country do not belong to any political party as well. They should function even when there is a change of government.

The opposition has an important role to play in a functioning democracy. The PAP is very resilient, but it is incapable of checking itself despite its attempts to project such an image. A credible opposition lends its voice to the voters to be the check against the ruling party.

### 8. The WP only criticises and never makes any proposals.

Individual WP MPs do offer proposals for improvements to policies. Throughout this book, I have given various examples as I described some areas I was involved in with greater details. Besides offering proposals in Parliament, I had also used my blog posts to offer more opinions, especially after I was no longer in Parliament. In Parliament, I used adjournment motion, speeches during the Committee of Supply debates on various ministries, and Parliament questions to push ideas. I took care to make sure that these proposals are aligned with the party's manifestos and, in some cases when they were new, to first collectively clear within the party's leadership.

Some areas which the WP as a party had pushed for in a bigger way include our alternative to the Population White Paper, redundancy insurance, and the decaying lease of public housing. These have been published as policy papers. Having worked with many of the current WP MPs before, I am confident that more areas will continue to be pushed by the party as it builds on the momentum from the increased Parliament presence since 2011.

### 9. The WP is too silent in criticising the government.

The WP that I was involved with took the approach started by Low to be a rational, responsible, and respectable opposition. Many have asked why the WP does not take part in protests at Hong Lim Park or be more active on social media when various issues crop up. Parliament is the preferred platform to raise issues as we have been elected by Singaporeans to use the Parliament processes. If the matter is to be brought before Parliament, we often prefer to use that platform rather than to be in the open with our arguments before Parliament sittings. Nevertheless, there have been a good number of times where the WP had issued statements online to state our stand on important issues and events even before Parliament debates. When necessary, the WP had also initiated debates on issues that may be uncomfortable to the PAP, such as the corruption case by Keppel Corp's officials or the poor handling of the criminal case brought on foreign domestic worker Parti Liyani.

I expect that under Singh, the WP will continue with the stance initiated by Low but with more engagement inside and outside of Parliament. However, one should not expect to see the WP going to Hong Lim Park to lead protests or start public demonstrations.

### 10. My career will be affected when I join the opposition.

I cannot speak for all. I was initially afraid too, and did not want to explore politics until I had sold my main business which had some 90 percent of its annual revenue dependent on government schools. Since joining the opposition, I continue to do business with schools. I was not shunned by friends whom I had already made prior to joining politics and continued to make new friends.

Nevertheless, there will be inconveniences and annoyances. I have been tagged as a politically exposed person. Once, I went to a money changer to change more than SGD $5,000. I had to show my national registration identity card and the moneychanger said that the system by the Monetary Authority of Singapore did not allow the transaction. I would need to have the transaction registered and approved first. I had to split the transaction into two separate transactions below $5,000 to get the money changed. Some local banks had also turned down my application for a business account before. When pressed for an answer, the officers would usually give some standard vague answers. However, after questioning one application processing officer several times, he sheepishly asked if I was a politically exposed person. That made me rather upset with the bank which I had some prior dealings with and yet turned down our company's application for a standard commercial banking account. In any case, I found another local bank which would accept opening our business account. In another instance, a company secretarial firm which I had used for many years declined to act for us after I had entered politics, citing fears of more supervision on their work on us.

In the next chapter, I will share about how the Distinguished Alumnus Award conferred to me was deferred for a year. When I was shortlisted to be the lead consultant for the Government of Bhutan in its Information and Communication Technology in Education Masterplan project in 2013, I was told during a casual conversation with a key member of the organisation leading the project that my suitability had been subjected to special scrutiny as the project was mainly funded by a foundation from Singapore. Nevertheless, I made it through the special evaluation.

My belief is that whether one gets shunned depends on how the opposition politicians portray himself or herself, and also whether the other party is being overly self-censoring. I do not believe that there are explicit instructions that government departments cannot award projects to opposition politicians or that financial institutions cannot deal with us. Some who chose not to because of the political affiliation of the person may do it out of self-censorship or fear of inconveniences. I also did not ask the buyers of my earlier business why they chose to rename the company only in 2011, not long after I had entered politics. The company was acquired in 2007. It will take some time to clear the ghosts that still haunt Singapore from the overly controlling style of politics in our earlier years.

# Part 3

# Reflections

# Chapter 9
# Whither Singapore?

## Sharing the Field?

In 2013, George Yeo, former Minister for Foreign Affairs, made a two-word post on his Facebook, "Whither Singapore", after the results of the Punggol East by-election. His post went viral. My blog post in reply to his post, with the same title, went viral too. Such was the interest of Singaporeans in what was happening in the political scene in Singapore. The past 10 years have seen wild swings in election results. Singapore is changing. This chapter contains my perspectives on Singapore politics in light of developments in the last decade.

First, a reproduction of my "Whither Singapore" post:

> Whither Singapore?
>
> (January 28, 2013)
>
> After the results for the Punggol East by-election was known, former Minister George Yeo made a 2-word post, "Whither Singapore" on his Facebook. Within hours, there were hundreds of comments. Whither is used in poetic language. It means 'to what place', or 'to what end or purpose'. I suppose George Yeo meant where Singapore politics is heading towards, given the unexpected defeat of a previously safe SMC[1] seat by a stunning 10.8% margin to the opposition in a 4-corner fight.
>
> When I plunged into politics 2 years ago, I never expected myself to be actively involved in a General Election and two by-elections, plus being a keen observer of a closely fought

---

1 Single Member Constituency

Presidential Election; all in less than 24 months. In election-deprived Singapore, we never had such election excitement since independence.

Many firsts had taken place. For the first time, a GRC[2] was lost to the opposition. The GRC is viewed by many as the impregnable fortress of the PAP[3], designed to make it difficult for the opposition to take down teams that are each led by 1–2 ministers. PAP also received its lowest share of the popular votes since independence. Three months later, for the first time, a presidential candidate favoured by the ruling party was elected by less than majority votes, and with a shocking razor-thin 0.3% margin as well. Then, after losses in Aljunied GRC and in the Hougang by-election, the PAP lost for the first time since independence in a multi-corner fight to a female opposition candidate.

To put matters into perspective, the PAP still has 92% control of the 87-seat house. Singapore is hardly a multi-party government system yet. PAP's 92% control is still a stunning success for any political party in a democratic system. Still, the progress made by the opposition after 46 years of near barrenness is remarkable.

I had used an analogy in my GE2011's[4] rally speech. I likened the PAP to an older horse, constantly winning races in the past, but it is now fast tiring. There's a new and younger horse in town, swiftly improving on its speed. Which horse would you count on to win? It is harder to call now. On nomination day, many would have given the race to the old winning horse in this 4-corner fight. It turned out otherwise, and by a winning

---

2  Group Representation Constituency

3  People's Action Party

4  2011 general election

margin that not even the most optimistic opposition supporter would have guessed. Two years since I first used this analogy, the younger horse has won 3 races in a row. I guess this is why George Yeo asked, "Whither Singapore." What's next? What now?

There are other significant points in the Punggol East election as well. Dr Koh[5] is the typical PAP candidate, well-educated and successful as a top surgeon. He's the technocrat that one can expect to come through PAP's tea parties, parachuted often at short notice into a contest. Picked for the job but not always willing initially because they are first and foremost, doing well in their career and lacking interest in politics.

PM Lee[6] highlighted Dr Koh as an example of the success of Singapore's system, as he came from a humble family background and succeeded through doing well in school and then in his job. PM Lee also cited WP candidate Lee Li Lian as another example of the success of the Singapore's system: went through N levels to polytechnic and then university. I suppose that while seemingly praising Li Lian for her 'success', the Prime Minister was subtly trying to tell voters to compare and contrast their intellectual capabilities measured by academic achievements. This is nothing new, just done more subtly. In 1984, the PAP publicly announced the stellar O level results of Mr Mah Bow Tan against the seven credits and one pass of Mr Chiam See Tong. That ploy backfired and angered voters. Mr Chiam got into parliament and put up a respectable performance in his 27 years in parliament and became well-loved by the residents of Potong Pasir. His less than impressive O level results

---

5   Koh Poh Koon

6   Prime Minister Lee Hsien Loong

did not seem to harm his performance as an MP.[7]

I like to think that Li Lian succeeded despite of Singapore's system. In 2011, I asked a parliament question for the number of Singaporeans studying in private universities in Singapore and overseas. We were told 41,000 Singaporeans were studying for university degrees in private universities in Singapore while the government did not track the number of Singaporeans studying overseas. The number of Singaporeans studying for higher education entirely at their own expenses is about the same as those studying at government funded local autonomous universities. Li Lian is one of the many Singaporeans who did part-time work while studying for a degree, without any help from the government.

Dr Koh was a 3-week old PAP member when he was introduced as PAP's candidate. In contrast, Li Lian joined in 2006 as a passionate volunteer and worked her way up the system, holding many posts in the party. All these while managing a demanding full-time job. Li Lian is one of the many volunteers and members of the Workers' Party. They are not paid for the tasks they do for the party but are nevertheless willing to slog it out to make sure things work. In contrast, the PAP has full control over the grassroots structure, funded with government monies. They get well-oiled machineries to get things done. In a way, having to work with little just makes one more resourceful. It also helps WP people to connect better with the ground.

---

[7] Member of Parliament

## Reflections

*MP-elect Lee Li Lian constantly reaching over the railings of the pick-up to shake hands with well wishers*

We have often been told by the PAP leaders that Singapore does not have enough for two teams. I strongly disagree with this damning analysis of the talent of our 3.29 million Singaporeans. I think we are looking for talents in the wrong places. When one is looking amongst the unwilling to serve, we will not find many. I had blogged about this previously ("Political sacrifice — Fishing for the unwilling"[8]) and had spoken about it in my speech on the debate on ministerial salaries[9].

For me, one of the exciting things about the Punggol East By-Election is to see 4 of our new members since 2011 speak at the rallies. We just had our Bricks in Blue concert earlier this month. The tagline is "Building for a new generation". Building up for the future is more than a brick and mortar building. It is building up the people for a future generation of WP. I am

---

8   Yee Jenn Jong, "Political sacrifice — Fishing for the unwilling", January 18, 2012, https://yeejj.wordpress.com/2012/01/18/political-sacrifice-fishing-for-the-unwilling/

9   Yee Jenn Jong, "My parliamentary speech on Ministerial Pay Review (17 Jan 2012)", January 17, 2012, https://yeejj.wordpress.com/2012/01/17/my-parliamentary-speech-on-ministerial-pay-review-17-jan-2012/

glad Li Lian won the By-Election. She is young and part of the new generation. So are the new people who have joined the party. And Li Lian's climb to become an MP is proof that we can widen the fishing pond for talent. It shows that with hard work and the right heart, one can make stellar breakthroughs.

People naturally have higher expectations of WP after the Punggol East win. As I said earlier, we still need to see things in perspective. WP now has 8% of elected seats in parliament. The young horse is galloping fast, but there's still some gap to catch up on the reigning horse. We need more people to step forward. Singaporeans themselves have to show that there's enough quality to form Singapore's Team B. Quality not just in qualifications and career successes, but quality of the heart too. It will take time to put people through the test of ground activities to see the quality of the heart. WP new member Associate Professor Daniel Goh summed it up nicely in his maiden rally speech:

> Many of my friends and family members asked why I joined the Workers' Party. Some were afraid for me. They asked me, "Is it really safe for you to do this?" But I told them life is too short and too precious, don't waste time being kiasu[10], kiasi[11] and kiagui[12].
>
> Some wondered about my motives. They say, "You are a professor, you got a comfortable life, if you idealistic, go join the PAP, change the system from inside." I told them change does not come from inside or from outside, but from the correct side. This is the co-driver side where we tell the driver he is heading down the wrong side of the road!

---

10 A Hokkien term describing a selfish attitude rooted in a fear of losing out.

11 A Hokkien term describing an attitude that is extremely afraid.

12 A Hokkien term describing someone who is afraid of ghosts.

Some laughed at me because they know I am not the slapping type. They say, "Hah, you can slap meh, you are a bookworm." I told them, even bookworms think of their children and would stand up for them.

Whither Singapore? It is still early days. I think it will be good that Singaporeans think deeply and determine what type of political parties and politicians that they will accept in today's political era. And the parties will need time to build themselves up to let Singaporeans judge and decide. Parties will each determine how it will draw in talent and build them up. I believe the days of a mono-coloured constituencies map of Singapore is over. We will have to deal with the realities of other parties sharing the field with the PAP. The different parties will need to figure out how they will play it out on Singapore's political field.

## The 2011 and 2017 Presidential Elections

Coming just after the poor PAP results in GE2011, the presidential election of 2011 was another thriller.

The Workers' Party (WP) had opposed the presidential election scheme. We are also a political party. As a WP parliamentarian and Central Executive Committee (CEC) member then, it would not be possible for me to openly campaign for anyone in the 2011 presidential election (PE2011), though I would very much had wanted to openly pitch for Tan Cheng Bock.

Why?

With my entry into opposition politics, I had by then entered into a whole new world of people interested in politics. I had friends who were staunchly on the PAP side as well as those on the opposition side. Even on the opposition side, there are those extremely anti-PAP and those who were the moderate ground supporters.

It was obvious to me from the start when the four Tans (Tony Tan, Tan Cheng Bock, Tan Jee Say, and Tan Kin Lian) were allowed to contest that Tan Cheng Bock was the only one with any chance of toppling the government's preferred candidate, Tony Tan. To me, the elected president (EP) is just another of the PAP's many creative inventions for control. I was far from convinced that Singapore needed it. I wanted to see the PAP's artificial machineries broken down so that we can have a fairer democratic system. Winning the government from the PAP was impossible in the short to medium term, given the dismal state of the opposition for many decades. Even with the PAP's worst general election results since independence, after GE2011, there were only six elected opposition MPs versus 81 of the PAP, a supermajority that would make any political party in a democracy jump for joy.

The best chance to dismantle one of the PAP's invention is to let it lose the EP. The government would not collapse. I believed the PAP had wrongly calculated when they created the EP system. It is far easier to lose one presidential election than to lose the government. I felt that Tan Cheng Bock was the candidate with the best chance against the government's anointed candidate. If Tan Cheng Bock won, it would send shock waves into the political side.

A large number of die-hard opposition supporters doubted if Tan Cheng Bock, being a former long-time PAP MP, would be too PAP-oriented for their liking or was planted there by the PAP. So this camp mostly voted for Tan Jee Say. This segment of voters was simply too small. Even if all the die-hard opposition supporters voted for Tan Jee Say, there would still be a far gap from those die-hard PAP supporters who would almost certainly go for Tony Tan.

Restrained by the party's stand, I could only blog occasionally to subtly indicate my personal support for Tan Cheng Bock. I anticipated that he could come close, perhaps short of a couple of percentage points to

## Reflections

win. I recall on PE2011 polling day, the WP had an event in the headquarters. Casual conversation touched on what the results might be. I shared my prediction. It would be Tony Tan, but Tan Cheng Bock would be a close second. I shared my analysis. I remember Sylvia Lim said that she found my analysis interesting and plausible.

The actual result was even closer than what I had predicted.

After all the excitement from the counting, I slept late but woke up early. I whipped up a blog post to analyse the results. I wrote the long piece in about 40 minutes and then went back to bed. I woke up again about three hours later and found that the post had gone viral. *The Straits Times* wrote to me asking for permission to publish my piece. Low Thia Khiang gave his permission. To date, this is still the highest viewed post on my blog. The piece is reproduced below.

> Analysis of PE2011 Result
>
> (August 28, 2011)
>
> Before polling, I made my prediction to close friends. I posted that prediction on my personal Facebook before counting results came in, at around 10 pm on polling night. I didn't post it publicly before voting ended because I did not want my predictions to influence voting. My post was:
>
>> Now that counting is underway and I am just back from shopping, let me share what I had predicted to close friends: $TT^{13}$ will take around 60% of PAP votes. $TJS^{14}$ will take 60% of $Opp^{15}$ votes. $TCB^{16}$ takes most of the rest (40% of both PAP and Opp). That means TT may win TCB

---

13 Tony Tan

14 Tan Jee Say

15 Opposition

16 Tan Cheng Bock

> narrowly. TJS will do reasonably well but hard to cross 25%. Winner will have less than 40% overall, maybe around 36%. Sorry, TKL[17]. You tried.

Based on the GE2011 results, that would mean 60% x 60% = 36% for Dr Tony Tan, 60% x 40% = 24% for Mr Tan Jee Say. Based on GE2011 3-corner fight result, I felt Mr Tan Kin Lian could garner around 5–6% of the votes only, which would have left Dr Tan Cheng Bock with around 34–35%, a close second.

The final result was amazingly close, closer than I had imagined.

I based my prediction on a fairly crude model. Being a political person, I now have access to many people who volunteered to tell me who they are voting. I must have met or had Facebook and email exchanges with over 100 people. I scanned the social media such as TOC[18] and TRE[19] to gauge sentiments.

I asked 2 key questions: (1) Who are you voting for and (2) which party do you normally vote for in GEs. In many cases, I did not even need to ask the second question as many that I interact with are in the opposition camp. Most volunteered to tell me the reasons for their choice as well.

While PE is not supposed to be a political contest, it nevertheless reflects the political desires of the people with proxy fights based on political ideologies.

The results were (after some generalisation of reasons):

1. I found around 40% of PAP voters going for TCB. Those who would go for TCB may have some

---

17 Tan Kin Lian

18 The Online Citizen

19 Temasek Review Emeritus

personal interactions with him previously or felt that he was truly sincere about his mission and had the heart for the people. They expressed reservations about why TT was in the race. Those who would go for TT felt he was best qualified or would simply vote for him because they knew he was the official choice of the PAP. I found no PAP supporters willing to go for TJS or TKL.

2. The opposition side is split between TJS and TCB. The moderate opposition supporters were inclined towards TCB. The vocal opposition supporters went for TJS. I met more TCB supporters on the opposition camp than TJS supporters. However, I knew my circle of interaction had more moderate supporters. From my scan of the vocal online media such as TRE and TOC and looking at TOC's survey, I felt after accounting for the more vocal group, around 60% of those who voted opposition in GE2011 would go for TJS. I found almost none that would go for TT (yes, I said almost none, because there were a small handful that felt PE should be about the person rather than political ideologies and they went for TT despite voting opposition in GEs).

3. I found few TKL supporters. He was the second choice of a number of people. Those who felt strongly that they could not support any former PAP senior members would pick TJS first and TKL second. Those who felt we should not have an aggressive president but could not support TT because he was the choice of the PAP would pick TCB first and TKL second. Unfortunately, there is no prize for being second in the one-vote system. Based on this, I used

the percentage from Punggol East 3-cornered fight in GE to predict a slightly better votes' percentage share for TKL than Desmond Lim.

4. Most of the opposition supporters' dilemma centred around choosing TJS or TCB. It was a fluid situation that changed with additional press and online reports, debates and media broadcasts. These were for votes from the moderate opposition camp.

The final result shows a number of things:

1. There is currently a base of around 36% who would support PAP rock solid. Hougang's result in GE2011 sort of reflected this. Hougang is the strongest opposition base with a young rookie PAP candidate contesting. Desmond Choo's 36% reflected the percentage of people that are solidly behind whatever PAP do. In Alex Au's Yawningbread recent blog, he shared a story of several elderly ladies in a coffeeshop talking about how they would vote. One said that it was simple. Just go into the poll and look for the lightning symbol! They do not care about the other candidates. Just go for the lightning. In this case, go for the person implicitly representing the party's choice. Hence, the clever use of unions and associations to support a candidate. It is a proxy to the party's choice and the mainstream media would dutifully publicise the endorsement. It is not to force their members to vote en-bloc but to indicate to the 'aunties' and 'uncles' PAP supporters who the establishment's choice is.

## Reflections

2. There is a vocal opposition group of supporters who will always choose the one who is the most anti-PAP. That vote went to TJS. However, given that TJS did have a good career track record, he pulled in some votes from the middle ground as well. However, by positioning himself as the opposition-type, he could not draw votes from the usual PAP voters, which meant it was impossible for him to win but he would finish well.

3. There's a moderate ground prepared to accept a good compromise candidate. TCB represented this middle ground. He could pull in voters from both the opposition and PAP camps. TCB marketed himself as an independent-minded guy with the capabilities to fit the office.

4. There is no fourth group. TKL appealed to none of the above groups as their first choice. Second choice does not count!

PE2011 offered analysis not possible in GE because:

1. There was only one 3-corner fight in GE where the choices were obvious: either for PAP or for the strongest opposition proposition.

2. The candidates in PE2011 have credible track records, having to go through a stringent PEC[20] qualification. Three of the candidates positioned themselves nicely into the pro-PAP, pro-opposition and middle ground. That is something we did not have in GE.

---

20 Presidential Elections Committee

3. Voting in PE is across the whole country making it like a referendum on the agenda presented by the candidates. In a GE, there are differences between political parties in their ideologies and also in the slate of candidates. That makes it more difficult to compare results across constituencies.

Having said all these, we follow the first-past-the-post election system. Even if it was by a single vote, the winner takes all.

Dr Tony Tan is the 7th president of Singapore. Let us congratulate Dr Tony Tan, whatever your political ideologies may be. He will enter the office with a burden to bridge the divide in expectations. It is useful to study why Dr Tan Cheng Bock was popular enough to garner 35% of the votes despite the tough 4-cornered competition that had damaged his chances much more than it did for Dr Tony Tan. TCB represents something significant for the people of Singapore — a desire for a president that has passion for the people and independence to check the government, when it is necessary. The fact that he could draw strong supporters and votes from both the opposition and the PAP camps was amazing. It showed that what he stood for had the chance to unify a [politically] divided country.

I did not vote for the late president Ong Teng Cheong because of political ideologies. But he won my respect during his term in office for proving that he truly could cast aside his political baggage and challenge the government when it mattered. I am prepared to do likewise for Dr Tony Tan.

To Dr Tan Cheng Bock, congratulations for putting up an honourable contest. You have demonstrated that it is possible to rally people from both [sides] of the political divide. I am reminded of Al Gore, who lost a bitterly close election to be

> president of the United States of America to George Bush. It must have been really shattering for him to win the popular votes but not the electoral college and even so by technical problems with the automated counting system. Yet Al Gore bounced back to make himself useful [by] championing causes he believes in.
>
> So, Dr Tan Cheng Bock, even though you are not our president, I hope you will continue in this work that you have started.

After the close PE2011, everyone wondered what the PAP would do about the 2017 presidential election (PE2017). Tan Cheng Bock was gearing up for a second run at the presidency. However, the Constitution was changed not long before PE2017. The post of President became reserved for someone only from the Malay-Muslim community. Now, Tan could not qualify to contest because of the race criteria. And the professional criteria to qualify was also raised. Two Malay candidates with a rags-to-riches life story were not able to qualify. At least one might have qualified under the previous criteria. And so, PE2017 was a let-down after the close PE2011 contest. I felt that democracy had died. Many felt so too. We shall see what happens in the 2023 presidential election when the post of President will no longer be reserved for a minority candidate.

How I felt about PE2017 was captured in the blog post below.

> PE2017 — A missed opportunity for EP to gain acceptance?
>
> (April 2, 2017)
>
> On Friday, former Presidential candidate Dr Tan Cheng Bock called a press conference to question why the late President Wee[21] and not the late President Ong[22] was considered as the

---

21 Wee Kim Wee

22 Ong Teng Cheong

first Elected President (EP). It was also an argument that Member of Parliament for Aljunied GRC, Ms Sylvia Lim had put forth in parliament as well during the debate on the changes to the elected presidency. Blogger Andrew Loh captured their arguments, as well as listed many evidences of how history and Singaporeans, myself included definitely, had always regarded President Ong as our first EP.

At issue would be whether the upcoming Presidential Election (PE) should be a reserved election for Malays because it pertains to whether 5 continuous election terms had passed without producing a Malay President. The government's unconvincing response so far has been that it was the advice of AGC[23] to consider President Wee as the first EP, thereby triggering the reserved election. However, the government would not publish the advice of the AGC despite attempts in parliament and by the online community to ask for it.

The AGC may well have their reasons for advising the government in this manner, but it is also the government's prerogative to decide if it wishes to accept. There are after all, good counter arguments against it. President Wee may have been given the powers and duties of an elected president but he was nominated for the position before the EP position was created. The powers of an EP were accorded to him near the end of his term as president until the first PE could be called. Hence, many Singaporeans are puzzled and remain unconvinced as to why the time should be counted from President Wee's term because there was never an election to get him into office.

The issue of EP has long been a contentious one. It was conceptualised as a safeguard of Singapore's reserves during the 1980s against a possible future 'rogue government' when the

---

23 Attorney-General's Chambers

## Reflections

opposition started to make inroads with the electorate. For the first PE in 1993, ex-banker Chua Kim Yeow openly said that he was persuaded by former DPM[24] Goh Keng Swee and then-Finance Minister Richard Hu to stand for election against the establishment's preferred candidate, former DPM Ong Teng Cheong, in order to give a choice to the people. He however, seemed reluctant to campaign Singaporeans to choose him. That irked me enough to write and have my first letter published in the forum pages of Straits Times.[25] I felt it seemed to be a contest for the sake of having a contest to give legitimacy to the first PE. Apparently, I was not the only one to have felt so because other forum writers and even journalist Bertha Henson also wrote to urge the late Mr Chua to show that he really wanted the President's job.

We next had two uneventful PEs which were walkovers because only one suitable candidate was available for both elections. It wasn't that there were no interests to contest. The barriers to qualify had been set very high and those who qualified were generally uninterested to offer themselves. Singaporeans generally lost interest in PEs until 2011 when four eligible candidates campaigned vigorously for the post.

After the nail-biting results of PE2011 in which President Tony Tan won Dr Tan Cheng Bock by just 0.45% with 35.20% of valid votes cast, the people's expectations had been set high for PE2017. Dr Tan declared last year that he would contest again in 2017.

Subsequently, just months before the upcoming PE, the government pushed through various amendments to the EP

---

24  Deputy Prime Minister

25  Yee Jenn Jong, "ST Forum Aug 14, 1993: Banker Chua must be confident he can be President", March 20, 2011, https://yeejj.wordpress.com/2011/03/20/st-forum-aug-14-1993-banker-chua-must-be-confident-he-can-be-president/

that include setting aside reserve election for minority candidates if no President of that minority race was produced after 5 consecutive terms, as well as increasing the qualifying criteria for the top executive of private companies. The top executive now needs to run a business with at least $500 million in shareholders' equity compared to $100 million in paid up capital previously. The previously very high barrier, has now been set to extraordinarily very high.

The government has now declared PE2017 to be a reserved election for Malays (counting 5 terms from President Wee). The candidate will be from a very, very short list,[26] and most likely from the public sector (i.e. political appointees).

I find it a big let-down that Dr Tan, who was found eligible to contest in 2011, contested vigorously, and who continued to show interest since then to contest again, is now disqualified on various counts.

The government had pushed for the clause to have reserve elections for minority on the reason that voting is very much race-based. Well, we had minority candidates winning in elections against the majority chinese race in single seat contests many times since independence. Recent ones include Mr Murali Pillai in the 2016 Bukit Batok by-election and Mr Michael Palmer in Punggol East in GE2011. Both won very comfortably.

Even opposition politician, the late Mr J. B. Jeyaretnam won in a 3-corner fight in the 1981 Anson by-election.

The government had never put forth a Malay candidate since the first PE in 1993, even when we had two consecutive

---

26 Danson Cheong and Pearl Lee, "Prominent names thrown up for Singapore's next president", The Straits Times, November 14, 2016, https://www.straitstimes.com/singapore/prominent-names-thrown-up-for-presidency

walk-overs with only one candidate each time. Now it has decided that it is important to ensure minority representation and passed the reserve election amendment.

There's nothing to prevent the government from recognising President Ong as the first EP and having the upcoming PE2017 as an open election. It can still put forth a Malay candidate. If it is as widely speculated to be Madam Halimah Yacob,[27] the current Speaker of Parliament, the government should have confidence that she can stand her ground in an open election. She has won comfortably in four general elections and has high standing in the eyes of Singaporeans of all races. Many Singaporeans, myself included, do want to have minorities as Presidents. It will be truly a missed opportunity if we do not allow a highly suitable Malay candidate to become president on his/her own merits in an open election. It will quell the constant speculation that Singaporeans are immature and will vote along racial lines. Imagine if President Obama had somehow (although so unimaginable in the context of USA) been engineered into the White House because of rules safeguarding minority participation in politics, would he have been the popular president of all Americans that he was throughout his two terms of office?

AGC may have their reasons for the recommendation but the government should find the courage to allow an open election, which it can if it considers President Ong to be the first EP. Then the EP office will be more respected. If it wishes to play safe and only have preferred persons to be in office, let's just dispense with the EP and revert back to having nominated

---

27 Terry Xu, "Why Chan Chun Sing's 'freudian slip' of Mdm President, is not funny at all", The Online Citizen, February 7, 2017, https://www.onlinecitizenasia.com/2017/02/07/why-chan-chun-sings-freudian-slip-of-mdm-president-is-not-funny-at-all/

Presidents, which had served us well for so long and had given us good and popular Presidents.

PE2017, with at least two interested and popular candidates contesting, would have rekindled Singaporeans' interest in the office of EP. Instead, the response by the government to Dr Tan's request for clarity and call for open election, is that Dr Tan's comments did not require a response.[28]

## Political Education

In my first speech in Parliament, I spoke extensively about reforms needed to our education system. I spoke about having political education in schools. In 2014, Low and I touched on political education in schools again. Then Minister of State for Education, Sim Ann, replied that what we had asked for is already taking place in schools. Sim said, "The concepts of citizen rights and obligations, democracy, our electoral system, principles of our Constitution, and the structure of government are covered in the character and citizenship education, social studies, and history curricula in primary and secondary schools."

Sim said that the Ministry of Education constantly conveyed the message that values matter, including the importance of the collective good. In her view, political education is covered in schools.[29]

My issue then, and still remains today, is about whether we meaningfully cover political education in schools and whether true diversity of thoughts is encouraged from a young age.

---

28 Leong Sze Hian, "Govt's response to Dr Tan Cheng Bock is that he 'has not raised any new points that require response'?", The Online Citizen, April 1, 2017, https://www.onlinecitizenasia.com/2017/04/01/govts-response-to-dr-tan-cheng-bok-is-that-he-has-not-raised-any-new-points-that-require-response/

29 Clarissa Yong, "Parliament: Pri and sec school students do learn about S'pore's political system: Sim Ann", The Straits Times, May 30, 2014, https://www.straitstimes.com/singapore/parliament-pri-and-sec-school-students-do-learn-about-spores-political-system-sim-ann

## Reflections

Below is a blog post I had crafted just before the 2020 general election (GE2020) relevant to this topic.

> Monopoly of Wisdom will Cripple Singapore
>
> (May 16, 2020)
>
> At a May 15 virtual forum on the topic, "What are the sacred cows that Covid-19 might force us to reconsider?",[30] a panel of academics and other prominent social commentators believe that the Covid-19 pandemic is challenging some of the Government's "sacred cows". These include the country's addiction to cheap, transient labour and what the [panellists] described as the policymakers' "fear of social responsibilities" and the idea that they hold "the monopoly of wisdom".
>
> Yes, I feel much needs to be done. Covid-19 has brought to the forefront issues which our society has been sweeping under the carpet for far too long.
>
> 1. We have a long entrenched and ever growing reliance on foreign workers. We were not like that years ago, definitely not under the first generation leaders who had repeatedly warned that we should never let ourselves become too dependent on low cost migrant workers. Those advice were swept aside in the chase for stellar annual GDP[31] growth when the 2G[32] leaders took over and grew worse over time. I have traced the 30 years journey of how we got to this mess today: https://yeejj.wordpress.com/2020/05/12/1-5-million-fw/. Just in case we think this is unavoidable, many

---

30 Wong Pei Ting, "Panellists call for Govt to rethink reliance on foreign workers, 'fear of social responsibilities', as Covid-19 exposes shortcomings", Today, May 16, 2020, https://www.todayonline.com/singapore/singapore-exceptionalism-expense-low-wage-transient-workers-sacred-cow-exposed-covid-19

31 Gross domestic product

32 Second-generation

developed economies such as Australia, Japan, Taiwan and Hong Kong have done far better especially in the construction industry compared to us by taking a different path. The productivity of their largely local-based construction workers are way higher than their counterparts in Singapore.

2. Assoc Prof Theseira[33] spoke about the myth of Singapore exceptionalism. Former NMP Sadasivan[34] said that the Government needs to come to terms with the fact that it "really does not have the monopoly of wisdom".

For far too long, given the vast success of our first generation of leaders in transforming Singapore and shutting down criticism, Singapore has gone deeply down the path of believing that only the government has all the wisdom, that we only have enough for one A team, etc. We have been conditioned since young, from schools to just follow rules. The government celebrates creativity and innovation only when they fall in line with what they like to see, but clamps down or [withholds] support when they feel ideas are not consistent with their views. There are many examples. Just to name one, graphic novelist Sonny Liew had his grant of $8,000 from the NAC[35] revoked on the eve of the official launch of his novel, The Art Of Charlie Chan Hock Chye for 'sensitive content'. He went on to become the first Singaporean to win at the prestigious Eisner Awards, considered to be the Oscar Awards of comics. He won not one, but three awards at that event.

---

33 Walter Theseira, Nominated Member of Parliament

34 Viswaroopan ("Viswa") Sadasivan

35 National Arts Council

## Reflections

Only the government can be right and all other views are portrayed as dangerous for society or 'irresponsible'.[36] As former veteran Permanent Secretary Ngiam Tong Dow had warned, many in government think they are little Lee Kuan Yews when they have not yet earned their spurs,[37] preaching and dictating others like they know-it-all, and even mocking other world leaders.

Bold change so far happens mostly when the ruling party feels their hold on near absolute power is being threatened, such as after GE2011. Unfortunately, group think has and will impede Singapore from innovating and moving forward. I believe too often, the false sense of exceptionalism will make us complacent, lazy to think deeply, just follow rules and unwilling to embrace divergent views.

I have long believed that only when the competition becomes stronger will the government be forced to be more innovative and more responsive. I remained even more convinced after GE2011.

Covid-19 has exposed that our government does not always know it all and that we do not always have the 'Gold' standard. We should be humble to learn from others, whether from other countries or from Singaporeans with differing views. Given the uncertainty of the 21st century, we need to learn to embrace diversity to continue to be relevant.

I would like to share a story that I have kept to myself for eight years. I share it now because I remain saddened by the lack of openness of

---

36 Asyraf Kamil, "'Irresponsible' to incite home-based businesses to put pressure on Government to grant exceptions, says Masagos", Today, April 27, 2020, https://www.todayonline.com/singapore/irresponsible-incite-home-based-business-put-pressure-government-grant-exceptions-says

37 "'I suspect we have started to believe our own propaganda.'", The Online Citizen, December 17, 2014, https://www.onlinecitizenasia.com/2014/12/17/i-suspect-we-have-started-to-believe-our-own-propaganda/

some who should be educating our youth to appreciate diversity and treat one another with respect.

In 2012, my alma mater Temasek Junior College was celebrating her 35th anniversary. Just a couple of weeks before College Day in May, I received a phone call from a senior teacher whom I knew well. We had served in the college alumni together.

He was unusually hesitant in the conversation. He asked if I had received a letter from the school regarding College Day. I was invited to College Day every year as I was active in the Alumni Executive Committee and was later a member of the College Advisory Board. I thought he was referring to the invitation to attend, for which I replied, yes.

Then he started apologising that the College had to delay the presentation of the Distinguished Alumnus Award to me. I was puzzled. He explained that a letter had been sent to me congratulating me for the award and that it would be given on College Day. However, the College had received instructions that Heng Swee Keat, then Minister for Education, was to be the Guest of Honour and he would be presenting the awards. Whoever instructed the College felt that it would be awkward for Heng to be giving an award to me, a non-constituency member of parliament (NCMP) from the opposition. I was told that I would receive the award on a later date. After the phone call, I found the letter in my mailbox.

I did not want to create an issue. I would have no issue with receiving an award from Heng. I am not even sure if Heng was aware that someone in his ministry stopped the presentation of my award. Nevertheless, I attended the event. The College had selected three individuals to receive the award that year because it was a significant milestone year for the College. I was supposed to be one of the recipients. That College Day, only two awards were presented.

I waited and I was not told to receive any award after the event. A few months later in September of 2012, there was a 35th anniversary dinner.

## Reflections

I received a Service to Education Award during that event. This award is automatically given to those who had served for 5, 10, or 15 years on school advisory boards. I thought the Distinguished Alumnus Award had been forgotten. I did not wish to make an issue out of it, so I did not remind anyone.

In 2013, I was presented the Distinguished Alumnus Award during College Day, a year late. There were no political office-bearers for the event, so I guessed it was considered safe for the award ceremony to go ahead. Even during the presentation of the award, when my contributions were listed out, my NCMP position was noticeably omitted. I did not mind. The event was attended only by the college staff, students, and some parents.

I received a Facebook message that evening from a former teacher of the College. She was my Facebook friend as well. She was told by her ex-colleague who had attended the event that my NCMP contribution was omitted. Both she and her ex-colleague were unhappy, so she vented it out by telling me. When the college alumni from the PAP were given the same award previously, their Parliament positions were proudly listed.

I thanked her for reaching out to me and told her not to be angry with the College. I was very appreciative of the award because I could only imagine what the College had to go through, first nominating me and then to be told to retract my award because someone higher up might not like the idea of me receiving the award from Heng. Definitely it was not something of the College's doing because they would not even have fought for my nomination in the first place. Perhaps some people might have even questioned why they wanted to give such an award to me.

Chen Show Mao was once "un-invited" for a seventh month event in his Paya Lebar ward and the incident went viral online. Like Chen, I had been "un-awarded" for an award I was to receive. I continued to serve in the College Advisory Committee until I had to retire in 2017 because I had served the maximum 10-year term allowed by the Ministry of Education for any board member of a school. It was only several years after the incident, in a casual conversation with another former teacher of the College, that I was told that after the intervention, the College decided to present the award to me in 2013. It did not come across as such to me at that time, nor did I pursue asking anyone after that phone call.

Our mindsets are too narrow. If we wish for Singapore to succeed in this new age, we must be prepared for diversity of ideas and opinions. We must be prepared for some messiness. We must be prepared to accept that success need not come from a prescribed route.

Yes, we have political education; in name but not in its true spirit.

## Political Office

Much has been said before about ministerial pay. Our first-generation leaders served with a mission for Singapore. Pay was relatively low then for the political office-bearers. In 1994, the pay was raised quite significantly because the PAP found it difficult to attract talent. It wanted to pay top dollars to match that of top talent in the private sector. Pay became a formula tied to the top four earners from six professions. Following yet another major adjustment initiated in 2007, the annual salary for the president reached a dizzying height of $4.268 million,[38] prime minister $3.1 million, and an entry-level minister S$1.9 million, on average, excluding special bonuses.[39]

There has been considerable debate about this online. In GE2011, there

---

38 Faris Mohktar, "Singapore President's annual salary tops S$4.2 million", Yahoo! News, March 11, 2011 https://sg.news.yahoo.com/singapore-president-s-annual-salary-tops-s-4-2-million-.html

39 Seth Mydans, "Singapore announces 60 percent pay raise for ministers", The New York Times, April 9, 2007, https://www.nytimes.com/2007/04/09/world/asia/09iht-sing.3.5200498.html

# Reflections

was much voter unhappiness about many things. Ministerial salary was one of them.

In an unprecedented move, within a week after GE2011, Lee Kuan Yew and Goh Chok Tong both stepped down. Goh was given an honorary title of Emeritus Senior Minister. Lee did not need any title. His name was strong enough to earn respect anywhere he travelled in the world, for anything that he needed to do for Singapore. Another week later, the government announced that ministers' salaries would be reviewed. That became the topic of my first major debate in Parliament. All WP parliamentarians spoke during that debate.

The following is the speech which I had delivered in 2012 for the ministerial salary debate. What I had said remains relevant today. My belief then, and today, is still the same. Singapore is fishing for talent in a small pond, with a narrow definition of who can become good parliamentarians and office-bearers.

My parliamentary speech on Ministerial Pay Review

(January 17, 2012)

Mr Speaker Sir, my party colleagues have touched on many aspects of the proposal. I wish to highlight the part that I have the biggest concern with. It is the way a minister's pay is pegged to the top 1,000 Singaporean earners.

The salary review committee was given the terms of reference by the Prime Minister to "take into account salaries of comparable jobs in the private sector and also other reference points such as the general wage levels in Singapore".

The assumption this government began with is that political talent is synonymous with career success; that office holders must have comparable pay with top private sector earners. So the committee arrived at the median income of the top 1,000 earners, less a 40% discount to "signify the ethos and sacrifice that comes with political service". It implies that our political office holders must come from this pool, or that their ability and job scope is equivalent to the top 0.06% of the working Singaporean population.

This sentiment has indeed been expressed by the Deputy Prime Minister and by various members over the past two days.

We have constantly used this mindset since 1994, when ministers' pay was first revamped to tie it to that of the top earners in the private sector. While the committee's new formula is better than that of the previous one which had been narrowly tied with only the top eight earners in six professions, it is nevertheless still an [elitist] thinking that only those who are top in their professional careers can make it to hold political office.

Running a company well is different from being able to run a country. Perhaps the government has treated running this country too much like running a business that we have often been referred to as Singapore Inc. So we also tie political work to that of running a very big company. I believe this is a flawed model.

In constantly drumming this message since 1994, we have created an expectation amongst potential political office holders that political office is a career progression for them, and that reaching a minister's position is like reaching the pinnacle of one's career.

It also creates an expectation amongst identified potential office holders that they need a safe route to parachute into parliament or they would not risk their career. This has made Singapore politics uniquely Singapore. It is a model of politics that despite years of attempts to justify and fine-tune, many have yet to accept. I for one, do not accept this model of politics.

I feel we have over commercialised the nature of running this country. We need to constantly remind ourselves that we have been elected by the people into this House. It is totally different from being headhunted to become a hired top management of a company. We should never forget it is a noble calling to serve the public.

I like to ask, what [inspires] a person to take the difficult route of politics?

Four years ago, I read with interest about how President Obama as a young student in an Indonesian school, stated that his ambition was to be the President of the United States of America. It was a noble aspiration for a child; an almost impossible ambition given his family background and then living half the globe away from America. Why would he have such an aspiration?

As a child growing up in post independent Singapore, I have been influenced by several of our first-generation leaders whom I had clearly seen have made lots of personal sacrifices and have made great improvements to the country by what they did.

I wonder what would [inspire] our next generation to become future ministers and the future Prime Minister. I certainly hope it will not be for career progression.

I share the Prime Minister's concern that Singapore needs good and high ability people to protect what we have. We have often heard that Singapore does not have enough talent for two teams. I do not agree with this thinking. I have more confidence in our people.

During the debate on the Presidential Address, I had called for political education in schools. It is to strengthen the knowledge of our youths in the functioning of parliament and of the government. I believe it is important that we [instil] this sense of public service and [political] awareness in our youths to give them a better understanding of issues important to our country. We should aim to create aspiring future politicians who will strongly believe in the importance of leading the nation, and that they wish to play a part in it.

Perhaps it is also how we constantly look for political talent from amongst a narrow pool of top career performers that has perpetuated lack of interest in political careers amongst the general population. I believe we have been talent ponding for too long, searching from a small pond for people that fit as career elites. We should instead talent flood with people from all walks of life.

The salary review committee describes the 40% discount as a sacrifice for political service. Personally, I do not like the word "sacrifice", a term that has been used by various members throughout the past 2 days. Being a politician should be an aspiration and an honour. It is the nature of politics all over the world that there will be public scrutiny; there will be challenges balancing family and work; and there will be set-backs such as electoral loss. The reluctant will deem these as sacrifice. Those who aspire to lead will welcome these as challenges to be overcome.

Singaporeans do not expect politicians to lead a spartan life with a religious calling. I believe Singapore politics has been more than fair to our political office holders in the past two decades. Even with the levels proposed by the Workers' Party, they can lead very dignified lives.

# Reflections

We sometimes hear examples of former US and UK political leaders earning a lot after retirement. I think life has also been fair to our political office holders after retirement. We can see that retiring ministers are sought after by our government linked companies and some by multinationals. I believe the experience they have gained while in office have increased their market value.

Several members have said that the Workers' Party's proposal supports the level of salaries proposed by the committee, just because we happen to arrive at roughly the same basic monthly salary level for an entry level minister. The differences are several, and important:

1. We start with the allowance for a member of parliament, because the minister is firstly a member of parliament. It is a reminder that we are elected by the people, not selected by a powerful committee to become ministers.

2. The base salary for entry-grade senior civil servants at MX9 grade[40] [is] less subjected to fluctuation compared with incomes at the 500th and 501st top income earners, which is the median of the top 100 earners. Over time, by comparing with the top, we could again see the salaries of ministers rising faster than are acceptable to Singaporeans.

3. We oppose the huge bonus payout. Again, I like to stress that while we like Singapore to be well run, Singapore is not just another very large company. As an entrepreneur, Mr Inderjit Singh is acceptable with huge bonuses of 13.5 months. That may be the

---

[40] In the civil service, civil servants are paid according to the Management Executive Scheme, where MX9 is the entry level for superscale salary.

practice of some very generous private companies. Politically, it is unheard of and unacceptable to the electorate. The bonus for any political party, comes at the ballot boxes.

I like to thank the Prime Minister for agreeing that the Workers' Party pay formula works out to less than that of the review committee's. I recommend that Mr Vikram Nair and Madam Halimah check with the Prime Minister how he arrived at the calculations.

In our computation, the benchmark point annual salary for an entry level minister with 13th month and 2.5 months bonus is $852,500, compared with $1.1 million as recommended by the committee. This is a 46% cut from 2010 annual pay. Furthermore, a portion of the bonus is deferred into a bonus bank. Under our proposal, the Prime Minister with 13th month and 2.5 months bonus will receive $1,534,500, compared with the recommended $2.2 million. This is a 50% cut from 2010 annual pay.

Before I conclude, I like to address a point that Mr Vikram Nair raised. Over the past 2 days, he had harped on what we have contributed to Gerard Ee's committee. With the permission of my colleague Gerald Giam, I like to share that Gerald Giam had spent more than 2 hours with the review committee. During the meeting, he had shared the deferred bonus, measuring by KPIs[41] and our benchmarking method, which are now contained in our proposal. We have no need to share everything with the committee. I wonder how many hours Mr Vikram spent with the committee.

---

41 Key performance indicators

Mr Vikram has said that by opposing the motion, we are supporting the 2010 pay levels. The parliament is the platform to debate the salary review and to come up with alternatives, which is what we are doing. I wonder if Mr Vikram Nair expects us to simply rubber stamp the review committee's proposal.

In conclusion, the annual levels we have proposed are not the same as that of the [review] committee's. More fundamentally, we object to the principles used to set the benchmark for ministerial salaries. Therefore, I oppose the motion.

## Opposition Unity

I get along reasonably well with members of other opposition parties. During the 12th Parliament, Lina Chiam's seat was next to mine. Chiam is from the Singapore People's Party (SPP). From time to time, we would discuss issues, especially if a bill or motion was particularly contentious. Once, a question which she had filed was slated for early in the session but she was not yet in Parliament. I rose to table the question for her. The Parliament's rule is that the member asking a question should be in Parliament to table it. However, the member can also request another member to table the question in his or her absence. Although Chiam did not ask me to, I thought it would be nice for opposition members to support one another.

Jeannette Chong-Aruldoss is a long-time resident of Joo Chiat SMC, and then a member of the National Solidarity Party. I became acquainted with her during my GE2011 campaign. In the 2015 general election, we could not get permission to visit homes in the condominium where she lived. Even though she was contesting Mountbatten SMC as a candidate for another opposition party at that time, she nonetheless organised a barbeque one evening in her condominium and invited many neighbours so that I could interact with them.

In GE2020, Chong-Aruldoss did not contest. Instead, she and her family helped as assentors with the campaign and as counting agents for us in Marine Parade GRC. She also acted as Commissioner of Oaths for various documents needed for our volunteers and candidates.

I have visited Tan Cheng Bock in his home several times, especially during his Chinese New Year open house. We have good conversations with other opposition members who were there.

I took part in three overseas gatherings of political parties: in Sri Lanka, Malaysia, and Armenia. Several of Singapore's other opposition party members went along, too. We got along well with one another on these trips.

In general, we try to avoid three-cornered fights. Nevertheless, they are not always avoidable. As the political landscape evolves, there will continue to be such three-cornered fights.

Anyone who has been in the opposition long enough would have met countless people who ask why the opposition parties cannot just band together to take on the PAP. It is as if all the parties merging together will oust the PAP.

In my opinion, joining all opposition parties together would be the worst thing to do for the opposition movement. The PAP would wish for this to happen. It would make their job of killing off the opposition so much easier. I would like to emphasise again, the thoughts expressed here are my personal opinions formed after observing politics close up from the opposition camp.

The reality is that there is no one type of opposition. Yes, the PAP is so dominant that it contests every seat all the time and wins with about 90 percent certainty at the moment. Every alternative party has to compete with the PAP, who are the likely incumbent other than for a small number of seats. Having the PAP as our common opponent does not make all alternative parties the same.

## Reflections

Each party has its own beliefs, value system, and way of functioning. When I was contemplating to be in the alternative camp, there were only two parties that I considered — the WP and SPP. I eventually excluded the SPP because I was uncertain how it would develop given the health of Chiam See Tong, the leader of the party. People join parties for various reasons, or move from one to another. Some have valid reasons to leave after finding that the party and people inside are not what they seem. The danger of joining an alternative party simply because it is against the PAP makes for poor ground to stand on.

There are good reasons why parties cannot merge easily. For any party to grow, I strongly believe that it cannot simply accept anyone who is anti-PAP. Soon, you will find that there are different ideals and ways of operating. Before I joined the WP, I read its previous manifestos. I needed to be assured of what the party stood for. I would not want to enter Parliament and start disagreeing with my comrades. This does not mean I do not have my own principles. My beliefs aligned quite well with those of the party. During my term in Parliament, I did not face any situation in which I had to compromise my beliefs to align with those of the party.

When Low took over the secretary-general position in 2001, he started shaping the party to have a clear identity of being a rational, responsible, and respectable opposition. In the process, senior members were offended as they were being passed over. Over time, newer people who joined identified with the new values and amplified them.

Political parties exist to contest elections. Only those that can figure out the formula to eventually win parliamentary seats will have long-term relevance. Parties that cannot win elections will still not be able to win elections if combined together in a coalition. Putting smaller parties under the branding of a bigger one would just cause the bigger one to sink. There will be too many wanting to be the chief, who believe that their ways are the best. Winning more seats from the PAP is already super tough. Bigger does not mean better.

Will there ever be a coalition? It depends on the situation. The only meaningful coalition is a coalition of parties that have won some seats in Parliament. There must be more to hold a coalition together than the fact that they are on the opposite side of the PAP. Being anti-PAP is a very weak bond that will not hold a coalition together for very long.

Can someone start a new party and make it big? In the past, we had Chiam who created the Singapore Democratic Party, which from 1991 to 1997 was the biggest opposition party with three elected MPs. Today, it is more difficult for a new Chiam to emerge on his own and start in a small way. The Progress Singapore Party (PSP) has shown that it was still possible, but the amount of resources and talent it had to gather in a short time was huge. The PSP made some inroads in GE2020 mainly because of the personal reputation of Tan Cheng Bock, founder of the PSP, and his network of talent and resources.

The opposition slate has grown stronger. Voters are now more demanding. There are now many candidates on the opposition slate who can match the credentials of those in the PAP. Given the evolution of the political scene in Singapore, we can expect that candidates with stronger profiles will continue to join bigger parties.

## A United Singapore

People sometimes ask me if we get along with PAP members when we meet them. And we see them all the time in Parliament. Occasionally, especially during an election, we bump into each other on the ground.

From time to time, there will be fireworks in Parliament. The occasional intense battle such as over the Aljunied-Hougang-Punggol East Town Council lawsuit and the PAP-owned company Action Information Management matters could sometimes feel awkward. We spar when we need to but in general, we get on well with PAP parliamentarians.

Most of the time, we see each other in casual settings in the Parliament

## Reflections

tearoom or in the library. Parliament sessions usually start at 1.30 pm, with tea break at around 4 pm. Light catered food is provided for tea. However, without fail at each Parliament sitting, Lily Neo, a former PAP MP, would put some nice snacks in the Parliament room before 1.30 pm for others to help themselves. Sometimes, when I went to Parliament without having had lunch because I was in a rush straight from work, these snacks and a cup of tea would come in handy because otherwise we would only get to eat at tea-time at around 4 pm.

My personality is such that I mingle about rather easily. Sometimes when debates were very intense, we preferred to sit in the tearoom with fellow opposition MPs. Otherwise, I did not mind chatting with anyone in the tearoom or in the library. I also got along well with a number of NMPs.

I do not know what it was like in the days of J. B. Jeyaretnam and when only Chiam and Low were in Parliament. I suppose the atmosphere could feel awkward in the tearoom when you were heavily outnumbered and when debates were confrontational in Parliament sittings.

I had shared earlier in this book that occasionally I used informal sessions to follow up with some political office-bearers on matters I had raised in earlier speeches or questions. Sometimes we were also asked in advance for our speeches or at least what we intended to speak about. Many issues were non-confrontational. Depending on the matter, I would reply to such emails with a brief outline of the points I intended to raise. I did this because it would help the office-bearer prepare a better response. If there was a need for the office-bearer to gather the information or think about the points I intended to raise, I felt that sending these pointers in advance would be useful in pushing my case.

Once, as a member of my alma mater's College Advisory Board, I was trying to raise money for the college's Adopt-A-Tree project. I knew that several PAP MPs were also alumni of the College. I approached all of them and some donated immediately.

From time to time, Singapore parliamentarians take part in regional or international parliamentarian gatherings. During the 12th Parliament term, I was selected for two overseas trips — to Sri Lanka and Mexico — with other parliamentarians. A PAP parliamentarian was always the leader of the team. We coordinated well with one another when we needed to speak at these conferences. Overseas, it is good to put up a united Singapore front. After all, we are a small country vulnerable to external threats.

In my maiden speech during the opening of the 12th Parliament, I responded to then Minister of State Teo Ser Luck's speech on developing the entrepreneurial spirit in Singaporeans and offered my willingness to work together on this. Not long later, I was contacted by SPRING Singapore (now Enterprise Singapore) and invited to be on the Action Community for Entrepreneurship (ACE) Subcommittee on Start-ups. From 2011 to 2017, I became involved in regular sessions as a panellist with fellow entrepreneurs to evaluate application for grants by Singapore start-ups. I also became mentor to a few start-ups in the education technology space. I continue to be in touch with and work with former panellists from the ACE Subcommittee.

Sometimes, we meet visiting parliamentarians from overseas in our Parliament House. I signed up to be on the list for meeting with European parliamentarians. I was involved in a few luncheons and meetings with visiting delegates. Sometimes, I attended functions of embassies in Singapore where I would also come across PAP politicians. All such meetings have been cordial.

If you have read this book from cover to cover, you might have noticed that I have cited meetings and conversations with friends and acquaintances very staunchly in the PAP's camp. I have even invited comments on this book from some of them. My belief is that even if I do not agree with their views, I can still meet with them if they wish to and have an intellectual discussion. I can even collaborate with them in

## Reflections

areas outside of politics, whether in business or in doing good for the community. Sometimes, opposition supporters accuse the PAP of groupthink or listening in an echo chamber. My belief is that I should guard against groupthink myself, which would happen if I listen only to people who support my views. It is better to hear the arguments on the other side and I can check against my own convictions to see how strong they still stand after exchanging our views. People should not have to resort to scratching the car or threatening the life of others who disagree with their political views.

Politics is designed in a manner in which there are winners and losers. I contest to win but I also believe that we need to maintain a harmonious Singapore, especially when it comes to defending our image and interests abroad.

During general election campaigning, we came across activists from the PAP from time to time. Before the start of an outreach, I often reminded volunteers to maintain a cordial relationship with residents who are pro-PAP and also when we come across a PAP group. Below is a post I had shared shortly after GE2020.

> Towards a United First World Singapore
>
> (July 12, 2020)
>
> During this General Elections, we came across the PAP's Marine Parade team several times during campaigning and of course in polling and counting stations. The exchanges have been cordial. While we fight for every vote and they do as well, the battle has been civil.
>
> On the eve of cooling day, one of the PAP's flyering team member at Kembangan bought my volunteers drinks from the nearby convenient shop. Much appreciated. I noticed too that some of my flyering team members and those at the PAP's side

# Whither Singapore?

at Kembangan that day were having cordial conversations when there were no residents around.

During my distribution of packed lunch and dinner to our polling agents at the stations, I also offered our packs to the PAP side at some stations.

Even as we challenged for disputed votes that were not clearly marked during counting, we were firm and civil.

I continue to believe we can have constructive politics even as we continue to put up a challenge to the super dominant ruling party. I hope this will be seen in the transfer of TC[42] management at Sengkang and also in how elected opposition MPs can have the direct and final say in how Community Improvement Projects funds can be used. Also elected opposition MPs should have access to PA[43] facilities so as to better serve residents who have elected them.

Even as I write this, my thoughts are with those early and brave warriors who championed on the alternative camp. Many were detained, lost their jobs, became bankrupt or were even exiled. Some returned to Singapore eventually, as ashes. May we never return to these dark days. Beyond going towards a First World Parliament, we should move towards a united First World Singapore.

---

42 Town Council

43 People's Association

## Chapter 10
# Concluding Words

My journey began with an email. It took me through three contests over three general elections during the past 10 years. It was a period of change in Singapore politics. When I entered the scene, our founding prime minister, who had defined our style of politics for the first three to four decades, was ailing. Change had been happening and was continuing to take place. I watched at first hand and participated in the push towards a First World Parliament and towards my hope for a more resilient Singapore which can flourish with a diversity of views.

In my Preface, I told the story of the primary school teacher who did not allow her student to write about me as a politician because I had failed to win in the general election. I have now failed three times.

Did I make a difference to Singapore?

By coming to this concluding chapter, you have read about my journey. I am privileged to have taken this journey. It was an unexpected journey, and not an easy one. Sometimes we live through life, wondering what if I had done this, what if I had done that? Before I wrote the email that sparked this journey, I too had wondered.

Mine was not a journey taken alone. I joined paths with many along the way. At some parts of the journey, I travelled along with others. Sometimes, the paths diverged at some point. My journey has made me richer in my perspectives. I was helped along in my journey and I trust that I was of use to others too.

This book is my attempt to add to political education in Singapore. I hope to share a different side to the stories that you hear from the victors

## Concluding Words

in history. I shall leave you to be the judge whether the teacher was correct: that we who did not manage to win have no stories to tell; that we did not make a difference to Singapore.

Singapore was founded on democratic principles. We had capable founding leaders who navigated the challenges of their times to chart a viable path for the then young nation. No dynasty or government in history has lasted forever. However pure and well a government had started off, there will come a time when decay sets in, and that government will not be capable of checking itself.

The alternatives to the PAP were killed off after the main opposition led the boycott of elections in 1968. There had been occasional bright sparks. For various reasons, most did not last long or grow to be a viable movement. Politics is brutal, particularly for some of the participants. The Workers' Party (WP), under the leadership of Low Thia Khiang, made the biggest and longest sustained progress. It did so at a time when the People's Action Party (PAP) was itself experiencing the transition from a post-Lee Kuan Yew reign after his passing. The breakthrough came in the 2011 general election and has so far continued despite dangerous pitfalls along the way. I am honoured to have played a part in the process and observed events from a privileged position. I had written this book to capture the stories of this ongoing breakthrough to provide others with a better understanding of events that had happened.

The story has not yet ended. The WP is still a work-in-progress. The movement towards a First World Parliament is progressing. How the WP and other opposition parties can develop will depend on how they adapt themselves to be relevant to Singapore. Singapore needs political education. We need a more resilient Singapore with politically aware citizens who can contribute to checking whoever is in power. I had shared several stories of the fear people have in politics and to be associated with the opposition. It is a fear we as a society should break

## Reflections

down because it is harmful for Singapore to have viable choices only from the so-called Team A, the PAP. No party has a monopoly of wisdom.

For each general election, all WP candidates are issued a badge with the hammer logo. We are required to pin it on our blue candidate shirt (blouse for ladies). Candidates can therefore be distinguished from other members so they are more easily recognisable by the public in our campaigning.

If you look closely, each badge is slightly different — different shades of red and gold, as well as being different in the finishing. I suppose they were from a different supplier each time.

I have collected three badges. Will there be a fourth?

They say old soldiers never die. Here is a quote from General Douglas MacArthur in his farewell address to the United States Congress:

> *"... but I still remember the refrain of one of the most popular barrack ballads of that day which proclaimed most proudly that 'old soldiers never die; they just fade away.'*
>
> *And like the old soldier of that ballad, I now close my military career and just fade away, an old soldier who tried to do his duty as God gave him the light to see that duty."*

Decades ago, when I first expressed my concern to want to have a better Singapore and a better world, I began by writing. It took me from the forum pages of newspapers and magazines to working in policy committees, to blogs, to Parliament and campaign speeches, and now in the form of this book. As long as I have breath, the journey continues, in one way or another.